BEARDED LADY

BEARDED LADY

ALLISON LANDA

Woodhall Press
Norwalk, CT

woodhall press

Woodhall Press, 81 Old Saugatuck Road, Norwalk, CT 06855
WoodhallPress.com

Cover design: Jessica Dionne Wright
Layout artist: Wendy Bowes

Library of Congress Cataloging-in-Publication Data available

ISBN 978-1-954907-38-6 (paper: alk paper)
ISBN 978-1-954907-39-3 (electronic)

First Edition

Distributed by Independent Publishers Group
(800) 888-4741

Printed in the United States of America

For Adam, Baz, Jack, and Maizie:
everything

PART I

CHAPTER 1

1985

Don't expect to understand my family. You'll have better luck comprehending the history of the Middle East, or a Rubik's Cube. The answers there may not be formal or finite, but they at least exist. When it comes to my family, there are few answers.

We live in northern San Diego County, a casually affluent burn zone decorated by waves of red-tile roofs. Here people think they can beat the inevitable by waving magic wands: money, image, designer dogs. Sometimes it works. Sometimes they wind up with their homes reduced to ashes.

My parents have charm. They use it as a strategy, a way to beat back the flames. A grin can flash into something darker or remain in sunshine. You never know.

My mother is Joan, but I occasionally call her Nails. She has talons the shade of blood and hair the color of rust. She is prone to crying fits and lengthy explanations. These ride on one premise: Once she had dreams, then she had kids.

She regrets moving here from the East Coast. She claims my father forced her into it so he could pursue his perversions. "He wants to do threesomes," my mother says, speaking in italics. "Wife-swapping. I tell him he can play a nice game of Hide and Go Fuck Yourself."

My father is Steve, but I often think of him as The Rooster. His combover flaps in the wind. In the outside world he is cordial; at home he can be every bit as aggressive as the barnyard animal. His eyes are black as midnight. When he yells they turn almost violet. Violet and violent.

Somehow these two came together to form me and my brothers. I am twelve. Middle—so-called because he is the middle child—is eleven. Jonathan is a year old. He is the accident, or, if you'd rather be more tactful, the surprise. When he pisses me off, I call him the Birth Control Poster Child. It doesn't seem to faze him.

Middle and I go to public school, but in the county's best district. In school, the teacher asks: What does your father do? My classmates answer: doctor, plumber, pro football player. Then it is my turn.

"He drinks beer," I say, "and watches *Hill Street Blues*."

Later, my mother explains: "Your father is an engineer." When I ask what that means, she shrugs. It's not that she doesn't know. It's more like she doesn't care. I imagine him at a desk doing something called paperwork, just as he does in his den for hours with the door shut and locked. Engineers must take home a lot of work. It must be important, just as our homework is important to us.

I know why work is important: It makes you money. Money means a lot to Nails and Rooster. It's how we have our house, and our house is serious business. It's a style my mother calls French Country Castle. She has a name for it: Jostaladjo—Joan-Steve-Allison-Middle-Jonathan. The house has a persona all its own. It is haughty in a laughable way, too big for its own britches. It is high on its own square footage. It prides itself on its prestige.

But inside it's a warren of small rooms with locks to close ourselves off from one another. The carpet is stained and sad, the victim of Rooster's dirty soles. When my mother complains he says, "What do you want from my life?" Then he slams into the den and does paperwork.

Our entryway is the biggest room. It's the size of some studio apartments and leads to a dining room with no carpet. It flooded a week after we moved in, and they never bothered to replace the flooring. Bare nails jut from the concrete floor. My parents closed it off and forbade Jonathan from crawling there.

By night my mother retreats to her own hiding spot far from that cold entryway and dangerous dining room, all the things she and Rooster have created but cannot maintain. She locks herself in my bathroom. There she smokes, tapping her ashes into an empty yogurt cup. She writes in her journal, filling pages with her classic longhand. After the last cigarette is smoked and the room vacated, I slip into the bathroom to read her written confessions. It's a different Nails than I know during the day, my tough-talking chain-smoker of a mother. This is a tender Nails, a rueful one. It's a Nails that makes me ache and want to read more.

I too write in a journal. It's nothing more than a spiral notebook, a series of blank lined pages. I use a ballpoint pen, pressing so hard that the imprint of my words can be found on the paper that lies beneath. Writing makes me feel safer than locking my door. It makes me feel freer than when Rooster is on a business trip. It makes me want to write more. I chronicle the events of the day—the credit card bill arrived and my parents fought—along with my goals. I want to meet Lucille Ball, be a cheerleader, have a boyfriend. I want to play first base on my softball team. I want to go roller-skating on Saturday.

Most of all, I want to be pretty. Pretty means a small waist like Scarlett O'Hara, and I love *Gone with the Wind*. Pretty means good hair like Madonna. Pretty means a nice smile with straight teeth, which I don't have because Rooster decided not to spend money on the braces my orthodontist recommended. I frown into the bathroom mirror, flanked by nicotine-stained walls. I resemble nothing so much as a human chipmunk, complete with fat cheeks and wide eyebrows that meet in the middle. My crooked teeth point in all directions. My eyes are small, my nose wide, my hair something out of *Return of the Jedi*. Jabba the Hutt, not Princess Leia.

Pretty means thin. Beauty is slim and angular, long and lissome. Everything about my body is curved and convex, rounded and generous. My breasts are already larger than those of most girls my age. So are my belly and behind. In the bathroom I run my hands along the arc of my hips, the swell of my thighs. My shoulders are wide like a linebacker. My upper arms bulge. Even my forehead looks enormous, a pale fleshy expanse. How will I do the things I want to do if I'm fat? Lucy won't want to meet a butterball. I wouldn't even be able to fit into a cheer uniform. And no boy will love a big girl. Even I know that.

I often vow to lose weight. The matter seems simple: Take in fewer calories than you burn. We learned that in health class. It's an issue of numbers, but I'm no good at math. When my parents fight, I fake a headache and skip dinner. Then I go downstairs after the table is cleared and consume chips, cookies, handfuls of cornmeal. I slather pieces of white bread with margarine and shove them into my mouth. I pour bowls of cereal and eat them dry. I belch and I smile. Sometimes I laugh. The cheeks of my face and butt are dimpled because eating makes me fat, but the food feels good. It feels familiar, like a grandparent. It also hurts, like nails going down my throat. Scratchy. Bloodletting.

While I eat and evaluate myself, my brothers find their own hiding places. Middle tucks himself in his room and watches pro wrestling, taking mental notes should he need to bust out a half nelson on the bully next door. Jonathan, just a baby, chews on teddy bears in his crib. Outside, the sun grows shy and the sky dark, wrapping us in nighttime as we dwell in our separate spaces.

I am in seventh grade. I sit on the floor of the Black Mountain Middle School assembly room, the hard linoleum stinging my butt. The place smells like hairspray and pre-adolescent sweat. Laughter and catcalls ping off hard surfaces, making it hard to hear even the person next to me. Maybe this is what they mean when they talk about being alone in a crowded room.

A voice behind me says: "A werewolf!"

A second voice: "Where? Lemme see."

Werewolf? That's way more interesting than the German rock band that's about to perform for us. The show's meant as a history lesson, an idea that appeals more to school administrators than to us. I want to see the werewolf too.

"There," First Voice says.

I hear the finger being pointed.

Laughter gathers, blooms, and spreads. I start to join in—and then I feel that flush. It starts in my cheeks, climbs to my forehead, and drops back to my chin. It makes my skin feel hot and prickly, itchy. *Dummy*, it says, *don't you know?*

I'm wearing a Wonder Woman T-shirt. It's pulled up and out of my jeans, exposing my lower back. I feel eyes. I reach back to pull the shirt down—and there's hair. It feels soft, but soft in this case doesn't feel good. It feels like a razor blade. Tears sting my eyes, but I don't cry. I bite my lip and feel my heart slam against my ribs. I can hear its drumbeat in my ears, feel it in the pulse at my wrists. It sounds like a warning.

On the bus ride home I glance down at my arms. Were they this hairy all along? I edge up the leg of my jeans: hair there too. Already my body feels different. A trap rather than a tool. An object of shame rather than a point of pride.

Werewolf. Something that changes into something else. I think of Michael Jackson's "Thriller" music video, his eyes going wide and dull, features shifting from human to zombie. I'd wanted change, but not like this. I wanted to be beautiful. This isn't beautiful.

I climb off the bus and walk down the driveway toward my house. It is a steep, sloping driveway marked by twin posts. It curves and dips and finally reaches its destination. In front is a basketball hoop and patches of dead grass. When my mother asks my father when we're getting a professional gardener, he counters, "When are you getting a job?"

I hesitate before going in. I stand in front of my house and think what an impressive mess it is, how the external can be so deceiving. Inside, I am not a werewolf. Inside, I am a smoothly manicured girl who fits into small-size GUESS jeans. Inside, I laugh at girls who look like me.

The key turns with a single smooth motion. The door works, why can't my body? I step into our massive expanse of an entryway. It is meant to impress and intimidate. *Enter this house. I dare you.* My Keds make a strange sucking sound on the marble floor. "Mom?" I yell. I wonder how she'd react if I called her Joan or, God forbid, Nails. She doesn't believe in corporal punishment, but my ass wouldn't stop stinging for a week.

I find my mother in the kitchen, smoking and working a crossword. "What's with you?" she asks. I turn my back toward her and slowly roll up my shirt.

Two days later we're headed down Interstate 15 South on the way to the doctor. My mother has a Benson & Hedges in her left hand and the radio dial in her right. She drives with her knees. "No reason to tell Him," she says. In our house there is only one Him, and it isn't God.

"Why not?"

"You're not supposed to be sick. That's why."

Sick? That would be excellent. I could take one of the antibiotics that makes me throw up and get a rash all over my body—and the hair would fall out. If it's as easy as that, I'm happy. Dr. Frye has white hair and an unlined face. He steeples his long, narrow fingers under his pointed chin. "She's hirsute," he says. I don't know the term, but I can guess. It has something to do with the fuzz on my back. And arms and legs. And, as it turns out, on my breasts, buttocks, and face.

Dummy, didn't you know?

But I didn't. When you see something every day, you don't really see it. Sometimes it takes an alarm, a call.

My mother puts a hand on my knee. Her grasp feels steady and almost too comforting. I want to tell her that the diagnosis itself isn't the problem. It makes me feel warm at the temples, the pit of my throat, in my heart as it pounds. But this doctor is going to help. He's going to fix me.

"We'll want to look into this," Dr. Frye said. "If she were my daughter, I'd get it taken care of as soon as possible."

No, the diagnosis doesn't scare me. What I'm worried about is the swing into action. My parents can't even remember to water the lawn.

"We'll run tests," the doctor says. He marks a small sheet of paper with his physician's scribble and hands it to my mother. She grasps it with her long red claws, wrinkling the center.

But instead of heading to the lab in the basement, we leave the office and head toward the car. My mother's posture is rigid, her mouth determined. She holds her purse as a soldier might wield his weapon. The sun shines on my hairy face and gorilla arms. Peach fuzz now, but what will happen in the future?

"What about the bloodwork?" I ask. I sound like a classroom goody-goody, a wannabe perfect girl. I was once called *the mother of the class*. I'm still trying to figure that one out.

My mother hands me her purse.

"Get my keys out," she says. She's always asking me to do these small things—get my keys; bring me a drink of water; hand me a cigarette, the pack's over there—and I never say no. The keys are jangly and jagged in my hand. I run my finger along a ragged edge. I do it hard enough that it hurts.

"Stop fucking around," my mother says, and snatches the keys out of my hand. She can curse, but I can't. When I ask why, her answer is the same as when I ask why she can smoke and I shouldn't. "Because I'm stupid," she says.

"I'm not fu— I mean, messing around."

"Neither am I. Get in the car."

She unlocks her door.

"Are you mad at me?" I ask.

"Mad? Why would I be mad?"

"I don't know. You seem mad."

"I'm always mad," she says. "I'm a mother."

She pulls her purse out of my hands and tosses it in the back seat. A bit of paper escapes and flutters to the floor. She settles herself in the driver's seat and beckons toward the passenger-side door. "Get in," she says.

I'm still standing by the driver's side. I don't want to get in. Getting in means driving away. Driving away means no lab tests. No lab tests mean The Werewolf is still alive.

"Get," she repeats, "in."

"No," I say.

I'm not the kind of kid who says no. Until this moment, I wasn't sure I even knew how to do it. It feels good. It tastes like triumph.

And like all sweetness, it doesn't last.

"I'm going to give you until the count of three," she says. "And at two and a half, you're getting your ass smacked."

I don't move, but already I know it's over.

"One," she says.

Why is she so insistent? Is there a reason I shouldn't take care of what's wrong with me?

"Two."

Maybe she wants me to be The Werewolf.

"Two and a—"

"Okay," I say.

She leans over and unlocks the door. I walk around the car and fit my fingers around the handle. In my mouth is the taste of rust, the sting of defeat.

"Don't worry," she says.

We eat lunch at Hob Nob Hill, surrounded by wood walls and cosseted by leather seats. My mother has the corned beef. I choose the fish fillet. I've decided to lose weight.

"You know," Nails says, "we can take care of this ourselves."

I nibble on a french fry. Losing weight can be a gradual process.

"You're not a freak," she says.

I look up and meet her eyes. A freak. Something out of a circus. Is she sure?

"You're my daughter," she says. "I love you."

Nails doesn't bust out those words lightly. She's not what you would call gushy. "Thanks," I say.

When we come home the house is quiet and oddly peaceful. Middle is in school. Jonathan is at a babysitter's house. My father is at his Point Loma office doing paperwork.

"Come," my mother says.

She takes me into my bathroom, her sanctuary. She retrieves a yogurt cup from underneath the sink and a cigarette from her pack. She flicks a lighter and inhales. "Let me look at you," she says. "I'm not going to bite."

"I might," I say.

"You've got an awfully big mouth for someone so little."

"I'm not that little."

"You're not that big either. Come here."

It's three o'clock in the afternoon. Ronald Reagan is in the White House. WrestleMania is in Madison Square Garden. My mother opens a cabinet, retrieves a disposable razor, then takes a can of shaving cream from the tub. I focus on the can's red and white stripes until they seem to pulse in waves.

"You might have to do it every day," Nails says, "or every other day. You'll figure it out. It takes time, but you will."

Is she going to shave my back? My legs? My arms?

"We'll start with the face," she says.

Of course. You can cover up everything else. It makes sense.

"First I'll do it," she says, "then you go on your own. It's pretty easy once you get the hang of it."

Then her mouth crumples. She sits on the toilet and lights a cigarette. It hangs from her crimson lips and smoke rises to frame her face. Eventually she puts it out in the cup.

"Sometimes I just realize how much I hate your father," she says.

I put my hand on her shoulder.

"Mom," I say, "don't cry."

She stands up, rips a piece of toilet paper from its roll, and blows her nose. The sound is coarse, a call to action. "Okay," she says.

She turns a mint-colored tap, and water cascades into the sink. Steam rises and spreads. "Here," she says. She hands me a towel. It's warm and wet. I press it to my face.

"Perfect," she says. "The water softens it."

I think of Rock, Paper, Scissors. If the water can defeat the hair, what can the hair defeat?

Nails pops the plastic cover from the disposable razor. She runs it under the steaming waterfall then snaps off the tap. "All right," she says.

She starts with my sideburns. Bushy and generous, running the length of my face from ears to jawbone. I've noticed them, but I always thought they were normal, like eyebrows or the hair that springs from my father's knuckles. I have hair there too.

"It's okay," she says. "You're not an ape."

"Or a freak?"

"Where did you get that word?"

"You said it—at lunch."

"No, baby," she says. "You're not a freak."

I watch in the mirror. I think about the men who get professional shaves in barber shops, the careful motions of the blade. My mother is similarly gentle. Her motions are usually

13

sharp with purpose, but this is a special occasion. In a way, I feel lucky.

Dinner is beef and broccoli with a side of television. We serve ourselves and my mother serves my father, who sits in the small dining nook wearing only his underwear. Middle and I serve him drinks. He communicates through grunts and hand signals, pounding his chest like an ape for emphasis. Even Jonathan looks disgusted in his highchair.

We take our places at the scarred bleached-wood table. I want to roll around in the wheeled dining-room chair until I vomit, but I load up my fork and put it to my lips. *Small bites*, I'd counseled myself in my journal. *Chew well. Trick your stomach into thinking it's not hungry.*

"I took her to Frye's office today," my mother says.

Rooster makes a *humph* noise.

"He said she was—"

"Do you mind?" He doesn't take his eyes from the screen. "*Family Ties* is on."

Forget about slow chewing. I shove my entire forkful into my mouth and swallow it near-whole. Things simmer and blow between my parents, but even when they come to a head it means nothing. There are explosions, but the pressure never dissipates.

My mother bites her lip and contemplates her silverware. The action is not contrite. She is plotting. It makes my stomach churn. I fold my paper napkin in half and tear it along the crease. I curl and flex my toes inside my Keds. I chew my own lip and feel it start to bleed.

"Such intellectual pursuits," my mother says, "from the man who whacks off to *TV Guide*."

I picture whacking off as an athletic activity akin to golf: ready, aim, whack off.

"Did I tell you to shut up? Shut up."

"You can't come up with anything better than that?"

He clears his throat, points to me, then points to his glass. "Speak," I say. He grunts in response. "That doesn't mean anything to me," I add.

"The hell it doesn't."

"Okay," I say. "At least you said something to me."

"You bet I did. Get me a goddamned glass of soda."

"No."

His look is more complicated than anger. It's disbelief mixed with just a touch of admiration. What if he'd been at the doctor's office this afternoon? What would his expression have been then?

"*The Breakfast Club*," he says. "A gang-bang. All of you against me."

On-screen, Alex Keaton threatens his younger sister in a loving tone. If she doesn't get off the phone, he says, he'll force-feed her the receiver. The studio audience roars its approval. I don't want to be Jennifer, a chunky teenager sitting cross-legged on the side table, blonde bangs forming a solid wall across her forehead. I want to be Mallory, her ditzy, cute older sister, the one who knows how to dress, flirt, and piss off Alex.

"Hey," Middle says. He's fifteen months younger than I am. Like Jennifer, he just wants to be normal. "I didn't say anything."

"You didn't have to," my father says. "I know where you stand."

"I'm sitting," Middle says, confused.

I wait for something to blow this moment clear to the sky: a phone call, a puking fit from Jonathan, a meteor. It just bubbles and boils.

What would Rooster say if he knew I was hirsute? If I told him that my mother taught me to shave this afternoon? Perhaps I should crawl into the television, broadcast myself to him.

I ask: "Dad?"

"Do you mind?" He forks some broccoli into his mouth and stares beyond me, beyond all of us. "I'm watching this."

CHAPTER 2

1986

When the alarm sounds, it is as if someone unreal is calling—an ancestor from another land, perhaps, or maybe someone more recent. My great-grandmother, who died last year. Maizie is beckoning from beyond the grave. I slap the snooze button and refuse to answer.

Ten minutes later my mother is pounding at my door. "You," she says, "up." Nails is not a morning person. She starts each day with a Sinutab and a mug of coffee liberally spiked with Sweet'n Low and flavored creamer. She likes flavors that sound like booze: Amaretto, Irish Cream. When I ask her why she says: "If you were me, you'd drink too."

Nails' monosyllabic greeting is my cue: She's out of the shower and the bathroom is mine. Thus begins one of the most difficult parts of my day: making myself presentable for school. I choose my outfit out of a pile of dirty clothes: a pair of Girls Plus jeans from Sears, a striped black-and-white sweater. Vertical stripes, of course. *Dress thin*, I write in my journal. Take attention away from the fact that you're wide. My socks and underwear are clean. My bra is negligible. It is my first, a white piece of cloth with lace at the top of the cups. I'll soon need to buy more. My breasts are large already and will get bigger. I can tell.

Boys like big boobs. But they like skinny girls. How can you have both?

I bring the pile of clothes to the bathroom and lock myself in. It still smells of my mother's cigarette smoke. Mornings are so fragile. How can she light up this early, while the light outside is still tentative?

In the mirror I look like just about any twelve-year-old kid. Chunky, sure; dimpled, okay; but normal. Except for one thing.

I run the water. I get it good and hot. I press the washcloth to my face and picture the hair vanquished, limp and dying. When I remove the cloth, though, it's as thick and black as ever. Twice a day I face this moment: once when I shave in the morning and then again in the afternoon, trying to keep the stubble to a minimum. The hair offers a challenge. *Get rid of me*, it says. *Cover me up. I dare you.*

No effort is ever enough. Run the razor under the steaming water, get it sterilized. Work against the grain, rinsing the blade periodically, starting with the sideburns and proceeding inward. The chin left for last, where the hair grows thickest, covers the skin in prickly rows. I've learned to pull the skin taut as I work, letting the blade come closer. A confident, steady hand avoids cuts. It's necessary to concentrate. It's inevitable to wonder why I can't just have a gimp leg, a lisp, any of those normal disorders.

Rinse, working carefully to remove all remaining shaving cream. Exfoliate with the rough edge of the towel, getting the skin as smooth as possible. Later, after showering, apply foundation to even the skin tone. Pay special attention to the shadow, which remains even after shaving. Dot and blend, using caution to not end up looking like a clown.

But these are all Band-Aids. Anyone can see what lies underneath.

Missy and I are walking down the hallway, toward our lockers, when it happens. There's a cackle from a shadowy corner, and I can tell it's made for me. I try to ignore it. I put one foot in front of the other, focusing on the transfer of weight from toe to heel, the swing of my palms through the air.

"There it is," a boy's voice says. It's not yet changed, this voice. It still squeaks and cracks, an instrument not yet properly tuned. I am neither girl nor boy. I have no gender, no female or male pronoun. I am something in the middle, a hybrid. I am not a living being. I am a thing, an object like this Southern California school with its murals and wide swaths of greedy grass.

Missy starts talking hard and fast about nonsense. She has a sweet protective instinct, a mother's character in a body. Her hand is on my back. She is pressing me forward, past them, beyond this.

Another voice, this one lower than the last: "Lookit it go."

You don't care what other people think, I'd written in my journal. *It doesn't matter.*

High Voice: "Nothing can stop . . . The Animal!"

The Animal is a battery-powered monster truck coveted by Black Mountain's male population. How I took on the name of such a hotly desired object is beyond me.

Other peoples' opinions don't matter? Who was I kidding?

"Just keep walking," Missy says. Her watery blue eyes are sharp with some emotion. I can't tell if it's anger or concern.

"Why don't they die?" I mutter.

"Someday," she says, "they will."

Ours is a California school, hallways open to the elements, the sun free to beat on our heads and cheeks. I am more comfortable in contained environments, segmented spaces like my own house, places to hide.

We reach our lockers, painted magenta and white to reflect the school colors. I wish I had enough positive feelings about this place for those colors to mean anything. I want to like school, to feel that I belong. *You can't always get what you want.* Was it the Beatles who said that?

"Maybe it left its razor in its locker."

"Hey, baby, you need some shaving cream?"

The Rolling Stones. I remember that now.

My lock is cool and reasonable under my fingers. I know the combination by heart but can't coax the dial into the right order. The numbers, known and trusted, fail me. I want to break it open and stow myself in the locker. I want to close the door behind me and stay safe in the cool, quiet dark. That's my idea of bliss: shutting myself apart from the world around me, letting life continue while I curl up within myself.

Missy puts her hands on my shoulders. I'm just grateful for her presence, her willingness to be seen with me. I don't want my freakishness to pollute her or anyone. Not even me. "Which member of Wham! do you like best?" she asks.

"You mean there's more than one?" I deposit my English book in my locker, pull out Algebra. I love math. I love the logic of numbers, the possibility of proofs. I like knowing that there are reasons for something, anything.

"Of course. There's George Michael and . . . and . . . Andrew."

"Andrew who?"

"Like anyone knows his last name?"

She slides something onto my wrist: a hand-braided friendship bracelet. It is magenta, white, and black—Black Mountain Raiders colors and yet not.

"You know what? I think it's too hairy to even be a guy."

"I wish I could grow a beard like that."

"No, you don't."

"Yeah. I'd never want to be like that."

"Man." A short, sharp cackle; pointed and glassy. "Can you imagine?"

I am more than an aberration. I am frightening theory. I am a case study. I am a warning sign. I glance at Missy, then at my new bracelet. My lips quirk. I am all these things, true, but I am also something more.

I see life in terms of story, of image and detail. Even as I cringe from these boys, I am trying to figure out how to slot this into my journal, or perhaps a novel someday.

My mother writes too. Like me, she keeps a journal. But unlike me, she doesn't think to hide it. She leaves it on a stack of *Cosmopolitan* magazines next to the toilet. When I'm in the bathroom, I pick it up and read it. I mean, if she wanted to keep it private, she wouldn't have left it out in the open, right?

She writes in a journal that Middle and I bought her from Natural Wonders, the only bohemian store at the North County Fair mall. Each page is decorated with seashells and butterflies, studded with quotes from *Walden*. She writes in a clear, light hand of which I'm jealous. It's the type of handwriting they teach you in school, the kind I could never perfect.

Nails uses some serious words. She describes my father as diabolical and our family as dysfunctional. I am an emotional tyrant, but I'm also precocious. *What will I do with her?* she writes. *I worry.*

She worries. What if she saw me now, red-faced by my locker? Would she regret making the decision to drive away from the pediatrician's office? The lab slip didn't leave the floor of the car for weeks. Occasionally we stepped on it. Eventually it was picked up and discarded, and from there it passed out of this story for good.

The bell rings, and the ridicule ends without ceremony. I don't even know the boys' names. I couldn't pick them out of a lineup. I only know that they know me, and that is more than enough.

"Hey," Missy says. "Don't listen to them."

"Hard not to hear it."

"Try."

Effort defines my life. I try to be good: as a student, as a friend, as a daughter and a sister. I try to be fair: in arguments, at home, during softball practice when it's time to share the best bat. I try to hide: my face, my stubble, myself.

But what happens when trying's not enough? What if the odds are so strongly stacked against you that it's impossible to put up a fight?

"Okay," I say. There's no point in arguing with Missy. She's just trying to help. It occurs to me that Missy has never once asked why I have a beard and moustache, if I shave, if I'm a guy or a girl—everything I've heard from classmate after classmate in whispers as well as shouts. Maybe she wonders but is too polite to ask. Maybe she isn't curious. Or maybe she simply hasn't noticed.

Could that be it?

I always assume that the hair is the first thing people see. That it's what people think about when my name comes up. That it is me. But what if that's not true?

Nothing can stop The Animal.

Oh, it's true. It's true all right.

We hug goodbye. Missy is thin, but her grasp is strong. When she hugs me, I feel hugged. She heads off to Social Studies and I to Algebra. As I walk down the hallway, I see my classmates: surfers in Billabong shirts, punks with black lipstick and greased hair, lovebirds grappling against walls. The world seems divided into two: the place where they stand and the spot where I hope to hide.

I reach class without anyone hollering. Inside is what you'd expect from a seventh-grade classroom: the posters, the bulletin boards, the pictures of famous mathematicians. It all feels innocent in a way, innocent and secure. I take my seat. Here I feel protected.

But later, waiting for my mother to pick me up in front of school, the feeling changes. I feel as if I'm standing in an open field, an easy target. It's a trap made of white stucco and lush lawns, marigold school buses and canvas Keds. Small details call out to me: a ripped leaf on a tree, a half-flat tire in the parking lot, the triangle on someone's jeans that says "GUESS?" Guess what? I have no idea.

The kids over by the bus stop are making fun of me. It's like a wave, a tsunami: one minute it doesn't exist and the next it's taking over your life. The ridicule rides on pointed fingers and open mouths. It surfs the roar of laughter. It emerges through faces framed by San Diego Padres caps and shaggy, unkempt hair. My ears are red, my cheeks flaming.

Then it's gone.

There are kids by the bus stop, sure, but they're not paying attention to me. They're not even looking in my direction.

Was it a hallucination? Some sort of waking dream? Or was it real?

My mother pulls up. She looks young and happy in her little Accord. I flop into the passenger seat. "Have I ever told you," she asks, "how much I hate your father?" Well, there goes that illusion.

"You've mentioned it."

She shifts into first gear and motors forward. I picture her toes on the gas and clutch: level off, balance. My mother favors ballet slippers and tennis shoes. Her feet are small and sturdy, determined. "He's the King of Fucktard Mountain," she says.

Nails has cursed in front of me for as long as I can remember. One time Missy had to take me aside to ask what the word *twat* meant and why my mother had used it to describe our teacher. *Twat* is one of my mother's favorite words. "Twat's twat," she'll say when in a philosophical mood, and that's that.

"Divorce him."

"Don't tempt me."

"I'm not. I'm saying do it."

On the hill there are houses you might call by flashier names: Mansions. Estates. They separate the occupants into wings: Parents. Children. Servants. They yawn across this land of barren brush: red roofs, white stucco, golf-course front lawns. Of course their occupants are as lost as I am. I'm still jealous. At least they look like they have it together.

My family? We're a shell. And it's cracking.

"I can't afford it," Nails says.

"Not everything's about money."

"Honey child," she says, "in our world it is."

My bedroom straddles the border between ridiculous and sublime. It's reached by climbing the curved cherrywood staircase, then turning down a long curving hall. Turn right by the cigarette-scented pink-and-green bathroom and you'll walk into a kid's paradise. Huge windows. A walk-in closet. A window seat whose wood reflects the sunshine. And a ladder that leads to a small upstairs loft.

I spend most of my time in that L-shaped space, locked away from the world and even most of my own quarters within it. I do my homework up there, leaning my notebook against my knee for balance. I read Jackie Collins, dog-earing the good pages, the ones with sex and fight scenes. Outside the window is the mossy pool and spa, which aren't cleaned nearly often enough. No one in my family really swims. My dad just chlorinates the water every so often.

I'm up in the loft when the phone rings. It's Missy. "Paul Castle threw up in class today," she says. "Mrs. Love told him to run outside and puke on the grass, but it was already too late."

I'm twisting a bit of string around my finger like they did in *The Breakfast Club*. The tighter I pull, the redder and more swollen it gets. "What happened?"

"The custodian brought in some sawdust to soak it up."

"*NAS*-ty."

"At least we didn't have to do it."

"What happened to Paul?"

"What do you think? They sent him home."

"He could puke there."

"Exactly."

Then her voice drops, goes low and confidential. "Can I ask you something?"

I hate when people do that. Either ask or don't, but don't ask if you can ask. It never leads to a question that I want to answer. "Sure," I say.

"Why do you . . . I mean . . . why . . . um . . ."

The string goes tighter.

"I don't know how to ask this."

Tighter.

"You know, what happened today."

I unwind the string and begin to chew on it. "No. I don't know."

"The guys. The ones who . . . you know, made fun of you."

"Can we talk about something else?"

She's trying so hard to be polite. I can hear her sweating. "Missy," I say, "can we drop it?"

"It's just that . . . I'm worried about you. Are you . . . sick?"

I don't like what she's getting at, and I'm certainly not interested in answering her questions. "I'm fine," I say.

"Allison," she says, "you're not." And that's when I hang up.

For a few minutes I sit very still. My only motion is the moving of my mouth as I chew: the string, my fingernails, the skin of my wrist. The string is wet and soggy in my mouth. I spit it out and it lies like a corpse on the dusty-rose carpet. That's what my mother calls it, dusty rose. But it's just gray.

A knock.

"Yeah?"

"You going to let me in?"

"Door's unlocked." For once.

Nails turns the knob and walks in. She's wearing a sweatshirt that says NEW YORK LAUNDRY and black leggings. My mother sometimes dresses like a teenager, and it suits her better than it would me. "Where the hell are you?"

"Up here."

I sit above the ladder and dangle my legs to freak her out. It works. "You're going to fall off that ridiculous thing," she says, sitting on my bed and lighting a cigarette.

"I'm fine."

"That's what you always say. Until you break your head. Come down here."

I climb down the ladder with slow, deliberate motion. Let her think that I'm being good to my body. That I would care if I broke every bone in it six times over.

"Sit down," she says. I perch on the window seat. I like lying here in the afternoon sun, lazily reading a book, feeling myself grow drowsy as I turn the pages. I look at her and realize that my mother is beautiful. She has long, feminine eyelashes and a ready smile. If she's hairy in any given place, I don't know about it. I certainly don't see any stubble on her face. How did she know how to shave, then? Did she read about it in some book somewhere? Did she look it up in the World Book Encyclopedia that our grandparents bought for us?

"What did you mean," she asks, "when you said, 'Divorce him'?"

My nails find my palms. My toes wiggle. She's asking me for my opinion.

"I meant divorce him."

"But what do you mean by that?"

You mean there's another meaning?

"I shouldn't be talking to you like this." She takes a drag and puffs out a lopsided smoke ring. "But you're precocious. I feel like I'm talking to a grown-up. I need your help, Allison."

She needs my help?

"Let's go for a ride," she says.

My mother thinks best when she's in the car, on the road, on the move. All possibilities seem to unfold themselves. Knotty problems unbraid, flow free with resolution. Maybe it's just the freedom of escaping from our house, that French Country monolith in the San Diego hills. We drive down Valle Verde and make a left on Espola, heading toward the 15 Freeway. Its landscape looks particularly barren today, almost stricken. Thin, pained trees. Reticent scrub brush. Dirt and dust.

Nails downshifts and takes a right onto Pomerado Road. Here the environment is more forgiving: sprays of flowers in the median with cheerful signs thanking the Boy Scouts for planting them, a few garish churches, a token senior center. Evidence of life and humanity. She merges northbound. The territory surrounding the road is a weird moonscape, ravaged every few years by fire, stampeded and tamed by rescuers only to bloom and burn again.

"You realize we won't live the way we do now."

"Competing with the TV? Being called from down the hall to find the newspaper that's lying right next to him? Getting yelled at because we didn't give him our used toothbrushes to scrub the bathroom tile?"

She laughs. It's a laugh that stings with so much more. There's grit, pain edged with grim humor. I take it as encouragement.

"We'll be fine," I say.

I should mention that my mother doesn't believe in seat belts. "What if something explodes?" she asks. "What if we drive into water?"

She takes an exit and points the car up a steep slope. I start to sweat. "We're on a mountain. There is no water."

"Use your imagination." She smokes and drives with a single hand. Sometimes she plays the radio and drives with her knees. She tells me to relax when I grip the dashboard. I'll relax when I'm safely home in my room, up in the loft, door locked, no one to come in, look, speak, intrude. I'll relax when my life is in my own hands. That's not going to be for a while.

"You want me to leave him."

"I want *us* to leave him."

"It won't be easy."

"Neither is living with him."

We're tearing up the mountain. There is no posted speed limit, but whatever it is, I know we're doubling it. At home she claims to suffer spontaneous heart attacks if we so much as misplace a dish. Somehow that never happens while she's scaring the shit out of us.

"Please slow down," I say. My voice sounds more grown-up than I am, husky somehow. It sounds as if I'm speaking somewhere extremely solemn—a funeral service, perhaps, or a wedding. Somewhere where you dress in black or white and carry flowers.

"We're fine."

"*You're* fine. I'm about to puke."

But that's not the feeling, not exactly. It's the same feeling I had earlier today, listening to the boys call me The Animal. It's a feeling of ridicule, of disrespect. It tastes like metal in my mouth. I have nowhere to spit, nothing with which to wash it out.

Nails jerks the car to the side of the road. "I don't think you understand. We need him. We may not love him or even like him, but we need him. Do you get that? That sometimes you need what you hate?"

"No," I say. "I don't."

She starts to turn the car around. We're at the crumbling edge of a steep drop-off. I picture the tires scrabbling for purchase on quickly eroding ground. I've seen a million horror movies like this, and not one ended well.

"Look," she wrenches the wheel to the right and I close my eyes to choke back the panic, "of course you don't get it. You're a kid. My job is to take care of you."

The laugh comes out before I can stop it.

She slams on the brakes.

This is it. Either her palm will flash across my face, sharp and stinging, or she'll indulge in a breakdown and we'll be stuck on this fucking mountain forever. She laughs too, ascending notes that resemble the graph of an earthquake, or perhaps the lie detector test of someone guilty as hell.

"You think you've got it real rough," she says, "don't you?"

Don't I?

"Other kids have miserable parents. They deal. You know?"

"Other girls," I say, "don't have a beard."

The word feels dirty. It's an intruder in my mouth. I don't want to use the word beard in relation to myself, but there's no other way to get the point across. After the words leave my lips, I wonder: *Am I the only girl with a beard? Are there others? Where?*

Nails hits the gas hard and I feel the tires spin in the side-of-the-road dirt. One false move and we'll wind up in Lake Hodges, who-knows-how-many thousands of feet below us. I expect her face to be grim, but she's smiling. This is her definition of fun. Living on the edge—the literal version.

"No, you're right. They don't. Which is why I taught you how to take care of it. You're doing a good job, actually. I can barely see anything."

"Maybe your eyes aren't as good as everyone else's."

I feel the tires spin, then stick—we're going down. I hope it'll be quick. I want to feel nothing. I pray the impact will be . . . gentle? Is that even possible?

"Is that right?"

And like that, we're back on solid ground. We're traveling downhill at a rate of speed that makes my heart feel like bursting out of my chest, but at least we're off the edge. I'll give her that.

"Forget it," I say.

Her hand moves in a series of small corrections, a blur of Florida Red nail polish. This is my mother, the one and only. I need to remember that.

CHAPTER 3

1988

I commit to lying my first day of high school. Standing on a basketball court, wearing baggy shorts and a frayed shirt. Thirty of us in this physical education class. I'm guessing about twenty-eight of them can dunk a better free throw—or whatever you do in basketball—better than I can. And that other kid? He's probably on crutches.

Our teacher is Ms. Sarver. Sharp of nose and rough of voice, she plays the part down to the whistle around her neck. She's a cross between an Olympic gymnast and Hitler. I like her. I like her honesty and her directness. I like how she doesn't play favorites. Most of all, I like how she's not like the other girls in this class, full of giggles and falseness.

What I don't like is how tough she is. When Ms. Sarver teaches PE, you're exercising. There's no getting out of it. First she has us do sit-ups—fifty, then catch your breath, then fifty again. Then come push-ups—and not girl push-ups either, the kind that allow us to rest on our knees. To Ms. Sarver, a push-up is a push-up, whether you're a boy or a girl, and there's no half-stepping it.

Then we run laps around the court. Running is my enemy. I am the anti-runner. If a physical activity were a person and I could kill it, running would be dead in the corner. I wheeze around the curves, wishing some sort of natural disaster would strike and save me. Fire? Earthquake? Hell, I'd take a good rainstorm, which counts as a natural disaster in San Diego County. Anything.

She comes out of what seems like nowhere. She's got teased hair and a viper's smile. She is blonde and blue-eyed and thin and all those things that everyone like me wants to be. She grabs me by the shoulder and we both stop running.

"Do you shave?" she asks.

For some reason I remember her name is Brandy. I'm not quite sure why that matters, but it does. Brandy will forever be a skinny-girl name, the name of someone who wanted to know something I didn't want to tell.

"No," I say.

I know that I'll need to be consistent with whatever I say. Saying yes would mean more explanations than I'm prepared to give. Saying no—well, they may not believe me, but what can they do about it? They can take my word or not, but I'm not going to give these people any more ammunition. Yes, the answer is no.

She smirks at me. My toes curl inside my Reeboks. A drop of sweat rolls down my back. My heart feels like a gun firing, *rat-tat-tat*. This was not the natural disaster I'd wanted.

"You two!" It's Ms. Sarver, blowing into her whistle from across the court. "Move it."

Brandy doesn't move, doesn't say anything, doesn't change her expression. Each second that ticks by is an accusation: I am a liar. And I'm not about to change my story.

"Girls! Are you deaf?"

Ms. Sarver's howling isn't affecting me the way a teacher usually would. All my good-girl instincts have been transferred.

I feel that Brandy needs to give me permission to move on. She must tell me it's okay to move.

But there's just her smile, and it's a trap. She's wearing lipstick the shade of a scar, a bruised pink. She doesn't show her teeth, but I picture them anyway: sharp little bits, something offering worse than a simple sting.

Her smile says, *Tell me the truth.*

"No," I say again. "I don't."

"Okay," she says, and starts jogging again. I watch her go. She wears red sneakers, and they kick up dirt with each stride. I feel those clouds entering my lungs, choking me. My knees are shaking and my teeth feel soft. I'm not sure what hurts worse: Brandy asking me the question or my giving her a lie for an answer. Lying feels like a block of concrete in my chest. It is stone, unreasoning. It is wrong.

But what am I supposed to do? Admit that I shave like a man? Not in a million.

I wait for her to gain a good lead, and then I begin to run too. Really it's less run and more shuffle. My shoes are white, not red, and I doubt I'm disturbing the dirt. I want to feel free, in flight. I just feel like I'm choking.

Once I've completed the lap I stop and pant. Why can't I run like the rest of them? "Allison," Ms. Sarver says, "come here for a minute."

Up close her nose is less sharp and her smile is soft. She puts a hand on my shoulder. "You okay?" she asks.

I'm not sure anyone's ever asked me that before. I don't know how to answer. I focus on her shirt. It says "NIKE" and has that swoosh symbol. The cloth looks comfortable, loose. I wonder what flaws it covers.

"Sure," I say. Lying to her is easier than lying to Brandy. Maybe I'm getting used to it. Maybe it'll continue to get less painful.

Everyone else is running another lap. Some are looking at me: Why did *she* get out of it? I worry that they'll label me the apple-polisher, the teacher's pet. That's not what I want. I want to be the troublemaker, the one who lives in detention. Those girls have style. They have flair. I'm not exactly sure what "flair" means, but I want it.

"Yeah?" The difference between her and Brandy is that Ms. Sarver is smart. She doesn't just take the easy answer and jog away. She sticks around and lifts the heavy weights.

Here's where I'm stuck. I could lie once more, have her question me again, and we could continue in this loop for the rest of the year. Or I could tell her the truth.

I hate the truth.

A shrill ring. It's a cliché for sure, but I'm saved by the bell.

Missy meets me at my locker, wearing sunglasses and a snarl. It's so unlike her that I want to laugh. I ask her what's going on.

"Mr. Wendt," she says, referring to her algebra teacher. "What a douche. He can't even spell."

"He teaches math. No one said anything about spelling."

"Whatever. He started yelling at us and told us that the way we were acting was a farce. Then he wrote it up on the board and spelled it out: 'F-A-R-S, farce.'" She shakes her head and her long straight hair swings around her cheeks. "I can't believe these are the kind of teachers we have."

"It's kind of funny, isn't it?"

She looks at me for a minute. I feel good. I feel like I just saw the lighter side of the world. I like pointing out the humor in situations. If you look closely enough, you'll always find it.

We take our lunch bags and head for the quad, finding a shady spot under a tree. Around us students mill around, eat, laugh. Are they as relaxed as they seem?

"Well," she says, "that's the highlight of my day. How about yours?"

There is no way in hell that I'm telling her about what happened during PE. Hopefully she's learned that I won't talk. She could threaten me with knives, guns, any weapon you care to pull out of your pocket. Take me prisoner, hold me hostage, starve and beat me. I'm not speaking about it.

I tell her about my English class, which is taught by something called Mrs. Love. It's tall and deep-voiced and looks like Julia Child. It is unlike any other person I've met. "That's why it's an it," I say, and immediately feel dirty when Missy laughs. Who am I to be calling other people *It*? Even if it feels good. Even if the joke's on someone else for a change.

The English class isn't like any other class I've attended. Mrs. Love had us pull our chairs in a circle. This is going to be a discussion, she said, not a dictatorship. We shifted and kind of laughed. I wondered how many people in that room even knew what a dictatorship was.

"Then she gave us our reading list," I say. The list had some of the screwiest titles I'd ever seen. *Flowers for Algernon. Slaughterhouse Five.* And a short story called "Yentl the Yeshiva Boy," which spawned *Yentl.* I didn't remember much about the movie except it had Barbra Streisand, who I always found annoying down to her sharp Jewish nose.

"Oh yeah," Missy says. "The one where she disguises herself as a boy."

Who would ever want to do that? Why would anyone want to deliberately put themselves up to be mistaken for a guy?

37

"She does it so she can study," Missy says. "They wouldn't allow girls into religious training."

"How do you know all this? You're not even Jewish."

"I watch HBO," she says, and I could swear there's a note of pride to that.

The Poway High School quad feels massive, transcontinental, like if you walked to the other side you'd better speak Russian and wear a muff to keep your hands warm. It's a series of alternating strips: concrete, grass, then concrete again. Planters, trees, picnic benches where kids flick french fries at one another. Far off in Siberia is the Drama Wall, where theater people congregate and emote. Nearby is the Filipino Wall, and catty-corner from that is the Jock Corner. How do I know all this on my first day? One word: observation.

"My parents had a fight last night," I say. I'd had no intention of letting those words leave my mouth. What let them loose?

"Yeah?" Missy asks. She unwraps a foil-covered peanut butter sandwich, grimaces, and takes a bite. She doesn't like what her mother packs her for lunch, but she's too lazy to make her own. I can respect that.

"Yeah," I say. I don't want to go any further. Right now I feel like I'd rather talk about *Yentl* and all its implications than go into everything to do with my parents. It's just too much. I don't understand all of it, and I wish I didn't understand what I do.

"They talking to each other?"

"No," I say. After the fight they populated their own corners of the house, much like the separate cliques here are doing today and more than likely do every day. Nails has the bathroom. Rooster, the bedroom. We, wherever we can hide.

She offers me a Devil Dog and I take it. In my mouth the sweetness tastes like comfort. The wall across from where we're

sitting is Peer Counselor Territory. They were the ones who
did our orientation this summer. They seemed so comfortable
with themselves, so confident and friendly. Maybe if I'm a peer
counselor, someday I'll be like that.

"What was it about?"

I don't want to tell her: It was about me.

When they fought, I just hung out by the top of the stairs and
listened. I couldn't help it. It's like I had no choice, and maybe
I didn't. He started the fight, which is unusual, not because he's
such a nice guy but because my mother usually does more of the
talking, which typically leads to more of the fight-starting.

He didn't use the word *freak*, but I knew that's what he meant.
What I didn't know was that my mother has the same thing I do.
She must not have it as badly, since I never noticed anything, but
maybe I just wasn't looking hard enough. It happens.

If she fixed herself, he said, I wouldn't be the way I am. But even
I know that wasn't true. She could never have prevented those genes
from being passed down. I know that. Why doesn't he?

CHAPTER 4

1990

Tina's house is a museum, but an oddly comfortable one. Plush carpet, china cabinets, and granite countertops on the kitchen's center island. Outside there is a pool, a barbecue, and a friendly dog. Anything seems possible in her parents' cushy living room with its expensive audio equipment, heavy bookshelves, and a mini-fridge containing all the Coke we can drink and burp up.

With her I am nothing like what I am with Missy. With Missy I am both considerate and considered, calm and seemingly collected. But Tina is different. She brings out the brass in me, the bitchiness. All my hard edges show around her—and I kind of like it.

We're the only sophomores on the Poway High paper, and somehow that's made us close friends. Tina is a booming Goliath to my short and stumpy David. Her femininity is an aggressive fragrance applied with a heavy hand, her bearing that of someone years older. It wouldn't be that hard to mistake her for thirty-five. Forty, even. And that's my parents' age. Old.

"Do you have confidence," she asks, "or don't you?"

She says it as if it were something you could check off your grocery list. Grapes, pasta, toilet paper—and, oh yeah, confidence. Something you could take off the shelf and tuck into your cart. An item with a price, payable at the end of a neatly contained shopping trip. A unit of exchange.

"You need to look at people straight on," she says. She leans back in her father's butter-colored recliner and slaps her ample thighs. The sound brings forth the family's standard poodle, the loyal and sweetly stupid Thor. The dog shambles in and nestles his snout in Tina's crotch.

"Come on," she says. "Let's practice."

"Practice what? Me staring into your eyes while your dog eats you out?"

"Don't be a moron." She slaps Thor away. "He's neutered."

I shrug and get up for another Coke.

"Diet Dr for me," she says.

"Since when?"

"I didn't tell you? I got approached at North County Fair."

San Diego can't call a mall a mall. Our shopping centers bear names like North County Fair, Fashion Valley, Horton Plaza, names that herald major architectural achievements when really all that's there are some yogurt shops and the Gap. "He was an agent for a plus-size modeling agency. I have my first shoot next week."

She's always coming up with drivel like this. "If that twat Tina said the sky was blue," my mother's fond of saying, "I'd check to make sure it hadn't turned purple."

Now I say: "If it's plus-size, you should be drinking two Cokes."

"Yeah, actually, you're right."

I come back juggling the three frosty cans.

"Okay." She taps the top of the can with a perfect acrylic-filled nail. She and my mother go to the same manicurist. "About this confidence thing."

"What about it?"

"Do you have it or not?"

How do you answer that? I've never been asked a question in such a point-blank way. But Tina doesn't waste time with tact. I hate that about her, but in a way I love it too.

"I have as much as you have."

"Well," she says, her eyes surprisingly downcast, "you may need a little help then."

She takes me into her pink-and-gold bathroom. Then she reaches into a cabinet and pulls out a salmon-colored tackle box. "First we'll wash your face," she says. "Give us something fresh to work with."

It's a makeover. The word makes my heart pump and my forehead flush. I don't want anyone deciding what color to paint my eyelids, my cheeks, my lips. I can't take the thought of anyone getting that close.

But how to tell Tina no?

She takes out a facial scrub called Mountain Sea Breeze. It makes no sense, but does any of this?

"I'll do it," I say. I don't want her washing my face. I don't want her touching my skin.

"Okay," she says, and hands me a washcloth.

The scrub is expensive and feels good. It smells of mint and musk, an odd combination that somehow works. I feel both ancient and refreshed, as if I'm about to become the world's oldest, cutest prostitute.

"Scrub it down deep," Tina says, looking in the mirror and squeezing a blackhead on her nose. "It'll get your skin clean."

"It hasn't worked that well for you, pizza-face."

"Keep scrubbing," she says, "bitch."

I'm scrubbing and she's popping, and at long last we're both done.

"Okay," she says. "Now, the philosophy."

Tina can't just reach into the tackle box where she keeps her beauty potions. She's got to give me the academia behind the image.

"There's a reason they say put your best face forward." I hop up on the counter and swing my feet against her bleached-wood cabinets while she expounds. "It's not just a saying. It's what life is."

"Mary Kay? Clairol?"

"Laugh," she says, "but yes, in a way it is."

I imagine the universe as a constellation of products: lipstick, eyeliner, blush. Instead of stars there are mirrors, a sky filled with reflection. In place of the sun is a giant eye. Everything revolves around judgment.

Tina puts on a serious face, which makes me want to laugh even harder. She looks like Miss Piggy when she concentrates— protruding snout, wayward eyes—and in the moment I like her for it.

"Allison," she says, "you've got to pay more attention to your looks."

In a way that's all I do. But how can I tell her that?

"You keep paying attention to my looks," I say, "and I may file a restraining order."

She's busy fishing in the tackle box, pulling out potions that will change my life. "You're a winter," she says.

"Aries, actually."

"Close your eyes," she says, "and shut the fuck up or I'll stab you with an eyebrow pencil."

Fifteen minutes later she says: "Look."

Reflected in her surrounded-by-Hollywood-lights mirror is . . . me. But different. Better. My eyes dance with color and mischief. My lips are rosy with promise. She's even combed and teased out my hair, giving it body and bounce.

"See?" she says.

For once I don't see the shadow across my lip and under my chin. For once I see myself as complete rather than a creature-in-parts, a jigsaw puzzle.

"Gosh," I say. The word has absolutely no power to convey my feelings at this moment. No word does. It's possible for me to be a pretty girl. Beauty is available to me. This opens an entire new world.

She puts a hand on my shoulder. I turn to her and smile.

"I can help you more," she says.

End of revelation. The world stops spinning on its axis. Fireworks no longer go off. I know what she's getting at. And I don't like it. *I can help you more.* It's the verbal equivalent of a stare, my daily enemy along the school halls. It makes me want to find a closet, shut the door behind me, and curl up in the cool quiet blessed dark.

"No," I say.

"You don't even know what I'm offering."

"I don't care. I don't need it."

"Allison," she says, "people see. They *talk*."

My picture of the universe shifts, becomes a series of lips pressed to ears, playing Telephone. *You see? She shaves!*

Tina reaches into her medicine cabinet. "Bleach," she says. "I bleach my moustache every few weeks."

"I don't want to talk about it."

"It's nothing to be ashamed of."

"Whatever."

This is shades of Missy, that apologetic voice on the phone asking what was wrong with me. Except here I can't hang up. I can't even walk out the door. I can't move.

"You don't have to do anything. Just sit there. I'll take care of it."

Who talks?

What do they say?

Do I even want to know?

Tina washes the makeup from my face. "Close your eyes," she says, and I feel her dot every problem area with cream. Then she sets the kitchen timer for fifteen minutes—longer than that and my skin might break out. As my mother might say, I need that like I need a pair of testicles.

To pass the time, we watch her father's tape of *Debbie Does Dallas*. The women in the movie have bad perms and bushy hair between their legs. The men have instant hard-ons and perma-smiles.

"Okay," she announces after the kitchen timer chimes. "Time to get that stuff off you."

"But the guy hasn't even *come* yet."

"Use your imagination."

She cleans me up, then leans down to inspect my face.

"Maybe you need a different kind," she says.

I check the mirror. Same five-o'clock shadow. I want to ask her to reapply the makeup, but it's clear she's lost interest. I call Nails to pick me up. When she gets there, she asks about my afternoon.

"Fine," I say. "Fine."

As we pull out of Tina's driveway, I notice that my mother is smoking with less vehemence than normal. Her jaw, normally taut, is so relaxed as to border on slack. The parts that make her up—lips, eyes, hands—move with confidence.

She flips on her blinker and makes the right turn onto Poway Road. "There's something your father and I need to talk to you about," she says.

It's got to be the hair. It's in so many places now: back, breasts, belly, in addition to the face. I'm betting they've consulted and come up with a plan. Maybe they'll take me to get the lab tests done. Maybe they'll talk to me about electrolysis, which makes me flinch even in concept. Maybe they'll just tell me they love me, that I'm not a freak. Nails told me that years ago, but I need to hear it now.

"Sure," I say. "What?"

"We'll wait until we get home."

It's going to be a team thing. That's unusual. They must be serious. I'm not sure whether to sweat or to be relieved. Something is going to change—that much feels clear—but I have no way of predicting what that change will be. The future is always uncertain, but today it is uncertain in a different way.

We drive past strip malls and community parks, car lots and fast-food joints. They call Poway the city in the country, but it sometimes feels more like a mouse of a suburban stripe. Civilization eventually gives way to a lift in the road and nothing on either side except sharp drops. From here we could go north to Escondido, east to Ramona. We turn toward the west, where the land and sun end. Ours is a withered Mercedes-Benz, a cream-colored sedan with a four-speed transmission. My mother shifts with what I could swear is triumph. What's *she* so happy about?

"We're not divorcing *you*." Rooster is crying. Crying! I'm not sure what shocks me more: his tears or the fact that this isn't all about me.

The center island separates him from us three kids. My mother stands off to the side, out of the picture. If she could hole up in the bathroom, or even the pantry, she'd do it. Her nails, so red and sharp as to be surreal, curl into her palms, yet she looks calmer than ever.

A divorce. Joint custody, weekends with Dad at some anonymous apartment crammed with all his stuff. Hiring of lawyers, arguments over who gets what. My mother will fight to the death for the Beatles records and Cat Stevens' *Tea for the Tillerman*. That I know.

He gestures to me and calls me *Igg-les*: the nonsense word I spouted so often as a little girl that it became my nickname. "You look upset," he says. "Do you want to talk about it?"

"I just want to know," I say, "what self-help book you read to come up with this spiel."

He cries *harder*. Ready—aim—*fire!* All that sparring practice with Tina has paid off. This is payback for the nights when we were shushed in favor of Alex P. Keaton, the days when he buried himself in paperwork so he didn't have to face us. This is the thanks he gets for yelling more often than speaking, for ignoring rather than listening. This is revenge.

I think about the phrase *broken family*. As if human relationships could ever fit together in a neat jigsaw to begin with. As if fragmented fighting belonged only to the divorced. Ours has always been a broken family. Now we're just making it official.

Now we stand in our kitchen, an ill-fitting place with all the wrong priorities. There are too many hard surfaces and not enough cabinet space, a huge center island with cheap cooking equipment. We have a walk-in pantry, but not enough spices, a bread box with nothing in it. Shiny image wins again.

We're five people bound by genes and something that can be felt, but not named.

Eventually Rooster's sniffles dry up. My mother disintegrates and reassembles somewhere far away. One by one, the rest of us do the same.

I don't climb into my loft, steadying myself with shaking hands. I go outside. Our backyard is a forgotten place that doesn't deserve the neglect. Leaves idle in the corners of our pool, congregate in our raised spa. Ants crawl along the built-in barbecue. Agapanthus bow their purple heads. They too have heard the news.

Out here the air smells different, less polluted. The intake of breath washes my lungs. The release cleanses them. There's a rhythm to the rise and fall of my chest. It's predictable. It makes sense.

The tears come as a shock.

Certainly this was expected. I can't ever remember a time when my parents were happy. Except I can. A flash of a grin in the car, a laugh overheard in the middle of the night. One time my mother fell ill at one of my softball games and my father helped her to the car, his hand in hers, his other at the small of her back.

They are the exceptions that prove the rule, but right now I'm not sure what that rule is.

I sit on the ground, on a patch of what my parents call stamped concrete. It's regular concrete gussied up with a pattern. Ours is made to look like brick. It may look good on its own terms, but you'll never mistake it for the real thing.

From my perspective I can see the back of our house. It's the bad side, the one where all the weird angles collide. Every house has its bad side. Edges have to meet somewhere. The patchwork is laced with a series of outside spotlights, small bulbs meant to be strategic. There is too much gray here, not enough green. Once we dreamt of vegetable gardens. At five, Middle happened upon a package of radish seeds and planted them. They were torn up months later when we put in the pool.

The light is on in his room. Is he thinking? Escaping into a magazine or wrestling on television? Staring at one of the many bikini models who decorate his walls? I don't know him well enough to figure out what goes on behind that closed door. We are not close, never have been.

Not like Jonathan and me. He's the brother I hadn't wanted, the brother I couldn't live without. I was furious when my mother announced her pregnancy, but then he was born and everything changed. Our bond began at the beginning of everything. From the moment I saw the red-haired screamer in his hospital cot, my heart fell into a new, yet-unintroduced place.

Was it sisterly?

Was it maternal?

Was it the meeting of two new best friends?

My belief in reincarnation began with the birth of my younger brother. I knew this person from back in the day, from another lifetime. God had recycled souls, and we were the result.

I should go to him, hold him, comfort him, at the very least tickle him to make him laugh. He is all of four years old. His world is changing, cracking, crumbling. But I can't bring myself to traverse the path between the backyard and his room. That's because, unlike Middle, I know what he's doing: the same thing I am. He is mourning in his own way. On his own terms. In his own time.

We live at the edge of a winery. Coyotes prowl there by night. They call out to one another, their cries rising and falling in the darkness. I know from my *World Book Encyclopedia* that they do this most often during the spring mating season and in fall, when the pups leave their families to establish new territories.

I let out a short, sharp moan. I wish it were my turn to go. I close my eyes and rub the lids with vicious fists. Behind them appears a laser-light show of patterns, an set of optical fireworks. I wonder if I am doing damage to myself. I hope I am.

Will I miss my father? The thought occurs to me mid-rub. It surprises me enough to make me stop and blink back into vision. He's leaving. What does that mean to me?

The first answer that comes to mind: *Not a whole hell of a lot.*

I can't figure out whether that's loathing or indifference. Maybe there's just a fine line between them. I pluck an agapantha from the ground and begin to strip its leaves. He loves me, he loves me not. It ends up on *he loves me not.* I snap the stem and throw it to the ground. I wish I could believe that, but I don't. It would make things easier, but that's not the case.

When I was eight years old, he stood next to me at Straw Hat Pizza. It was my softball banquet. I held a pepperoni slice in my hand, the grease tumbling, staining the web between my thumb and forefinger. My father ran his hand over my hair, his fingers tangling in the dark wayward locks. His touch felt sincere and more than a little scared, as if he weren't used to this, the show of affection.

I pluck another agapantha from the ground and bring it to my nose. It smells of nothing.

After the banquet ended and my father walked me to the car, anger twisted his voice. Why? Does the reason ever matter?

I throw the flower into the pool—let it lie there with the leaves.

As a child I wanted things: piano lessons, braces, therapy.

"Next year," my father said with each flip of the calendar.

"Not now," he said when I pressed the issue.

I picture him in his underwear at the dining-room table, scratching himself like some sort of rhesus monkey, belching like something out of a John Waters movie. He wanted to turn up the television, drown out reality.

Let him go. Let him go to hell. I don't mean that. Yes, I do.

I run my hands through my hair. How can the stuff on my head be so soft but what grows everywhere else so rough? So many sides to everything. How to tell which one is real?

"My mom's keeping the house," I tell Missy. We're sprawled out in my loft eating kettle corn, idly flipping through issues of *Tiger Beat*.

"How's she plan to do that? She doesn't have a j-o-b."

"Alimony," I say. "And something else."

Nails is going to do something honorable. Something that will give back to the community. Something unique.

She's becoming a real estate agent. She's going to buy a ritzy car, put on some pretty clothes, pick up a sharp haircut and get a regular mani-pedi. She's going to sell houses.

"Your mom couldn't sell hairspray to Madonna."

"Never know until you try."

"No," she says, "in this case I already know."

Missy likes everyone except Nails. It dates to the time my mother forgot to pick us up after school and we wound up walking three miles home in the freezing—for San Diego—60-degree cold.

"What's your dad doing?" she asks.

"He's already rented a place."

She already knows where. He's taken an apartment at The Boulders, where everybody's father goes to live during the divorce. I'll bet my beard he doesn't last throughout the yearlong lease. Rooster likes room, a place to spread his wings and crow.

"You see the place yet?"

"No. We're going this weekend." A Saturday afternoon surrounded by boxes, eating Kraft Macaroni and Cheese, watching snowy television on his rabbit-ear black-and-white. I can't wait.

Missy concentrates on a kernel of corn, drops it in her mouth with a delicate touch. I notice her slim fingers, the sharp cut of her jaw. Missy's growing up. She's becoming a lady. "You talk to Tina lately?"

"No." I'm lying. Missy's jealous of our friendship. The envy makes me feel good, wanted.

"She's kind of . . . low-class."

"Where'd you get that phrase from?"

Missy waves a copy of *Tiger Beat*. "Oh, bullshit," I say.

This isn't the first time she's brought up the idea of class. I'm not even sure what that word means, only that it means a lot to her.

My mother puts a premium on class too, but something tells me that her vision differs from Missy's. Nails thinks of class as existing within the confines of custom-home developments, the places where she takes me for driving lessons. There are ulterior motives at work. She's also trying to get clients.

"Speed up," she told me during one lesson. "See that Rover in front of us? Follow it."

Range Rovers are a novelty. They mean money. *Money* signals class.

"See how they're crawling past the big houses?" she asks.

"This is The Trails. They're *all* big houses."

"Then keep following, smartass, and don't lose them."

I find myself telling Missy this story, relating how the Rover pulled over beside an outsized gate flanked by palm trees.

Beyond it could be a dirt lot for all I could see. That's the appeal of The Trails—not that there are beautiful homes, but that there are beautiful homes you need to buy to see.

"Stop here," she said.

"Jesus." Missy rolls her eyes at this part of the story. Something tells me she would've reacted just as I had.

Nails yanked up the emergency brake and we flew against our seat belts. Then she stepped out of the car and approached the Rover. I cringed in the driver's seat and imagined how it went down: She slapped on the charm, no doubt. My mother is good at the stranger approach. I'm sure she worked them, welcoming them to the neighborhood, asking about their beautiful car and the dog licking its empty sac in the backseat and whether they've been considering working with a Realtor (this word is always capitalized, even in speech) to find their dream home.

Maybe she really felt the spiel. Maybe she felt she was offering a type of bedside manner, something more commonly found in psychiatric clinics and shoe stores. *This*, she thought, *is a way of helping people.*

She got back in the car and closed the door. It shut hard and solid in that German-car way. *Thwack.* "I've met someone," she says, and she starts to weep.

I pull out the choke, turn the key, and concentrate. Left foot on clutch all the way in. Right foot poised over the gas. Level off.

"And that," I tell Missy, "is the first I heard of Bill Sullivan."

Bill Sullivan. The name comes into our home like an unwanted act of God, a tornado perhaps, a hurricane. A monsoon, and there are no life rafts.

It begins in the way I will later begin my own relationships, with disdain. "He's twenty-four years old," she tells me the day my brothers and I are supposed to visit our father. We're standing in the kitchen, my mother smoking with abandon. No one to hide it from now. "Less than a decade older than you. And still not enough brains to come in out of the rain."

Bill recently joined her real estate office. He is dark of eye, fair of skin, incipient of muscle, the owner of a Saab with expired Alabama tags and a cat named Vampire. I met him once and wasn't impressed. "He tells me things," she says, "but I don't really listen."

Again there are tears. Hard and fast, unexpected, they hail from a sky that has yet to even turn gray. I know better than to say anything during one of these storms. I focus on the pictures that hang on the wall: my great-grandmother as a young woman, my great-grandfather with a straight back and mischievous eyes, my parents' wedding photo, looking like what they were: two kids dressed up at the local JCC. There's me missing a tooth and Middle missing four, and Jonathan, the baby, the charming afterthought, two hours after he emerged.

Nails reaches into a basket and pulls out one of my father's socks. I hadn't thought he left anything behind, so methodical was his packing and pullout, but here is evidence. She uses the bit of cloth to wipe her eyes and blow her nose.

"He needs someone," she says, finally. "Anyone."

I picture him as a giant baby, a backwards-baseball-cap-wearing infant rocking and burping on her shoulder, settling down to a series of quiet hiccups. Do they make diapers for people old enough to vote? Sure. They're called Depends.

"It's just platonic," she says. "In case you're wondering."

I'm not. Platonic or not, who cares? She could be this guy's goatherder and she'd still be totally obsessed. I picture Nails as one of those gushing girl reporters in *Tiger Beat*: Sources say BILL needs a home! He needs somewhere, ANYWHERE!

"His landlady is sexually harassing him," Nails says.

I snort.

"You don't believe me?"

I snort again.

"All right. If I wanted your editorial opinion, I'd beat it out of you."

My mother has hit me once in my life. I was twelve years old, spinning around on one of the kitchen chairs, mouthing off. Nails asked: *What kind of drugs are you on anyway?* I answered: *Wouldn't you like to know?* She hit me so hard I spun around twice.

Now I turn on one heel and walk away.

Bill's possessions arrive before he does. Boxes piled in the garage. "He just needs some storage space," my mother says. "It's not like we're putting the stuff in your room."

"Not yet."

"What do you want from my life?"

Today my brothers and I are going to see our father. It's been a week since he officially moved out. I say "officially" because the process seemed to take a year. He filled up his hatchback, pulled out of our curving driveway, rinse and repeat. He left an empty space, and now Bill has claimed it.

The kitchen phone rings. Tina.

"Is Mr. Pennzoil there yet?" That's her nickname for Bill. It stems from his hair. Too many products and not enough result.

"Nope." My mother is over by the sink lighting a cigarette. She looks young and radiant. Divorce as a makeover.

"Call me when he gets there. I'm coming over. This I have got to see."

"Circus act," I say, and immediately regret the metaphor. Freaks. Bearded ladies. My mother glares at me and draws a red talon across her throat. "Got to go," I say.

"Queen Latifah getting pissed?"

"Something like that."

I replace the phone in its receiver. Nails takes a long puff and chuffs out a line of smoke. "If that twat Tina said the sky was blue," she says, "I'd look outside to make sure she wasn't lying."

"Good to see you kids getting along."

"Don't be sarcastic." She studies her reflection in the back of a spoon. "It's unattractive." She peers closely at me. "Come here."

"Do I have to?"

"Get your ass over here."

I walk over to her, feet dragging with reluctance. What does she want to lay on me now?

She takes her hand and tips my face upward. "Razor burn," she says.

I flame from forehead to chin.

"Are you shaving like I taught you?"

I push her hand away.

"It's ugly, Allison. Ugly."

"What do you want from my life?"

She raises a hand. Shades of twelve years old, a kitchen chair out of control beneath me. "You'll break a nail," I say.

She mutters something under her breath.

"You got something to say?" I focus on her hand, still raised, as I speak. "Say it."

Her lip quivers. She looks like a disappointed little kid at Christmas, one who received a gift certificate to a store that went out of business.

"Oh yeah," I say. "Cry. Because that helps."

57

The first tear is a victory strike. So are the second, third, and tenth. She looks like a rhesus monkey now, a sobbing zoo creature taken out of its natural habitat.

When she hits me it feels like a relief, like something I've been anticipating. Let's go. Break it open, bring it on.

"You made me do this," she says.

My cheek hurts. Shit. She clocked me.

"You and all the abusive husbands in the world. What a cliché."

Her cigarette is still smoldering between her fingers—fortunately not in the hand she used to hit me—and it singes her. She tosses it to the tile floor and steps on it, grinds it with her heel. That'll leave a stain. A memory. Every time I want to revisit this moment, I can look at the burn mark on the floor. Does tile even burn? I will remember without the reminder.

"You," she says. "Always you."

"Yes, Mommie Dearest."

"Always with a quip. A hard line. You're hurtful. You walk around like you have spikes sticking from your skin."

The phone rings again. We both ignore it.

"You're not owed anything in life," she says. "You're not entitled. You're a kid. You're under my roof. You're subject to my rules. If you don't like it, you can leave."

"I'm tempted."

"Go, then." She's contemplating hitting me again, I can tell. She walks away. My mother is not intimidating when she walks. She looks like a little kid shuffling along the street. I don't feel empathy for her. I'd be incapable of empathy for anyone at this moment. I can't even feel sorry for myself. She was right. Always a hard line. Always a nasty thought.

Speaking of which, it's time to go see my father.

Rooster shows us around, clucking. His two-bedroom
apartment is lined with boxes along every wall. Most of these
will never get unpacked. My father doesn't know how to
limit, take what he needs and leave the rest. He grabs eighteen
toothpicks when we leave a restaurant, twenty mints. He needs
everything, so long as it's free.

"This is just a temporary thing," he says. "I'm house-hunting
on the coast. I'm done with living inland. We did it for the
schools. That was your mother's thing. No more for me."

I stand in his living room and count off everything that used
to live in our house: the ugly plaid couch where Middle and I
sat and played Nintendo; the glass-topped coffee table that once
featured a picture of me as a baby; a print of foxes playing poker.
It'll never get hung on the wall, I can guarantee you that. I'm not
even sure why he took it. My father doesn't like art of any kind,
even the bad stuff.

He's placed a barbecue on the small balcony. "Do you know
how to use that?" I ask.

"No. But I'll learn."

I haven't seen the bedroom and don't want to. I know what's
there: the bed in which my parents used to sleep, the television
on which we all watched the World Series play-offs when the
Padres were contenders, and, of course, their Beatles records.
They had an enviable collection and most were still in the
original shrink-wrap. My father will never listen to these records.
He may never sell them either. He may just keep them and crow
over his triumph—they are now his alone.

He has never addressed the facial hair. Does he not see it?
Does he not care? Or is there some strain of sensitivity, of tact,
that prevents him from bringing it up?

I remember a conversation between him and my mother after they'd returned home from a company party. I was six, spying at the top of the stairs. "Chuck thinks someone should talk to her," he said. Chuck was his boss, a guy with a moustache and a white sports car, a bit of a David Hasselhoff rip-off.

"And what exactly are they going to say?"

"They're going to say, 'Peggy, you have a beard.'"

My mother said in an *I-need-a-cigarette* voice: "Like she doesn't already know?"

I think about Bearded Peggy, my father's colleague. Did she know, or was she like me before someone pointed out the hair on her body? What would even be the point of doing that? Why did Chuck care?

Maybe it bothered him to see a bearded lady every single day.

My brothers sit on the plaid couch, looking lost. My father's home may be cluttered, but it offers no distractions from the awkward tension. There are only boxes and packing peanuts, not even the bubble wrap that you can pop. My father takes a seat in his battered recliner. I perch on a folding chair, the kind you bring to a kid's baseball game, low like that.

"I want you to be honest."

Yes, I think, *you are an asshole.*

"Whose fault is the divorce? Mine or your mother's?"

A vein throbs in the middle of his forehead, a sure sign that he's going to blow his cool if given the wrong answer. We don't say anything. Middle pretends deep interest in his thumbnail. Jonathan investigates the bottom of his shoe. Me, I just bite my lip until it bleeds.

"Well? You deaf?"

Hear no evil, see no evil, speak no evil. How are we supposed to take sides?

"I don't want to talk about it," Middle says. We're all startled. He's never the one who speaks up. He's the middle kid, the quiet one, the one whose pressure is internal, simmering, waiting to blow. I see my mother in him at this moment, the youthfulness and femininity. I wonder how long it would take for my father to beat it out of him. I'm surprised he hasn't already.

The vein throbs harder. "What does that mean?"

I want to see him as wounded, vulnerable. I see him as ugly. In his being, in his soul, where these things count the most. He is tainted and tortured. He is emotionally bereft. He is the stock from which I come.

A cough. Then a gag. And then Jonathan throws up on the carpet.

My father's fist slams on the coffee table. A familiar sound, a familiar feeling. You couldn't spill a glass of water in our house without him doing that and then yelling—as he does now—"God*dammit.*"

Then he breaks down.

He's crying again. Seeing him do this makes absolutely no sense. It's like a Jewish star atop a Christmas tree. Sure, you can put it there, but there's something wrong about it. None of us kids say anything. We don't approach him. We don't offer comfort. I find some paper towels and a bottle of Resolve and tackle Jonathan's mess. By the time I'm done, so is my father.

"Okay," he says, and blows his nose. "Okay," he repeats, and honks into the tissue once again.

I'm not sure what's worse: feeling sorry for someone or *wanting* to feel sorry for them. Wanting has that special form of guilt: the *if-only-I-could.* But I can't.

I expect the house to feel different when we get back. Rooms rearranged, perhaps, or the scent of skunk. But it's that deceptive type of normal, the kind where the stench is perfumed over by a squirt of air freshener. You can still smell the rot underneath.

And there's a duffel bag in the entryway. It's got an elephant on it. It says "Big Al." The University of Alabama mascot, and I know this only because I pick the bag up and examine it from all angles. Carefully, gingerly, as if it were a dangerous parcel set to explode.

"An elephant," Middle says, and raises his foot to kick the bag. At that moment, my mother walks in. She's not somebody I recognize. She too is papered over, hidden and brittle.

"Down," she says, as if talking to a dog. I open my hand and drop the bag with a *thunk*. My brother, startled, forgets to put his foot down. He looks like a karate master frozen in the moment.

"Good," she says. Then she turns on her heel and leaves. My brother finally lowers his foot. I look at him, arch my eyebrows, and hum the *Twilight Zone* opening theme.

"This is fucked," he says and stalks off to his room. Jonathan follows. It's just me and the duffel.

I drop to my knees on the marble floor and begin searching through it. Suntan lotion, hair gel, a sweatshirt that says "BUM"—truth in advertising—and a gold mine.

His journal.

Bill writes? Really? I imagine there aren't enough crayons in the world to contain his vacuous thoughts. I zip up the duffel, palm the journal, and hustle up the stairs. As I pass the master bedroom, I hear them whispering.

"You wouldn't have to leave," Nails says. "There's plenty of room."

"Your kids hate me."

"They don't know you."

Not yet, I think. *Not yet.*

CHAPTER 5

1991

Senior year means planning for college. This finally gives Missy and Tina something in common. The three of us are sitting in the school's career counseling office, listening to Ms. Stark give a presentation. As far as I know, Ms. Stark has no first name. She also seems to have no neck. I pass Tina a note with this observation. She writes back in her loopy scrawl: *Probably has no vag either.*

"This isn't just college," Ms. Stark says. "It's not just the next four years. It's your future."

I swallow a smirk. My future? When you're on the college track, the word *future* gets crammed down your throat so much that it becomes a mantra. Say it enough times and it loses its meaning. It becomes just another two-syllable word.

She passes around a handout called "Mapping Your Future." *Original,* I sneer to Missy in a note. She raises her eyebrows in response.

"The first step," Ms. Stark says, "is to look at yourself."

I start to laugh, but at the last minute it comes out as a cough. Missy kicks me under the desk and Tina smirks in my direction. If Ms. Stark notices, she doesn't comment.

"You have to know yourself," she says, "to understand how you want your future to look. You're all different, of course. One of you may want to go into business. Another one of you might want to fix cars. And one of you may even want to be a career counselor."

She smiles. It doesn't really save her face—her teeth are too yellow and her cheeks too red—but it does humanize her.

She looks like Frankenstein's monster. I'd put a bolt in her neck if she had one.

Unfortunately, Tina's note makes me laugh—for real this time. And this time Ms. Stark notices. The smile becomes a hard grin. She says nothing, just fixes me with her eyes. I notice for the first time that they are a deep brown, so dark as to be almost be black. Eyes like Rooster.

"I'm sorry," I say.

I'm not sure how to look at myself. Do I use smoke and mirrors, or can I handle a clear vision? I glance down at the handout. It tells me to assess my skills. Ms. Stark has us break up into groups to begin the process. Tina, Missy, and I pull our chairs into a circle.

"Skills," Missy says.

"Mad skills," I say.

Tina chews on an acrylic nail.

"We've got to come up with something," Missy says.

I sweep the room with my eyes, pretending to be lost in thought. The thing I notice—that no one can help noticing—is the posters. They're everywhere, sponsored by every school. At Duke, students congregate on a patch of grass, clustering over a book and laughing. At Brandeis, a blonde girl is ruminating amidst blurry classmates. At Harvard, a co-ed group kicks a soccer ball.

I am not scared of leaving home. I am. I'm not.

"What are we good at?" I ask.

"Not speaking English, apparently," Missy says, curling a strand of thin, straight hair around her finger.

"It's called colloquial," I say, "bitch."

Across the room Ms. Stark glances at me and clears her throat. Man. Does she have *radar*?

"Let's make lists," Tina says.

I fiddle with my pen, chew on it, tap it on the desk. I know I'm being irritating, but really, I'm just filling the moment. Tina and Missy scribble on their sheets of paper. They have something to say. Why don't I?

Writing.

It's not something I think about. It's nothing I consider a skill. I'm not counting on it to land me a job, and most of the time I forget that I even do it. But I do. I write short stories and poems. I write confessions to myself. I rip up what I write. Most of it, anyway.

Writing tops the list. What else?

If I can write, I can communicate. And if I can communicate, I can think. Right?

Somehow I doubt all this is what's going to get me into college. They want to know your grades, your awards, the clubs you were a member of. Or, for Missy, of which you were a member.

I blank momentarily. I've gone to Poway High the last four years, and I can't remember a damn thing I've done.

Time's up.

Bill writes too. He fills up pages with a third grader's scribble. But his tone is not juvenile. It is grandiose and callow. He has an observation about everybody: Middle is a *pussy*, Jonathan a *brat* and my mother *pathetic*. I'm *the hairy-backed little toad*. When I first read that, I gasped audibly. How did he know?

My mother probably told him.

She tells him everything. They are constantly wrapped in conversation: in the master bedroom, the kitchen, sitting at the base of the stairs. There are days I practically trip over them and they ignore me. Those are the days I go and steal his journal.

I've been reading it for more than a year now. I stop after a few entries. What I read makes my stomach hurt. He has insane ideas. He wants to own an airplane, buy In-N-Out Burger on a generous monthly payment plan. He wants to date models. He wants to *be* one.

How do we achieve our dreams? How do we reach our goals? Give it your all? Or write it down and hope for the best?

"You want to be a writer," Ms. Stark says, "but for what? A magazine? A newspaper? You need to be specific. That's where success comes from: specificity."

You may not have a neck, I think, *but your ass more than makes up for it.*

"Just saying you want to do something isn't enough," she says. I feel rather than hear Tina snickering next to me.

"You asked us what we're good at," I say. "I answered the question."

The room is silent. Even Tina's laughter stops. Sure, you can snicker behind a teacher's back, pass notes and ridicule her, but you don't dare pose a direct challenge.

"Skills are not enough," she says. "It's how you use them. It's how you plan to take the opportunities when they come."

Opportunities. The word sounds unwieldy, a jumble in the mouth. It sounds as though it has one too many syllables, as if it's trying to take too much on. Like it's trying too hard.

Missy raises her hand. "I want to be a veterinarian," she says. Missy, the peacemaker. Missy, for whom confrontation is like kryptonite. She's trying. But for some reason, I've dug in my heels. I *want* to fight with this woman.

"I'm going to write," I say, "for myself."

It's as if I've spoken in Bulgarian.

"It's not a job."

"It can be."

"Allison," she says. I'm not sure how she knows my name, and it doesn't sound quite right coming from her lips. "You're fooling yourself."

"Why? Because I want to do my own thing?"

"No. Because you don't even know what that thing is."

And the thing of it is, she's right. I know what I have, but not how to use it. Even my mother says I'm a good writer. "And you're going to take advantage of it," she told me during a rare conversation in the kitchen a few weeks ago. "Not like the one upstairs."

They were having a fight. It happened every so often.

"Why not?" I asked. "He's taken care of."

"Not for long."

The first time she issued this threat I got excited. Now I've heard it multiple times, and it's lost its luster.

Now Ms. Stark is looking at me with the eyes on her no-neck head. "You're right," I tell her. "But I'll figure it out."

College. It has a ring to it like a gong, a call to action. It terrifies and excites me, often in the same breath. It feels unreal, untouchable, a mirage.

I will go, of course. I was raised with the idea that college was not an *if*, it was a *when*. I'm not sure how I'm going to do it, though. Once I had a college fund, but I have a sinking feeling that most of it is going to San Diego's finest legal counsel.

Divorce. The word is part of our daily vocabulary. It's like a rock band that stopped being good years ago but just won't die. My parents' marriage was never good, but the divorce started out excellent, full of drama and promise. Now it's just getting old.

My father asks me about my plans over Chinese food. I watch him fumble with his chopsticks and debate how to answer. Do I go smartass and tell him I've decided to eschew school for pole dancing? Or do I get serious and ask him if there's any money left to finance it?

Finally I say: "I'm applying to a few places."

"Like?"

"Well," I say, "I haven't gotten that far yet."

I'm confused by the catalogs. Glossy and gorgeous, they make every place look ideal. Students flocking to classrooms, athletic fields, dorms. The latter scares me more than anything. How am I supposed to shave when my room is shared and the bathrooms communal? Where are you supposed to find privacy when you're all living on top of one another? The catalogs don't say anything about that.

Lunch is just my father and me. Middle's off playing hoops with his friends. Jonathan's at home. Neither wanted to come. I can't blame them. But I'm the one who feels a sense of obligation. I'm not sure why. I just do.

"How do you plan to pay for college?"

The kung pao goes sour in my mouth. Well, there's my answer. "I'm not sure," I say. The words feel thick, cotton between my teeth.

"There's big trouble in River City," he says. "I'm just giving you a heads-up."

Since when did my father start talking like a dime-store cowboy?

"There's no money," he says. "None. It's getting eaten up because your mother won't go to mediation. You know how much it costs every time we go to court? Plenty."

No money for college. None. I will either go into debt or I won't be able to leave San Diego. And despite my apprehension, I want to leave. I want to pack and buy a college pennant. I want to stay up late cramming for finals. More than anything, I want to leave my family's mess behind.

"Okay," I say.

"That's all you have to say? 'Okay'?"

"Yes," I say. "That's about it."

"You're on your mother's side."

"What about *okay* means I'm on her side?"

"You've always been on her side. All of you. The Breakfast Club."

For a moment I try to look at life from my father's perspective. Bitch soon-to-be-ex-wife. Ingrate kids who won't even stand by him in his moment of need. Out to get him. Breakfast Club.

Or does he see the world in a softer way?

"Dad," I say, "I'm not out to get you."

We sit in the silence that follows. Around us there is conversation, laughter, perhaps a raised voice or a yawn or two. The restaurant's white walls are closer to beige, the floor a flowery linoleum. I am on my own.

CHAPTER 6

1992

I am eighteen.

I find the baseball bat by the side of the mattress. Bill's mattress. He's placed it on the floor of what was once my parents' bedroom. Now the room lies bare apart from a crooked picture of my mother's family—my grandparents, Bernie and Dolly; Nails; my Aunt Eileen. My father took most everything, no matter whether it was nailed down, but he didn't want *that*.

I take the bat in my hand. There is a piggy bank at my feet.

I lift and swing.

One thing about that moment: It's just a moment. My life doesn't roar through my ears. The highlights don't flash before my eyes. The regrets don't make my cheeks grow rosy, don't cause my ears to roar. I'm not about to stop *breathing*, for crying out loud. I'm not dying.

I don't so much kill anything as set it free, break it wide and open.

My mother and Bill meander outside. I see them from the bedroom window, two small stick figures roaming the adjacent winery. Insignificant, both their lives and mine, so pinheaded and inconsequential. Why should they or anyone care what I do next?

I hit the pig spot-on. No equivocation, no trembling, no regrets. It explodes, barfing out coins. Pennies, nickels, dimes, and quarters. I drop my weapon and collect my reward.

Bill hasn't been in real estate for years. Now he's a server at Red Lobster. When his tips come in coins, they go into the pig. He must be a lousy waiter, because he seems to receive *all* his tips in copper and silver. That pig must hold a couple hundred bucks.

Now it's all mine.

The pockets of my jeans can't contain all of Bill's change. I'm plotting a stealth trip downstairs for a grocery bag when I hear the front door swing open and thud shut. That movement steals a puff of warm, stale air from the outside. The heat flows over the entryway floor, up the curving cherrywood staircase, along the hall, and through an arched doorway before slipping through my nostrils and into my lungs.

They're back.

The pig's a goner. His snout lies at an angle across the room. The ruins of his chin rest on his crushed front paws. Where are his back legs? I have no idea.

I kick him once, then again. I kick him for spite; I kick him for revenge. "Take that," I say, "you damned—*pig*."

My mother and Bill move further back into the house, toward the kitchen. They're not going upstairs. That buys me a little more time. I pluck up a few final handfuls and stuff them wherever they fit: my bra, my pockets, a few in my mouth, where their taste stings.

This is almost certainly the worst thing I've ever done. Trespassing, stealing, assault on a ceramic animal. Still, I hadn't expected to feel guilt. I especially hadn't expected to feel the kind of guilt I'm feeling—crushing, as if an army of football players was perched on my chest.

It's supposed to be revenge. It's supposed to be what's coming to him. Two years he's been here, and while it's a little too easy to say things get worse every day, it's accurate enough to say they haven't improved. Not long after he moved in, my mother gave him the master bedroom suite. She spends nights on the living-room couch watching television, staring at the wall. She won't smoke in front of him. Ever.

They are wrapped in an incomprehensible relationship marked off by stakes and spikes, fencing off all outsiders. It is neither friendship not romantic connection. It is not even in that murky in-between. It is a place and passion all its own.

I should bust it up. Throw down the gauntlet and maybe a few of the pig's smashed limbs. Demand that my mother in fact *be a mother* and that he *leave this house this instant.*

Yeah, that sounds good.

I hide in Jonathan's room. Lock the door. Pick up the phone. Call Tina. "I'm fucked," I say. "Save me. If I take my car, she'll report it stolen."

By the time Tina's magenta Ford Escort with the laughable sport package pulls into my driveway, it's all over.

Before that, my mother finds me. She's wearing one of her rictus smiles, teeth lined up like one of those old-fashioned black combs Rooster likes to tuck into his back pocket. That smile tells me one thing: *You're dead.*

"When you leave," she says, her enunciation deadly, "you will *not* come back."

"I wasn't *trying* to steal," I say, regretting the words before they even leave my mouth.

"Pack. Take everything."

"No."

"Do I need to do it for you?"

Jonathan stands just outside the kitchen, his little feet steadying him on the small landing that leads past the walk-in pantry and toward the center island. He's seven. He's got a red-headed bowl cut, broad shoulders for a kid, eyes greener than the rest of ours. "Where's she going?" he asks.

"Out." My mother's voice is ice, ceramic. No sadness, no second thoughts.

"She's *throwing* me out."

"Jonathan . . . upstairs . . . now."

He says: "Don't leave."

Tina arrives. I hear her stereo, Guns N' Roses. In the kitchen, she tries to reason with my mother. She keeps calling her by her name: Joan-Joan-Joan. She presses her every Speech and Debate Club skill into service.

"Take her," my mother says.

"Joan, Joan. You don't mean that, Joan."

"Get her *out* of here. I don't want to *look* at her. Jesus, would you?"

And there it is: the lesson. You can find and target anyone's weak spot. It doesn't take a genius, just observation and a little luck. Narrow down, zero in, fine-tune your crosshairs. Pull back your hammer. Trip the trigger, watch it fly, see it connect, revel in the impact.

"I tried to help her," she tells Tina. I stand near the walk-in pantry and watch my mother's lipsticked mouth quiver. I want to fold myself in there and shut the six-paneled door, hide and snack on Triscuits and matzoh until all this blows over.

"She's not *normal*," Nails says. "That's *her* problem. She makes it everyone else's problem. Does she ever do that to *you*, Tina? Make it your problem?"

From the adjacent living room, a series of *bleeps*, *bloops*, and the occasional morbid musical note: the Nintendo. Two sets of laughter, one childlike, the other only slightly less so. It's not just Jonathan in there. Bill is sitting on the couch next to him. They're competing at something with pixels and already-outdated graphic design. They're developing a rapport.

"Let's go," Tina says. I've already packed a bag. I shoulder the duffel and follow her. I can hear my mother planning a smoke, that treat she allows herself and thinks is so secret. She doesn't say anything as we leave. Neither do we. Yet it feels like something final, a closing of something that can never be reopened in the same way.

Tina starts the car and turns down the stereo. Guns N' Roses doesn't sound right muted. It's like caging a bison. She takes a curve, downshifts, and shoots me a stern look. "Your mother's *fucked*," she says. "That's pretty much all *I've* got to say."

No one's ever put it quite like that, but if there's someone to do it, it would be Tina. Fucked. Really? Does that mean she's the villain? I never saw her that way. Maybe we're programmed not to give up on our families. As much as we want to, as hard as we try, biology won't allow it.

"Fucked," Tina says now, again, as she turns onto Espola Road. This is Poway's backbone. It leads to everything: school, my mother's real estate office, and eventually Tina's house. She lives on the other end of town, a fifteen-minute drive away. Long enough for me to catch my breath. Hopefully.

"You don't think I screwed up?"

She lays her hand on my arm: friendly acrylic talons. Through the rolled-down windows come the scents of jasmine, of azaleas: summer. "Define 'screwing up,'" she says.

At summer's end we will go our separate ways: Tina to Angelo State University in Texas and I to the University of California, Santa Barbara. It is a three-hour drive up the coast. I will be putting three counties—Orange, Los Angeles, and Ventura—between my family and me. I'm not sure it's enough, but UCSB gave me a good deal on financial aid. It also has a great student newspaper. I envision myself as a collegiate cub reporter, nailing down the UC Regents in a single series of questions. I will be front page. I will be big news.

Missy got into Berkeley. That didn't come as a surprise to any of us. Gentle, smart Missy, my sweet friend. Yet I chose Tina to save me in this moment, possibly because gentle and smart could easily break me at this point. I need a hard edge to work against, to sharpen myself. That's Tina.

When we arrive at her house, her parents are sitting in the kitchen and smoking. Tina can get on my nerves at times, but I love her parents. They want me to call them Harry and Andrea, but I sometimes still think of them as Mr. and Mrs. Matier.

"Allison's spending the night," Tina announces. "She got kicked out."

I feel my eyes roll practically to the back of my head. Did she *have* to?

"Allison," Harry Matier says, "sit down."

I take a seat at the spacious glass table. Tina's father is short and stumpy, hairy and friendly. Her mother is blonde and cool with a wicked sense of humor. When they fight, they scream, but somehow it doesn't scare me.

"All right," he says. "What's going on with your crazy mother now?"

Tina's parents don't like mine. Never did, still don't. When they talk about my family, they use words like *self-centered* and *neglect*. It doesn't occur to me to be offended. I can handle the truth.

"She—" Tina can't contain herself.

"Look, girlie. I didn't ask you. I asked your friend."

I restrain a grin. Tina's father can slap her down better than anyone else I know.

"Well?"

"I'll deal with her," I say.

"Want to tell me what she did?"

"Kicked me out."

"I hear. Can you expand on that?"

I like how Mr. Matier—Harry—talks to me as if I'm a grown-up. After all, I'm eighteen. I kind of am.

"I kind of—smashed a pig."

"Smashed a pig."

"Yes," I say, and start to laugh. It's funny. How could I not have realized that this whole time? Using a baseball bat to smash a piggy bank that is shaped like a pig. Stealing money that some waiter got by slinging cheese biscuits. Oh yeah; it's funny.

The laughter gets louder, more high-pitched. The problem is that I'm the only one who's laughing. It echoes within their white walls and bounces off the granite countertops. It pings off the ceiling and bounces back to hit me in the head. Finally, I stop.

"Smashed a pig," Harry says.

"Well," I say, "sort of."

"A ceramic pig," Tina offers.

"Girlie," her father says, "I'm warning you."

"I'm just trying to help."

"Save it," he says.

Andrea Matier lights another cigarette and puffs out a sleek line of white smoke. "I don't care what you did," she says.

She doesn't?

"You're a kid," she says. "It's your mother's job to take care of you."

But she doesn't. I can't say I've accepted that, but I've gotten used to it. I see the panic in Nails' eyes when she's called upon to do something motherly, like writing me an excuse note when I've been absent from school. As graduation neared, she didn't even do that anymore. I wrote the note myself and then I signed her name, and nobody could tell the difference.

"She doesn't know how to do that job," I say.

I look first at Andrea Matier, then at Harry. Both sets of eyes search me, looking for some sort of answer. I can't provide it. I'm not even sure of the question.

I sleep where I've slept so many nights throughout high school and now in this summer of change: the pullout daybed in Tina's lipstick-colored boudoir. I sleep, but I do not sleep well. I dream intermittently, waking with my fist wrapped around the iron headboard, clutching.

She threw me out. I have no money and nowhere to go long-term. For a panicked moment I try to remember if I brought my toiletries with me: Do I have a razor? Then I realize the answer is yes and I relax, but not enough to sleep.

It is June. I leave for Santa Barbara in September. I don't know how I'll get there from here, but I'll have to figure it out. I think about a little girl I saw in a cafe a few weeks back. She wore a yellow slicker and a huge smile. Her father steadied her on a chair, danced with her. She grinned at him with all the trust in the universe. I once had that trust. What picked up a baseball bat and smashed it to bits?

Tina sighs and shifts in her bed. I experience a wash of feelings about her that I can only know, not name. It's not jealousy and it's not friendship. It's not anger, but neither is it warmth. Perhaps the best word for it is *ambivalence*, that state of conflict. I am ambivalent.

The alarm screeches us into morning. It is seven o'clock, and Tina must get ready to go to work. She has one of those faceless temporary office jobs, something to earn her enough cash to put posters on the white walls of her dorm room. Before she stirs, I barricade myself in her candy-cane bathroom. It's one of those Jack-and-Jill types, a long sliver sandwiched between two bedrooms. Double sinks, a built-in makeup vanity, even a telephone.

I've finished shaving my chin and am about to start on my upper lip when the door opens. Dear God. I'd only locked one door, not both.

Tina claps both hands to her rosebud mouth. "Oh, nutsacks!"

She's caught me. Red-handed, red-faced. Dancing around the subject is one thing, but her *seeing* me with a razor to my face is exponentially worse. My feet go tingly and my ears flame. Why couldn't she knock?

"I'm sorry," she says.

I'm still standing there with shaving cream on my face and the BIC in my hand. "Why?" I ask. My voice sounds like a blade, a quavering thing. Not only can it nick, it can also cut.

"You shouldn't have to go through this," she says.

I take a towel and press it to my face. I toss the razor in the trash. I want to erase all signs of what she's just witnessed. I want to cover up and stay covered. She's right, but what does that matter? I *am* going through this.

"Thanks," I say. I have nothing else to offer, no words that will pass through my throat and across my lips. I am tapped out. I am depleted. My knees buckle under me, and I find myself sitting on the floor. It is cold and yet safe down here. Tina offers me a hand and I take it, but reluctantly.

"Al," she says, "I have to take you home. I don't want to, but I've got to work."

I need to leave. I can't stay here.

"The cleaning ladies are coming today. It's going to be chaotic when they're working."

And it's not chaotic at home?

"Al," she says, "I'm sorry. That's just how it is. You can come back when I'm home from work. They should be gone by then."

When did she start calling me Al? Al is a man's name, something hairy and hard. I don't want to be a man. I don't even want to be a woman. I want to be a girl. I want to enjoy shopping, to be able to put on makeup without coming out looking like a clown.

"Sure," I say. I seem incapable of putting more than one word together at a time. The words that are available to me come out leaden and hard, verbal bullets. They hurt as they leave my mouth. They sting my heart with their miserly nature. Why can't I put words to how I feel? Why can't I ask for what I need?

I don't want to leave here. I don't want to go home. More than anything, I don't want to see the look in my mother's eyes. I'm not sure if it will be disgust or strange, wayward affection. Maybe it will just be ambivalence.

After Tina drops me off, turns her magenta car around in my driveway and heads out past the posts, I let myself in. The house is just a house, fresh and quiet, a clock ticking somewhere in the wash of morning light. But my stomach is a concrete pit, a valley. My heart is a metronome. I am scared as hell.

I can't make it past the entryway. It is cold in here, a place of marble floors and cherrywood railings. Yet somehow it feels like a point of safety. I can't be hurt here. I can't be rejected. I can't be buttonholed, because I can always turn around and leave.

And go where?

The house feels like a stranger. It is a sick and sad being, a cancerous soul. It looks shiny, but there is rot at its core.

I cannot stay and I cannot leave. I don't belong here, but I have nowhere else to go. I am trapped. I am stuck—in this house, in this body. I feel fenced off from escape, locked in by cause and circumstance. And I can't get over the feeling that somehow I put myself here.

Ms. Stark's voice looms large in my head. *Opportunities*, it says. *It's how you plan to take them when they come.* They are coming. In September I will start school. I will settle in a dorm room and scribble notes in class. I will stay up late exchanging confidences. I will walk the beach at midnight, pondering Nietzsche or perhaps just the guy in my astronomy class.

My life is changing.

It has already begun.

The confidence flushes my cheeks. I can *do* this. I've only got to make it until the fall, and then I'm out of here. Right? Right.

But how to convince my mother not to throw me out again?

Laundry.

That's always been my task. Rarely have I done it to her satisfaction. I can't blame her for being frustrated. I rarely did it at all. I'd let the clothes pile high, backing up the laundry chute, and then I'd do a half-assed job of washing and drying and folding, just enough to get by.

But this is a different time. There are different needs. There is an urgency to the task now. I need to do this right so my mother feels that she needs me in the house. If it takes folding some T-shirts, who am I to argue?

Ms. Stark's voice looms again: *How do you know that's going to work?*

"Oh," I say out loud, "shut up." My voice echoes in this large empty space. For the first time I realize just how immense this entryway is, what a complete waste of square footage. It's bigger than our kitchen, than our living room. Why?

"Come on," I mutter to myself.

The laundry room has an industrial sink and front-facing window. From here I can see Bill's Saab parked in the driveway. I think about his doomed piggy bank, his journal. I try to imagine his parents. Nails once told me that his mother was a drunk and his father nowhere to be found. Does that make a difference? Does it matter?

I don't hate him, but I don't feel sorry for him. He too put himself where he is. Of course, that happens to be the master bedroom of a 5,000-square-foot house, so somewhere along the way he made the right stumbling motions. Or maybe he just got lucky. Luck is an odd thing. It doesn't play favorites. It just touches down like lightning and hits whoever happens to be standing in its way.

Inside the dryer are several fluffy towels, a few mismatched socks, random pairs of underwear. I toss in a few sheets of fabric softener and let the machine roll for a few minutes to give it that fresh scent. Then I reach inside and pull out the load.

I set aside the unfamiliar items, Bill's articles of clothing that have made it to our family's dryer: a Nike crew sock, the BUM sweatshirt. I fold everything else. Let him take care of that himself, or more likely let my mother do it for him. I press my face into the clean, folded pile. It smells like gardenias, which is how I imagine Santa Barbara smells on a clean cloudless night. I wish I were already there. *Three more months,* I tell myself. *Just three more months.*

On a whim I reach for my duffel bag and pull out Bill's change. I lock the laundry-room door and count it out into comforting piles of nickels and dimes. It adds up to several hundred dollars. No kidding. He must've been saving his tips for months, a year, perhaps more. Maybe he *is* good at his job— efficient and personable, a skilled actor, manipulative, good at getting what he wants no matter what stands in his way.

I think about what I could do with that money. I could rent a hotel room, buy a bus ticket. I could strike out, piece together my movements one at a time, a jigsaw that could move me from Point A to Point C. I'd make up Point B as I went along. Opportunities.

For once I want to fix what's wrong, fix my situation, fix myself. Standing in that hallway at 8:15 in the morning, my hands folded around fresh laundry, I grasp at an emerging sense of focus, clarity, purpose, cleanliness.

My back's never been against the wall as it is right now. I can practically feel the plaster pressing against my spine. It's weirdly invigorating. It makes me want to move forward, to help myself in ways that my parents wouldn't—or couldn't.

Adversity, Ms. Stark says in my head. *Skills are not enough. It's how you use them.*

I feel my strength for what seems the first time. I feel it in the straightness of my shoulders, the erectness of my back. It resonates in my curled toes, in what feels like my determined line of a mouth.

I can *do something*.

Right now that means taking this pile of laundry and climbing the stairs. It means finding my mother and facing her anger. It means doing what I can—what I must—to have a place to stay until I can strike out on my own. That might be next week or next month or this coming September. I'm not sure of my next move. I just need a place to hunker down and plan.

I leave the laundry room and start up the curving staircase. At the top there is a closed door. Once my parents' room, now Bill's quarters. My mother doesn't sleep in there with him. Her passion is far from platonic, but so far as I know, it's unreciprocated.

I find her in my room.

"You're *back*," Nails says. Morning light streams through the windows, playing rainbow havoc on the window seat.

"I didn't *ask* you to come back," my mother says. She is fully dressed and sitting on my bed, my childhood canopy, draped in raspberry-sherbet colors. The bed is made, dust ruffle and everything. She's been doing bills. Her glasses are pressed up onto the top of her head. There is a calculator by her knee.

I look at her and there is that pleasant mom-feeling: Underneath everything, this is the woman who cried into the void and gave me life.

"Leave," she says.

The word registers at the top of my skull and there only, ruffling my hair, smoothing it with a tarnished hand. Eventually it works its way down to the nape of my neck, playing with the strands of my shoulder-length blunt cut.

I am transported to a pizza banquet a decade earlier, a paternal hand, a tender touch. Then the parking lot and yelling, that radical shift.

Danger, Will Robinson. Do not be fooled.

"I did laundry," I say.

A twitch at the corner of her mouth. A softness, an equivocation of sorts. Uncertainty, an opening.

"Go to a friend's," she says, "or go to the park. Sleep in the grass for all I care. Go anywhere. Do anything. But get the hell out."

The order registers in my ears and feet. I feel them redden and grow warm. Jonathan is sleeping on the window seat, his little body covered with the blanket my mother hand-stitched while pregnant. I hadn't even noticed him there until now. He is on his side, his peaceful face turned toward us, and I want to rush him, grab him up, stuff him in my backpack along with the dirty cash, and make a run for it.

Would Nails even protest?

Jonathan sighs and turns onto his stomach. He is seven years old and as seemingly normal as any kid could be in this situation. He was happy to play video games with Bill yesterday while my mother tossed me out.

Maybe it's not him who needs saving.

I place the laundry at the foot of the bed. It's the only thing I have to offer. "Get a hold of yourself," I say, channeling my father. She's not impressed.

"You have until noon. That's four hours. Get on the phone and do what you need to do. At noon, I call the cops."

Thing is, she can. I'm eighteen.

"I'm going to go pee, if I'm still allowed."

She snorts: *Go ahead.* Still wearing my backpack, I find my way into my pink-and-green bathroom and shut the door. I lean against it momentarily, catching my breath. The door is strong against my back, solid. When I open my eyes, my vision is clearer. I'm okay, I think. I look in the mirror and tell myself that. I think I believe it.

When I look at my reflection, I usually go straight to the hair. Not today. Today I'm looking at my eyes. They're determined, calm even. The eyes of someone capable of doing something, getting somewhere.

Oh, the hair's there. The shadow on my face is so obvious, so dark and apparent already, just an hour after shaving. I run my hand along my chin and it is smooth. How is that possible? How can it feel so right and look so wrong?

But that's not the problem I'm looking to solve right now. That's not my most pressing issue. My biggest concern is where I'm going to sleep tonight. Should I go back to Tina's? Call Missy? Book a room at the La Quinta down the road?

I call my grandfather in Los Angeles. I don't need to leave the bathroom for this. My mother installed a phone in here just as she'd had one installed in every possible room: no need to run for a ringing phone; no need to leave our sequestered spaces and cross paths with one another. My family crest should be a locked and barred door.

I cradle the receiver. It is not pink to match the toilet or green to pair with the tile. It is beige, and the ordinary familiarity of that color comforts me. On the other end I can hear Bernie— smoking? Can't be. He hasn't done that since my grandmother died of emphysema two years ago. Maybe it's him spreading Smart Beat butter on a low-carb piece of toast.

"You talking about that Bill Solomon?"

"Sullivan," I say. "Bill Sullivan."

"And you smashed his cat."

"His pig."

"He has a pig living in the house?"

Jesus! "A fake pig. It had money in it."

"Well, why didn't you say so?"

I hear a trilling at the other end of the door: Nails has come knocking. My heartbeat starts preparing for the three-minute mile.

"Put her on," Bernie says.

Nails rattles the bathroom's faulty handle. The last time she did that, some crucial piece of hardware fell off, trapping me inside the pink-and-green cavern. I wound up cooling my heels for three hours, sitting on the toilet, waiting for the repairman to spring me loose. I can't afford to waste that time today.

I open the door, surprising my mother. She must have expected more fight from me. She takes the phone. "Daddy," she says, and I leave the room. It doesn't matter what he says, how she responds. What matters is the bottom line, whether he can talk her down. I don't want to wait around to find out. I need to pack and prepare.

Yet somehow I find myself in my mother's office, that place she inhabited after she decided to play the real estate game. The walls are painted dusky rose, a color that purports to mix pink and gray, sunshine and fog. The desk holds folders, files, a three-month-old *Cosmo*, and a picture frame turned on its face.

It's the five of us at Middle's bar mitzvah: my mother smiling her Ipana toothpaste smile; my father with the bushy mustache he would later shave; me grinning wide in hopes that the stubble would not show; Jonathan wearing a small blue bow tie; Middle awkward above a Torah scroll.

I tuck the photo in my backpack, where it sits kissing the

change Bill Sullivan has earned over time. It is fifteen minutes before nine in the morning. Outside the light is changing, hardening into a glazed summer heat.

"You can stay," my mother says. She's standing in the doorway of her office, her hands perched on her hips. I realize with a jolt that she is no longer young. She is a middle-aged woman playing at being a teenager, complete with a crush and black leggings. But she's still beautiful. I can say that even now, with my vision blurred by anger and fear. She is beautiful and smart, funny and outgoing. I love my mother. I am grateful that she will allow me to remain in the house.

"But," she says, "I have conditions."

Since she's sleeping in my bedroom and Jonathan is sleeping on the window seat, I will sleep in his bedroom. I will get a job and contribute to the household expenses. Most importantly, I am not to talk to Bill. I am not to address or even look at him. "You can't be trusted," she says.

I nod. I can't be trusted. Yes.

"You're going to have to earn that trust back. If you can."

Of course.

"You understand?"

I do.

That strange twist comes to her mouth again, that twitch at its corner. It could mean any number of things, of course: anger, vulnerability, boredom. I want to hug her, tell her it'll be okay. We'll be okay. Somehow we will.

"You hurt me," she says. "Don't do it again." Then she turns on her heel and walks away. I glance over at the mirrored closet door and there I am. I can't escape. I don't want to. I want to see myself, not strategic bits and pieces.

And there I am. What a funny thing, mirrors, reflecting you back at yourself. When you look in them, are you looking inward or outward? What pose do you take to reveal your truth?

As it is, I'm not posing. I'm sitting on my mother's wheeled office chair, short legs swinging a good two inches above the ground. My face is square, my hair sun-streaked, the color of caramel in summer and chocolate in winter. It falls to just below my chin, wavy on good days, frizzy on bad. My nose is wide, my lips thin. I grin at myself just to do it. There it is—my mother's smile, the charmer, the runway queen.

There is the hair. But I don't want to focus on that. I want to acknowledge it, but not make it my sole center of attention.

Because there is more. I am dressed simply—a Tom Petty T-shirt and faded jeans paired with sandals—but I carry myself well. My shoulders are straight, my chest strong. I am thick through the hips and belly, but I know that under my jeans my legs are slim and well-shaped. I am ready to begin my life. I am ready to begin.

Three months pass. A quarter of a year, a slice of a lifetime. My mother's conditions grow more plentiful.

Thou shalt ask permission before using the car. Laundry room. Kitchen. Phone.

Thou shalt make thyself scarce when not asking permission.

Thou shalt not address Bill. Even if you've tripped over his cat's litter box. Again.

Even if his weights and his Walkman and all his workout junk are scattered all over the kitchen, making it impossible for you to find a place to eat dinner. Even if you've received permission to use the kitchen.

Even if he and your mother are sitting on the stairs, engaged in conversation, blocking your path.

Thou shalt never address Bill.

Even when his cat disappears. Vampire and I never got along. She was a slinky little creature who liked to hiss, bite me, and then run away on fleet black feet. I don't like cats. I don't trust them. They always look like they're up to something.

"You let her out," my mother says. "You let her escape."

"I didn't," I say. I'm in the bathroom, straightening the tie on my work uniform. I work at the Mann Movie Theatre, the one that used to be the class act in town and is now outclassed. It smells of burnt popcorn and that sticky red syrup that seems to populate movie-house drinks. The air conditioning is always ten degrees too cold. The theme song to *Star Wars* plays all afternoon over the sound system, I sneak sodas and mini Baby Ruths just to stay awake, but at least I'm earning money.

Nails is standing in the doorway. Her talons look ragged. Her eyes are turning into something concrete—hard and impenetrable.

"Just tell me," she says. "Tell me and you'll get less trouble for being honest."

I am being honest. It's not that I didn't want to do something to Vampire. I did. I wanted her out—of the house, of our lives. Just like her owner, who I taunt with kitty noises each time I pass him in our hallways. But she's gone now, too far away for me to chase.

My mother's eyes move down my face, scanning every inch. Then her gaze sweeps upward to meet my eyes, and my face flames hot with the scrutiny.

"Look at yourself," she says.

"I do on occasion."

"I can't believe I gave birth to something like you."

Something. I am back to being twelve years old, back to being The Animal. I am an It.

"Neither can I," I say. "You sure as hell don't act like a mother."

I don't see her hand as it strikes my face. I only feel it.

"Don't worry," I say. "I'll leave soon."

She is crying. "Not soon enough," she says.

Vampire never returns.

"Probably a coyote," I tell Missy. We're sitting in her blue-plaid bedroom. Every time I walk in here I feel as though I've entered a flannel factory, but it's as comfortable as the cloth itself. There are books on the shelves, clothes tossed on the floor, a poster of Johnny Depp on the wall. A typical teenage girl's room, a typical teen's life. She leaves for Berkeley later this month. Soon after I go to Santa Barbara.

We are drinking mango tea. I've doused it with lemon because that's how I like it, tart like that. The taste clings to my lips and the corners of my mouth. I imagine them twitching like my mother's, that confusing motion.

"Bill's probably bummed."

"Like you care?"

Missy allows a sly, ugly smile to slip across her face. I don't recognize this girl, but I kind of like her. "Let's just say," she says, "I'm hoping."

I laugh. It stings and cleanses at the same time. I don't want to be the person who celebrates someone else's loss, but it feels good in a dirty, sneaky way. Like stealing. Like destroying. Like wrecking something that can never be put back together, risking the wrath of consequence.

"Seriously," she says, "your mother should be ashamed."

I try to put the two together. Nails. Shame. The pieces don't fit.

"She can't take care of her kids," Missy says. "She doesn't even try."

The protective instinct hits me like odd lightning. "Knock it off," I say.

"Why? It's true."

"It's not true."

Missy's lips are a tight line that defines the rest of her face. The word *righteous* comes to mind, a near-religious fervor. Her skin is pale except for her cheeks, which flame bright red. "Really?" she asks. "You want me to go there?"

No. Not really.

"You should see yourself right now. You look sick."

It's as if the tea is curdling in my stomach. If I vomit, it will taste of mango and lemon.

"Let's talk about something else," I say. "Anything else."

"Why are you defending her?"

"I'm not defending her. I just . . ."

She watches me, expectant.

"It's hard," I say.

I remember hanging up on her years ago. She tried to go somewhere I didn't want to follow. She's doing it again.

"What's hard?" Missy's lips grow thinner. It seems they might disappear. "Living? Being a parent? Getting your kid the help she needs to—"

"Stop it. Now." My voice is a tone I don't recognize, a knife-edge that I like.

"Stop what? Someone needs to talk about it."

"Like talking does anything?"

"It's the way things start."

And there I am—crying. The tears flow over my cheeks, cooling their hot glare. They are a revelation, a confession of sorts, an admission of the vulnerability I never want to admit.

She's trying to help.

"Fine," I say. "Go there."

Swimming lessons. Age six, the backyard of a home on a street called Salmon River Road. A boy who painted his toes just because, the laughter childish and slightly derisive, the flush of his cheeks. A bathing suit that fits too tightly, the pull of Lycra atop the skin.

The lesson: Diving—holding your breath, taking that leap. Just go.

"You need help," Missy says. No preamble, no warning. Straight to the point, an arrow to the chest.

Am I one of the men who hold signs at the side of the road in downtown San Diego, the ones my parents always called warnings? Don't study, don't go to college, and you'll wind up like them, waving us into parking spots and then bumming a dollar for the kindness. What would my sign read? Will shave for food?

"Help," I say. The word tastes like cotton candy in my mouth. Soft, sweet, no structure. Apply too much pressure and it will dissolve.

"No reason to be ashamed."

"I'm not." Lie. *Lie.*

She takes my hand. Her eyes are the color of oceans, wise and deep. I am back in junior high. Once again Missy is my skinny, smart, loyal protector. She pulls me into a hug. Her grip is strong, familiar. She doesn't hug often, but when she does, you remember it. She releases me and we sit in silence for a moment.

93

"I'll miss you," I say.

"I'll just be up the coast."

But it won't be the same. We both know that.

"Promise me you'll take care of yourself," she says.

"Stop talking like you're dying."

"I'm serious. We're grown-ups now. If we can vote, we can fend for ourselves."

"What does that mean for me?" Asking the question makes my heart slam against my ribcage. I want the answer, but I don't, but I do.

"You've got to kick ass," she says. "You've got to be strong. You've got to do for yourself what needs to be done. You've got to find the help you need."

"But what the hell does that *mean*?"

"Allison," she says, "you have to go to a doctor."

A doctor. Another physical exam, another white coat. Eyes that peer, hands that invade. Wet palms in the waiting room, a gown that barely covers my butt. No thanks.

"I'll think about it," I say.

There's nothing to think about. I'm not going to subject myself to inspection in the name of help. What help? What's it going to do for me? What did it do the last time?

Missy looks me up and down, sweeping my face from forehead to chin with her eyes. "You look like you're about to burst into flames," she says.

"Well," I say, "talking about this isn't exactly like eating cotton candy."

"Sugar's no good for you," she says, and we both laugh. Then she turns serious again, too soon. "I know it's hard for you to talk about this."

"Yeah." I say. It's all I can say right now. My teeth are gritted, my nails digging into my palms. If I open my hands, there will be a line of half-moons in my skin, hot pink, burning.

"That's why I want to help," she says.

Help feels like a hug from an armadillo. Sharp claws, leathery skin. Easier to retreat. Better to tuck away, to hide.

"I need to pee," I say.

The door clicks behind me and I lock it: safety. Missy shares her bathroom with her brother, and his razor sits on the sink. I pick it up and hold it in my hand. Its weight is negligible, its blade sharp. It can cut hair, skin, veins. Not that I'm thinking about that or anything.

I take the long way home from Missy's, something I've done with more frequency over the last few years. She lives in Rancho Bernardo, a place of red roofs and retirement homes. If I turned right out of her driveway, I could get to my house before the radio could play three songs in a row. I turn left. I pass rows of ranch houses, expansive lawns, picket fences. Normal life, the suburbs. Comforting.

My car is a 1984 Toyota Celica. It is the color of champagne and has a sunroof. I'm very proud of this sunroof. A sunroof means I have a sports car. A sports car means I'm cool. I need to be cool, especially right now.

I love the car. It's my escape. It's a temporary escape to be sure, but temporary is better than nothing. I won't be taking it to college. Middle will inherit it, and then it will be his escape. I am rueful, but I also understand. School is my path to freedom. Let him have his.

I drive until I reach Walmart. Then I pull in and park. I have my mother's credit card. She gave it to me last week when I

95

asked her to go shopping for school supplies with me. "You're a big girl," she said. "You can shop for yourself."

I was amazed when she gave me the card. After the debacle with Bill, I never would've thought that she would trust me with any source of money. But she just handed it to me, no caveats, no apparent reservations. I bought clothes, linens, a poster that said, "College 101." "Blow it off," it advises. "Party naked." Will that be me in college? Will I be the girl who blows it off, who parties naked? Will I forget my blue book, do some serious drinking, and crash?

For a minute I just sit in the car, keys still dangling from the ignition. For the first time in my life, I can be someone else. The idea keeps me on my ass for a single intense second before getting out of the car and slamming the door.

I walk through the parking lot with shoulders thrown back, head held high. It is the opposite of the feeling I had in Missy's bathroom, that defeatist weight. There is no thought of harming myself in this moment. There is only excitement.

A new city, a new beginning. A new school, a fresh start. A new life, unstained, unsoiled, unsullied. That much-vaunted clean slate lies ahead of me. It is up to me to determine what to inscribe upon it.

As I walk through the automatic doors and am hailed by the Walmart greeter, Missy's voice echoes in my head: *Promise me you'll take care of yourself.* That's part of that clean slate too. If I'm going to write on it, I'm going to write myself a good future, one in which I help myself.

I am so happy right now. I am so happy it's frightening. It feels false somehow, saccharine. But I want it to feel real. I want it to make sense. I want it to be something I can achieve.

I find myself in the Books section. It's a melancholy mix of the secular and the spiritual, with a smattering of Harlequin romances thrown in for spice. I am particularly drawn to one book. It's called *God Calling*—the kind of book my parents would label as *goyische*, of the gentiles. I thumb through it first out of amusement, then with interest.

Bury all thought of unkindness and bitterness, all your dislikes, your resentments, your sense of failure, your disappointment in others and in yourself, your gloom, your despondency, and let us leave them all, buried, and go forward to a new and risen life.

I've never given God much thought. He or She or It is a foreign concept, a being in a far-away land. I'm not religious. I don't pray or attend temple or do anything else you're supposed to do. And this is not a moment of conversion. I'm not seeing any light. I'm not about to become a nun. I don't even look good in black.

But someone's talking directly to me. Is it God? Is it someone else? Is it whoever people mean when they talk about spirituality? I never imagined faith would hit me in the face at the Walmart, but here I am, leaning against the shelves, thumbing through the book, contemplating its meaning.

The helping hand is needed that raises the helpless to courage, to struggle, to faith, to health. Love. Laugh. Trust on, love on, joy on.

I want to cry, but my eyes are dry, too dry. I rub them, hoping to provoke some tears. This seems the time for tears. It seems the place for an outburst, a sudden and violent reckoning. I just watch the lumpy butt of the woman at the end of the aisle. She's flipping through a book on something called personal vibration. It takes all kinds.

Packing isn't easy when my mother is living in my room. I leave for Santa Barbara in two days, and only my books have made it into boxes. The rest feels all over the place, uncontrolled. What to bring, what to leave? Everything seems symbolic. If I take my yearbooks, I'm clinging to the past—but to leave them means abandoning memories. I'm not sure if that's a good thing or not.

This afternoon I manage to make my way into my room. My mother and Bill have gone—somewhere. They never tell us where. Middle is outside playing hoops with his friends. Jonathan walks in while I'm sorting through my clothes. "Can I have your room?" he asks. He's got messy red hair and hazel eyes. He is eating a Popsicle, and it's getting all over his shirt.

"Ask Mom."

"Why?"

"It's hers now." I pull a sweatshirt that says "PHS TITANS" from the shelf. Am I ever going to wear this in my new life? I toss it on the floor to decide later.

"Where are you going?"

"College."

"Why?"

"You know what?" I say. "I don't know."

"We're having dinner with Dad tonight."

"Shit. I forgot."

"You said 'shit.'"

"I said it. You can't."

"Why not?"

"Because," I say, but can't think of a reason to elaborate, so I don't.

"Shit," he says. "Shit, shit, shit."

I toss the Tom Petty concert T-shirt into a box. I'll take this one. "Whatever," I say.

"You don't want to have dinner with Dad, do you?"

"I don't care."

"Why do you have a mustache?"

A classic little-kid maneuver: Skid sideways into a whole other line of conversation. It leaves me feeling dizzy and flushed. "I don't know," I say. "Why do you still piss your pants?"

Missy said I need help. She's right. I hate that she's right. I hate that I need help. More than anything, I hate the idea that getting help means sharing my problem with someone else. I pick up a flannel shirt and run my fingertips over its soft surface. Then I toss it to the floor.

I'm still thinking about it—the shirt, the exchange—as I sit in a large booth later. Jonathan's sitting next to me. Middle is next to Rooster, and he doesn't look too happy about it. My father is wearing something loud and Hawaiian. It doesn't look like it fits him in any way. I imagine him shopping in some anonymous store, trying to figure out how to become a different person. How to change his identity too.

"You're leaving," he says.

"She's going to college," Jonathan tells him.

"I hear."

He's already told me that I made the wrong choice in schools. Santa Barbara's a party school, he says, that it cares more about surfing than academics. I'm running away, he says. I should be here for my family in this time of—what can I call it? Turbulence? Tragedy? Let's just call it what it is: divorce.

"How you getting there?" he says now. My father recently shaved his mustache, and his face looks like a wide moonscape, not enough to occupy it. It is an empty face, a lonely one.

"Mom's driving me."

"Her friend coming?"

"What friend?"

"Bill," Jonathan says helpfully.

"See? At least he's honest. Unlike the rest of you."

We've tried to keep Bill a secret—not so much out of protecting our mother, but to protect ourselves. The middle is no place to dwell, particularly between two people gunning for each other with lawyers in tow.

The waitress comes to take our order. I think about Bill in his waiter days. Did he simper, make suggestions? Did he bring the food promptly and offer enough refills? Did he talk at all? Our waitress has wide eyes and a surprised smile. I can't figure out if her hair is the type of blonde that occurs in nature or only in Southern California.

My father changes, puts on the charm. He orders for the table—no side salads or sodas allowed—and slips her the coupon. If this were the 1950s he would pat her on the ass as she walked away, but as it is, he just rapes her a little bit with his eyes.

"Leave me alone," I mutter under my breath. Apparently I don't mutter well enough, though, because a vein starts to pulse in his forehead.

"Look, smartass," he says. He has a slight Bronx accent, and it comes out in moments like this. I associate New York with anger and accusation. "I'm not the one who shacked up with some . . . some . . . dumb bunny."

I almost laugh in his face. He can't come up with anything better?

The waitress brings our waters. She sets them down on the table, and the *clunk* is huge. My mouth is dry, like a cotton field. I pick up the glass and drink, then drink some more. My thirst is an animal unsated by time or temperament. It is a wild thing in the woods gone crazed with abandonment, driven mad by temptation. I drink until I feel the water back up in my throat. I come close to choking, to gagging, but at the last minute I swallow down the liquid. It traces a line through my throat down to my stomach, where it resides in a chilly swirling motion. What I'm trying to say is that I'm nervous. My father's presence scares the hell out of me. I don't know what he'll zero in on next, what he'll choose to criticize. It feels as though I can't escape. Sometimes I wonder if I'll ever be able to.

Middle clears his throat. My father looks at him with an expression of—if I didn't know any better, I would classify it as hatred. Hatred of him, of us. I know what hatred looks like, and I could swear this is it. It's a laser-beam look, a thing of stupid brutality. It is also misguided. Middle is quiet, gentle. I would use the word *inoffensive* if it didn't have such dishwater-dull connotations. And my brother is not dull. He is an introvert. Come to think of it, he's the type of personality my father most loves to attack: someone who is least likely to fight back.

"Shut up," my father says. Why does he have to be such an asshole? Can't he pretend to be a human being for a single night?

"I didn't say anything."

"Yes, you did."

"I coughed."

"That's saying something."

Our food arrives. My father beams at the waitress. This is his way: Strangers get one type of behavior; family gets another. Ours is always the rough end of the stick. Why?

"Well," he says, forking into his chicken Parmesan, "good to know someone has the time for road trips. I'm the one working to make money to support her and her monkey."

I eat the free breadsticks one at a time. I fill my stomach and feel it expand. I chew and swallow. Then I repeat the motion. I am churning inside. I picture my guts as a washing machine, an agitator switching direction. I want to come clean in the end.

Later we stand in the parking lot. Rooster bends to give me an awkward half-hug. His body feels like a stranger's in my arms—plastic, not quite real. The palm trees on his shirt brush stiffly against my cheek. He straightens sooner than I'd like.

"Good luck," he says. Then he climbs into his Toyota and drives away.

PART II

CHAPTER 7

1992

I wake up in a dorm room steps from the ocean. The walls are bare and blue, no character here yet. They need thumbtacks, Scotch tape, posters. There are two sets of light pine furniture: two beds, two desks, two matching chairs, two closets that swing open to reveal mirrors.

There is no privacy here.

That prospect dogged me all summer, and now it is real. This is not my childhood home, with its doors and its locks, its separate spaces for all purposes. There are no places to run here. No nooks in which to hide. For a moment the homesickness is so real that I feel it in my throat, my heart; lumps that block the body's business, interfering. There was no time for this when I was packing, pondering my imminent escape. All I felt was excitement. Now I am here, and the emotion is settling upon my shoulders. My life has changed forever. I am a grown-up. I am on my own.

But am I really? It's not as though I turned eighteen and got my union card. I went to college, a place with only a certain measure of independence. I'm living in a dorm room cleaned by maids. I'll be eating food prepared by kitchens, not by my own hands. There are no pets, no overnight guests without permission, no open flames. It's that weird middle ground: not a kid, but not quite a grown-up.

Yesterday my mother dropped me off and drove away, tears streaking her makeup into mush. I hadn't expected the display of emotion, and it felt strong in all directions: the pain of watching her suffer, but also the pleasure of watching her realize what's been lost. I've made a vow to myself: I will never go home again, not to the place where I grew up, the home that now belongs to people I don't know and can't recognize. I will find my way in this midway place. I will make myself a home.

But how can this be a home when I still hide within it?

The dorm room is pocket-size, but this is where I'll have to engage in my grooming rituals. There's no way I can use the communal bathrooms with their shared sinks. I can't put a razor to my face there, not unless I want someone walking in on me.

And speaking of that someone—where is she?

I know only two things about my roommate: Her name is Iris, and she's from Los Angeles. I do know this, though: Unless she's blind, tapping her cane within the tight confines of these walls, I need to be careful. I can't get caught.

I think about the girls I saw heading into the dorm tower, bearing Caboodles and dark tans, some more attractive than others. It's not the blatantly gorgeous ones who scare me. It's the normal girls.

Will Iris be gorgeous or normal? Or will she be—like me?

I pull open my closet door and face the full-length mirror. Eight years after the doctor's visit, I'm still fleshy, with dark Brooke Shields eyebrows and chubby cheeks. My fashion sense no longer runs to pop culture, but my jeans still sometimes sport holes in the thighs.

I pull my equipment from my suitcase.

I heat water in my little four-cup Black & Decker coffeepot. The machine sends a thin cascade of water into its little carafe. When it's done, I pour the water into a UCSB mug.

I press the plastic button on the shaving cream. It's cool, smooth, soothing.

I follow my mother's instructions: Use the razor with a confident hand and it will glide, not bite. Wash and rinse your face; there, the cream's all off now. The shadow is subdued, but not gone. The foundation stick appears in your hand. Dot judiciously. Blend with a careful forefinger. Stand back. Observe. Not so bad. Not so bad.

There's a dance going on in nearby Storke Plaza, a gathering that sends techno and hip-hop wafting through my open window, mingling with the scents of jasmine and eucalyptus. Who are these dancers? Do they have stories that are more interesting than the usual abortion and rehab tales? All the cool kids got pregnant and shot smack. That doesn't interest me. What interests me is the role of luck in life, for them, for me.

My father wished me good luck before he drove away. It was appropriate. In a way, my entire childhood was about luck. Luck is accidental. Luck either falls from the sky or worms its way up from the earth, and in either event it has nothing to do with your needs being met. Luck lies at arm's length. It is a distant relative, the one who thinks you're eight when you're really fifteen. It is real, but it is not real enough.

I'm sitting on my bed pretending to read, waiting for my roommate to arrive. You can't concentrate when you're waiting for something: a door to open, a phone to ring. My book is a blur, and I couldn't even tell you the title.

Iris is neither ugly nor gorgeous. She is what I feared: unextraordinary, cute and feminine, small and nimble—a total that is more than the sum of its parts. She's Korean, from Los Angeles, a Mariah Carey fan.

Her hair is straight, dark, and fine; her skin, pale. She has brown eyes and pink lips. Her eyebrows are bushy like mine, and for this I like her. She holds out a slim hand with bony fingers, and I shake it carefully.

Her parents come in behind her. Her father is fat in the face and loving, putting his arm around her even as he shakes my hand. Her mother flashes me a smile and moves to make Iris's bed.

I'll bet she was never called *The Animal* in junior high, or *It* in high school. I don't see her scoping out corners in which to hide. Lucky girl.

I offer to help bring in boxes. "Sure, sure," Iris says. On the way downstairs, her father puts his hand between her mother's shoulder blades. I want to tell them about my parents' pending divorce, how they broke up three weeks before I left to go to school, but I can't find the words.

I ask: "What's your major?"

"Business."

Her slim body in a suit, her delicate fingers clutching a briefcase handle. I can see it. "Cool."

We walk through the lobby, cutting a path among all the other nervous students and box-bearing parents. Outside is ocean-colored sky, the sound of lapping azure waves. A party school. Surfers. "You?"

"Communication."

"That's . . . interesting." Sure, sure.

We reach a dented white minivan. Her father hits a button on his keychain. There is a beep and the sound of doors unlocking. He reaches inside the van and hands me a box. I can tell it contains books. It's just that kind of weight, solid and literary. My arms ache, but I don't complain. Inside, there is a line for the elevator and instead we take the stairs. My heart pounds but I say nothing. I am ashamed of my excess weight, the bulk that despite well-meaning diets and stringent exercise programs will not budge.

I've read up on my condition. Most women with hirsutism are also overweight. Iris is neither fat nor hairy. Neither are the girls I've seen walking around in shorts and tank tops. By the time we reach the fourth floor, I am sweating. Fat, hairy, and sweaty is no way to go through life, but my breed of luck left me little choice.

Fortunately this is the only trip. Six boxes contain all of Iris's worldly goods. I'm living with a minimalist. Finally something in common. I like my environment orderly and free of excess distraction, books alphabetized with spines aligned, posters symmetrical on the wall. You can't achieve that when you have too much to work with. Things spin out of control.

Iris places a family photo on her nightstand and a Bible in her drawer. She lifts a teddy bear from its cardboard container and lays it on the now neatly made bed. Meanwhile, her mother arranges her toiletries in a turquoise Caboodle: electric toothbrush and floss, apricot facial scrub, shampoo and conditioner called Bed Head. No secrets here.

Of course I am jealous. Jealousy tastes like battery acid, that bite along the throat. I am sucking on my lip, digging my nails into my palms, pretending that I am not watching as they work. If only I hadn't unpacked when I'd arrived, arranging pens in holders, angling picture frames neatly on well-dusted surfaces. If only there were something to distract me. I worry that they smell Nails' cigarette smoke left over from yesterday afternoon when she dropped me off. I begged her not to light up, but she just laughed and cranked open the window.

I don't fit in here. Literally.

It's the first day of class and I'm in Campbell Hall, the school's largest lecture hall. The seats have attached desks that swing out and down in front of whoever's seated in them, much like a tray table on an airplane. But my stomach is too big. The desk can't lie down flat in front of me. It balances on my fat like a book sloppily canted on a shelf.

I don't like playing the victim, telling myself that I'm the only person who experiences pain in this world. I know that's not true. But I don't see anyone else—and there are 860 seats here, most of them occupied—who can't fit behind their desk.

What if I had a choice between being thin and being hairless? I'm pondering which brand of normalcy I'd pick when Carol sits down next to me. I don't yet know her name is Carol, of course, but I will soon learn.

"Do you ever feel," she asks, "like a freak?"

The question is not accusatory or cruel. It's asking for confirmation of her own feelings.

"When don't I?"

She smiles and holds out her hand.

After class we shoulder our backpacks and head to the University Center—the UCen, in UCSB parlance—for coffee and cynical conversation. "Like we even need a lab for an anthro class," she says. "Look around you. It's a jungle in here."

Not everyone is stunning or shorts-clad or wearing sunglasses indoors. There are plain girls here, chunky boys. I struggle to find the words for why I feel different—a freak, in Carol's parlance—and fail. It's not just the hair or the weight. That's too easy.

Maybe it's because they don't feel they have to hide. I do.

Carol is different. She's a freak largely of her own making. She believes her interests are not that of your typical eighteen-year-old: ancient Russian history, role-playing games, beading.

"Okay," I say. "History I get. I mean, Barbie dolls don't like history. But Dungeons & Dragons? Beaded necklaces? Come on.

I bet half the girls in here eat that shit up."

"Somehow," she says, "I doubt it."

Carol is beautiful. Her hair hangs down to mid-back, black and glossy and curly. Her eyes are the color of the ocean on the clearest of days. Her skin is pure even if her thoughts are not.

"Why," I say, "if you're such a misanthrope, did you bother talking to me?"

"You're cool," she says. "I can tell."

We exchange phone numbers and dorm-room information—I live in San Nicolas Hall, she lives a five-minute walk away in Anacapa—and agree to meet up later for dinner. As we part, I feel my shoulders relaxing. I'll have someone to talk to over my veggie lasagna. What a relief.

I won't be hanging out with Iris. It's obvious. Our few attempts at polite conversation grew stilted enough to make my heart pound, so nervous was I about finding each bridge to the next sentence. Here there were no breadsticks to eat while trying to fill the silence, simply that well-meaning swamp of trying to get to know someone with whom you share very few traits and no interests. Iris is a runner, a religious girl, an early riser, and an only child. Sometimes I see her in the cafeteria with her tray loaded down. How can she eat so much and weigh so little?

"Genetics," Carol says one night.

"Dumb luck," I say.

"Same diff." She slides an amber-colored bead onto a piece of wire. Her dorm room is anything but symmetrical. The books are not alphabetized. They're not even placed on the shelves for the most part. They spill onto the floor, where they reside with bobby pins, mismatched throw rugs, and discarded scarves. Surprisingly, the space puts me at ease.

Carol's roommate turns from where she's hunched over her Mac Classic. Sandy looks like a top-heavy bird: broad shoulders, large breasts, scrawny legs usually clad in torn black leggings. Peacock feathers are her main design element, followed closely by Japanese anime. "Not really," she says. "There are no accidents."

"Sandy," I say, "what's your egghead–English major brain cooking up this time?"

"The universe aligns itself as it should," she says. "That's all."

I picture my DNA, beaded together like the necklace Carol will soon clasp around my neck. Is it aligned as it should be?

"I don't buy it," I say.

"You don't have to buy it to be subject to it."

Well, she's got a point. I'd have to shave twice a day regardless of what I believed. Still, I can't accept the idea that the universe has chosen this path for me. Did it also decide that Helen Keller deserved to be a deaf-mute? That Stephen Hawking should spend most of his adult life in a wheelchair? If there are no accidents, then who assigned me the part of Bearded Lady?

"Tell me what you think," Carol says. The necklace lies tucked along my collarbone as if it belonged there.

"It," I say, "was meant to be."

It's the week before Halloween, shorts weather. Iris is wearing a tiny flowered tank top and cutoffs. Her small face is determined and slightly nervous. "I'm moving out," she says. She pronounces "out" in three syllables: *ee-yew-ut*.

My ears flush in surprise. "Where?"

"I'm going to live with Janet."

Janet is our next-door neighbor. Demographically she is like Iris—Korean, from Los Angeles, a dedicated Mariah Carey listener—but that's where the commonalities end. Janet is convex where Iris is concave, ribald where Iris is demure. I like her better than Iris, actually. She's got personality, a spirit and light. Hell, I'd rather live with her than with Iris.

But I can't help wondering: Why is Iris leaving?

Does she sense I have something to hide?

Over the three weeks that we've shared Room 4214, I've managed to time my grooming activities to match her schedule. She wakes to go jogging at seven and is in class by nine. I'm not exactly sure how she spends the balance of her day, but I've never seen her return to our room any earlier than five in the afternoon. By then the five o'clock shadow is vanquished and my life's a semi-open book.

Does she feel I'm too pushy?

I wanted to be friends. Even as I wrote her off, I still made overtures. *Come have dinner with us. Want to study together at the library? We're going to the movies, want to come?* Each was met with a polite smile and a refusal.

Or are we just not compatible?

That's the hardest one to swallow. I'd wanted to become best friends with my roommate. I'd wanted someone with whom I could share confidences in the middle of the night. And maybe, just maybe, unburden myself of some of my harshest secrets.

Oh, who am I kidding? I'm a closed door.

"Janet," I say.

"Yes," she says. "Janet."

"I'm sorry," I say. I *am* sorry. I'm sorry we couldn't find common ground. I'm sorry I'm closed but needy. I'm sorry to be rejected, even by someone with whom I would never choose to share my space.

I tell myself it isn't all about me. Maybe she wants to live with Janet because they share an ethnic background. Because they literally speak the same language. Because I just don't get the beauty of Mariah singing "All I Want for Christmas Is You."

It's luck, that slippery son of a bitch. At times we all feel him wriggle out of our grasp.

"I'm sorry too," she says. Then she picks up a picture frame and wraps it in the opinion pages of the *Daily Nexus*, our student newspaper.

"Do you need help?"

"Sure, sure, sure." Silently we work alongside each other, in an odd way closer than we ever have been and ever will be. We fold and roll, and within a half hour her belongings are back in the same six boxes. She never recycled them, just kept them under her bed. Maybe she knew all along how this was going to end up.

I help her carry the boxes down the hall to the room where she and Janet will live. Already they're rearranging the modular furniture, lofting beds above desks. Sweat prickles at the back of my neck, but I don't allow myself to breathe heavily. Today, just today, I will not be the fat lady. I will be a good friend.

After Iris moves *ee-yew-ut*, I extend my sense of order to her side of the room. Textbooks sit arranged according to size order. Pencils and pens are neatly arranged in separate cups. Blankets lie tucked around mattresses. Now that this room is mine, I can display all my uncool stuff, my "College 101" poster, my *Cosmo* centerfold of Burt Reynolds looking like a human shag rug. He was hairy and hot. How unfair. Guys with hair on their bodies are true men, robust and virile. Women with hair are just gross.

I'm contemplating that as I hang upside down from my lofted bed, lower torso and legs prone, toes hooked on the mattress, head dangling over the desk, face growing red with blood. This is my thinking position. I picture myself as a bat, teeth sheathed, wings hushed and ready.

Carol walks through the unlocked door: "What the hell are you doing?"

Dear God! What if I'd been shaving?

What does it look like I'm doing?" I ask.

"Being really, really high on acid?"

"I'm *thinking*."

"Right."

She perches on Iris's former desk. Carol has blue eyes and a well-shaped body. I wonder what it would be like to look like her even for a day. Would it change how I moved in the world? How the world, in turn, pressed against me?

I want to ask her why she just walked in, but I can't bring myself to do it. I tell myself it's a sign of familiarity, that it's something I should be comfortable with. Open doors are not invitations to violence. They're just open.

I say: "Want to ditch tomorrow and go down to State Street?"

"Can't. I've got a gyn appointment."

Gyn? I'm not sure I should ask. But she picks up on my confusion.

"Gynecologist? You know, as in girl parts?"

I've never been to the gyn. What would it be like to wear a paper gown, place my feet in stirrups? What would they make of me? What would they say?

"Enjoy," I say. The sharpness of my voice makes me cringe. Jealousy tastes bitter under my tongue, corrosive and biting. The word comes like glass, a short sharp shard that slices and burns.

Confusion creases her features. "It's just a doctor's appointment."

I was fifteen the last time I saw any sort of doctor. It was a dentist appointment, and I spent the entire cleaning hoping that they wouldn't comment on my stubble. They didn't, but they did lecture me on my flossing habits.

"I know," I say. It's not her fault she's normal.

After dinner I go to the student center and buy a bag of chips. Ruffles, Cheddar and Sour Cream flavor. I walk up the four flights to my room to justify what I'm about to do. Scents and sounds drift out of half-open doors: incense, Wu-Tang, laughter. I reach Room 4214 and fit my key to the lock. No one to walk in on, no pair of eyes to see, no fear other than that of being alone.

The phone rings. Carol.

"You were quiet at dinner," she says.

"I'm cool."

"Would you tell me if you weren't?"

Would I?

I've never talked to anyone about the hair. I never wanted to address it, never wanted to hear my voice saying the words. Somehow it seemed safer unacknowledged, an unlit and inert stick of dynamite.

"It was PMS," I say. Better to blame it on being a woman, to throw out a condition to which she can relate. She doesn't have to know I haven't had my period in years.

"Sucks, huh?" I can't tell if she believes me or not. I also know it doesn't matter. I can't talk to Carol. Some days I can barely talk to myself.

"And how. I'm totally bloated."

"Feel like the *Good Ship Lollipop*?"

"Setting to sail, ma'am."

When we hang up, I look in the mirror. I see myself in parts that refuse to come together as a whole. My eyes are hazel, brown shot through with green. My nose is small, my lips rosy. My ears are unobtrusive and lie close to my head. My cheeks are flushed. I wouldn't be bad-looking if you took away the five-o'clock shadow. Even with the excess weight, which shows less in the face and more in the body. My broad shoulders make me look like the world's shortest linebacker. My hips are ample, my stomach obvious. There is too much of me, and my body feels like a pushy alien.

I turn away from the mirror and toward the bag. It crinkles as I open it. It sounds like love.

CHAPTER 8

1993

Carol and I are shopping at the Isla Vista Food Co-Op. It's a little more than two blocks from campus, but two blocks are another world when you're talking about the difference between campus and IV. Campus is manicured lawns and commemorative plaques, landscaped pathways, and well-maintained buildings. IV defies description. If a garbage dump featured cafes, burrito shops, and a place called Dogshit Park, it would be the college town in which I live.

"This place is dusty," I mutter to her as we walk in. "I feel like I need a mask or something."

"You looked at your bedroom lately?"

I moved here after the end of the school year. Carol, Sandy, and I found a place on Camino Pescadero. Translation: Fishmonger Street. It's between Picasso and Abrego Roads—a painter and a southwest wind. I sometimes wonder who named these streets, who if anyone designed this place of pizza and the occasional peace march. It feels random and reckless, as if whoever named it was as drunk as the residents.

We live in Apartment Zero, five blocks from the beach. That might as well be another country so far as this college surf town is concerned. I'm okay with that. Isla Vista may not be for the weak of stomach muscles or those who lack a decent tan, but

I don't feel as out of place as I might have expected. This little enclave is 80 percent clones, and that makes for a 20 percent freak show. There's room for me.

See, a freak finds its way. On the face of it, there's not much choice. Figure out how to walk in the open or spend your days in the bell tower. Modern-day bell towers are no place to spend your time. There's no pizza delivery. No satellite TV.

"What the hell is an Oatmeal Wheat Free Snackimal?"

"A dollar's worth of love, that's what."

So the freak climbs down into the world.

The world. That warren of rocky pathways. The freak learns to navigate, bumping against dead ends, tripping on fallen branches. There's the occasional twinge of the funny bone, the high sweet sting, a flashing warning, a lesson.

Today's lesson: Organic Cheerios cost five dollars. Why am I doing this?

Because I want to lose weight, that's why. I want to be healthier. Left to my own devices, I wouldn't go to this co-op. I would take the bus to Lucky, a place of everyday low prices and familiar goods. They don't have the kind of cereal and bread I like here. They don't sell Ruffles. Good thing, though, since I'm not supposed to be eating that stuff anyway.

"These coffee filters are called If You Care. What if I don't care?"

"Then you get the ones that ruin the environment. And shut up while you're at it."

We're in the bulk foods aisle when the blonde approaches. She's maybe thirty-five, with wavy hair that brushes her shoulders and a warm, inviting smile. I would trust that smile. I could fall into it. She wears a tailored jacket and matching slacks. Other than Ronald Reagan, I couldn't think of a more ill-fitting customer for this place. This woman looks like she should be shopping downtown at Lazy Acres, browsing for free-range poultry on her way to the cappuccino bar.

She walks up to me as if we've known each other somewhere in a past life. She was Lady Godiva and I the horse.

She walks up to me as if she had the right.

Her mouth never opens. She doesn't speak a word. She retrieves a silver holder from her jacket pocket. She handles it with long polished nails, a subdued version of my mother's talons. She flips the holder open and retrieves a small, square card.

My reach is a reflex.

The card feels stiff and substantial between my fingers, a tactile testament to her professional expertise. In an instant her smile disassembles and walks out the door. Part by part, the rest of her follows. All that remains is a shampoo scent, something the marketing people might call Fresh White Rain.

I look down.

I see one word: ELECTROLOGIST.

I heat up from the inside out. I turn to steam. I could vaporize.

Carol takes the card. She pulls it from my grasp. She rarely smiles, and when she does it feels as if it's for you and you alone. She is not smiling now. She runs her finger along the raised lettering, then folds the card in half, creasing it. She reminds me of Missy in this moment, forceful and protective.

The market smells like a mixture of incense and plastic, a blend of the phony and the overly familiar.

I watch her ragged nails with their torn cuticles as she rips the card along its crease. She tears it in half, then in fourths, and throws away the remnants.

I'm munching some carrots and Follow Your Heart hummus when my mother walks in. She doesn't bother knocking. She doesn't trouble herself with preliminaries. "Garfield?" she sniffs, gesturing toward a poster on the back wall of the living room. She smells of cigarettes and a single squirt of Jean Naté.

"Hello to you too."

"Where did you get that thing?"

"You bought it for me."

"Weren't you six or something?"

I indulge in a deep sigh. This is our attempt at reconciliation. She'll be here for three days. She's staying downtown. I'd like to show her the campus, the corners where I like to hang out, the classrooms where I take notes, the patches of grass where I nap in between. We'll probably go shopping.

Both my roommates are missing in action. Carol is down on State Street with her jarhead boyfriend, who's up for the weekend. Sandy is off taking part in something called a role-playing game. I don't get it. She once asked if I ever wanted to be someone else. I never have.

Nails paces around the apartment, taking in every inch. I find myself looking at it through her eyes: an odd glass front door covered by blinds; ostrich feathers in a tall blue vase; Carol's beading equipment and sewing needles on the coffee table; a hanging ivy plant with its long tendrils taped across the ceiling. Eclectic doesn't begin to cover it. Not my mother's taste. She is given to fluffy area rugs, framed portraits of seascapes. Every so often she would get it into her head to repaint a room or two. She would make a federal case out of the matter. It took her months to select the right color, to place the dropcloths just so. I'd never seen anyone painting with a cigarette in one hand, but that's Nails' style.

She huffs and drops into a ragged armchair. This place came furnished. We took what we got. "So," she says.

"So," I repeat.

And she bursts into tears.

With Nails, this could mean anything. My heart picks up speed. My palms grow moist. My face starts to flame red and I stare at my cuticles. Anything to distract.

Then the door opens: Sandy.

She looks for all the world like a human stork. She's wearing a Sailor Moon T-shirt and ripped leggings. Her long hair is lush and brown—her best feature, really—and scraped back into a ragged ponytail. She carries a bag of oranges and an Oscar Wilde book.

My mother looks at her through the tears and says, "Who are you?"

"I *live* here."

"I don't know you."

"I know you," Sandy says, "but only from pictures."

I only have one picture of my family, actually: the one I took from my mother's office the day she threw me out, the one I found face-down on her desk. In that picture she is smiling her ivory smile, teeth on display for the world to admire. I don't know how Sandy recognizes her. She looks nothing like that woman now. She is wrought and distraught. She is stressed. She is weeping.

"Mom," I say, "this is Sandy. My roommate."

"Oh," she says, and honks into a tissue.

Sandy gives me a *look*. It is a mix of horror and humor, pity, and something I can't even name. *I thought I had it rough with my family*, it says, *but you hit the jackpot.*

"Pleasure to meet you, Mrs. Landa," she says in a voice I don't recognize. It's a good-little-girl voice, a polite tone, a Catholic schoolgirl's cadence. Then I realize: She's making fun of my mother. And I can't blame her either.

123

"Yes," Nails says. "Pleasure."

Sandy sits down on our ugly plaid couch and cocks her head. "Are you here for long?"

"Three days." Another honk into the tissue.

"Beautiful weather we've got, don't we?"

"Yes," my mother says, "gorgeous."

It's an assault of small talk. I've used it myself. When you want to drive someone crazy, you Weather Channel them to death. And by all indications, it's working.

Fifteen minutes later we're headed toward the freeway in my mother's car. She bought a red BMW convertible after the divorce. I don't like convertibles. I don't like the way my hair blows back from my face, exposes my skin. I don't like all the hype. They're supposed to make you feel free, young, and fabulous. They just make me feel vulnerable.

My mother rummages in her purse and fishes out a cigarette as she's merging onto the freeway. "Try driving with your hands," I say, "not your knees."

"Try talking with your mouth," she says, "instead of your ass."

Highway 101 rolls before us in a blur. The other drivers seem like they're out for revenge. This freeway feels dangerous, fraught. "What *was* that?" my mother asks, her cigarette jutting from the corner of her mouth.

"Huh?"

"That . . . girl."

"My roommate. And she has a name."

"She was as boring as frozen shit."

"Can we talk about something else?"

"Sure." But then she's silent. The wind tears through the car's open top, tangling our hair. I think about how long it's going to take to brush out these knots. If I asked her to put up the top, would she comply?

We marinate in her silence all the way to State Street, Santa Barbara's main drag. Put Rodeo Drive at oceanside and you've got State. It's a wash of white buildings, a Mediterranean feast of high-rent shopping. Shopping is a sport in Santa Barbara, and people play to win. Nails pulls into a garage and snuffs her cigarette in the ashtray. I look at the twisted and crumpled butt—once needed, now discarded. "Let's go," she says.

We have lunch at Aldo's, which serves classy Italian food at manageable prices. I've been there a few times, and the manager greets me by name. He remembers my favorite dish. He knows that I like a Diet Coke with no ice, and if that's not service, what is? We're seated on the outside patio. It reminds me of everything I like about this town: lush greenery, plush surroundings, sunshine spilling over the stone-topped tables. I watch my mother page through the laminated menu and realize that somewhere along the way my mood has improved. Sometimes you don't have to wish for it. It just happens.

I want this moment to freeze. I want to preserve it in ice, keep it under glass. I know it won't last, but I wish more than anything that it would.

"Your brother totaled his car last week," she says.

"And you didn't bother to call me?"

"I'm telling you now."

My mother's face is dramatic from eyebrows to chin, a countenance that manages to be both angular and rounded in the right places. Her eyes are wide-set and oddly innocent, her nose perky, her cheeks soft and giving. Her smile is toothy and broad, a compelling sight that makes you want to grin back. But she is not smiling now.

"What happened?"

"I told you."

"Want to be more specific?"

The waitress comes to take our order. She has big hair and bigger earrings. I order chicken Parmesan and my mother gets veal piccata. We both order meat sauce, not marinara.

"What do you want to know?" she asks after the waitress brings her big presence to another table. She taps her talons on the table. It sounds like a slow, steady rain.

"He totaled the car. How?"

"Drove down an embankment, through a backyard, and into a house. Wound up hanging upside down from the seat belt. Anything else I can tell you?"

She's threatening to cry again. I take a sip of my ice water.

"He's out of control," she says. "He's just so . . . angry."

I curl my toes, flex them, curl again. I suck on the inner part of my lower lip. "Angry," I say.

"You wouldn't believe how much."

"You know," I say, "that was my car. Not his."

"You left."

"It was still my car."

"Now it's gone."

"What did you do?"

"Me?"

"You. There had to be something."

"You know your brother. Always with a hair up his ass."

No, I don't know my brother. I don't know that side of him, at any rate. Adam has always been the most sweet-natured of the three of us. Then again, what do I know? I left.

"What got that hair up his ass?"

She goes to light a cigarette. "Don't," I say.

"What are you, my nanny?"

"There's no smoking allowed in the courtyard."

She's already chuffing out smoke. "Fuck them," she says.

The waitress arrives with our salads. "Ma'am," she says, putting the plate down in front of my mother. "Sir," she says, offering me mine.

For once it really doesn't register. "Thank you," I say.

"See?" Nails says. "She didn't stop me."

"Maybe she just doesn't care."

"Works out for me," she says, "doesn't it?"

In my mouth the lettuce is crisp and cold. I chew and chew and chew some more. Did my mother even notice what the waitress said? "You have no idea why he was angry?"

"If I did, I'd tell you."

"Come on."

"Smartass. Tell me."

"One word," I say.

"This isn't charades. Just say it."

"Bill."

Nothing could cut the silence.

"You asked me to tell you. I did."

Not a word.

"Did you want me to lie?"

She reaches across the table. At first, I think she's going to put out her cigarette in my plate, but she's just ashing onto the ground. Her hand is elegant, unlined, capped by ruby-colored talons.

"I don't want you to lie," she says. "I don't want you to speak."

Our entrees arrive. They are ebullient, hearty, bubbling with sauce and cheese. They grow cold on the plates. Eventually they are removed.

My mother intimidates me. Why?

"Find me a hotel," she says. "Make it a nice one. I still have one of your father's credit cards."

There's the Montecito Inn, Spanish-style lodgings in the ritziest part of town. "That'll do," Nails says, and turns over the engine. The top is down and I think about all the small discoveries I've made here, all the places I'd like to show her: Hot Spots, a twenty-four-hour coffee shop a block from the beach; El Paseo, a shopping arcade with metal figures lifelike enough to greet; the Santa Barbara Mission at night, its twin bell towers spotlit against a starry black sky.

But the conversation at Aldo's lingers. The air between us feels as if it could be shattered by the slightest motion. My mouth is dry. My body hurts, that type of deep muscle ache you get when a cold is approaching. I wish I were getting sick. I want to be able to blame this feeling on . . . something. Anything but its true origin.

The air could shatter. And what if it did? Would that be such a bad thing? Break some eggs, make an omelet. That old chestnut.

"Can we talk about—"

"No," she says in a *that's-it* voice.

We drive down State Street. Groups of students flock to bars and bookstores. Mothers carry coffee and push strollers. Lovers amble hand in hand. How would it feel to have someone's fingers laced through mine? Comforting or clammy?

I think about the waitress. Does it matter that she thought I was a guy? I was able to blow it off while sitting at the table. Maybe I could learn from that. Maybe it doesn't matter how other people see me, what other people think.

Oh, come on. Who am I kidding?

We reach the ocean and make a left. The smells and sounds of Santa Barbara drift through the open convertible top: salt water

128

and caramel lattes, grunge music, and female laughter, light and tinkling as wind chimes. Games of beach volleyball, tourists browsing at vendor stalls along the water's edge.

"Keep me company," my mother says. It's a refrain from my childhood. When I was a kid, it meant accompanying her in the car while she drove aimlessly, in the kitchen while she made Chinese chicken salad, in the bathroom where she smoked and chattered, only halfway expecting a response.

"What do you think I'm doing?" I say.

"No," she says. "I mean at the hotel."

Oh, *Christ*. I don't want to spend the night with her. I want to sleep in my own bed, that narrow mattress supported by a light-oak frame. I want to spend the night in my apartment, even if that means fighting Carol's military dude for the bathroom in the morning. I want to look up and see my posters: Rhett Butler, some idyllic scene from some random beach with some random inspirational quote that I *like*, the maligned Garfield.

Besides, I don't do unplanned sleepovers.

"Not tonight," I say.

"I see you how often?"

"Don't blame me. You're the one who booted me out." I sound petulant to my own ears, sullen and juvenile. If only I could let the anger go, peel my fingers off the resentment and start anew. I don't know if that's possible. I only wish it were.

We stop at a light. She turns her smile on me, full-watt. "Come on, Igles," she says.

Something loosens in my chest. At first I fight it, then I realize it's what I've wanted. Forgiveness. Just that little wedge in the door, that spill of light through the crack.

"I need to get a change of clothes." And my razor.

"I can loan you something."

"That's okay." My mother's taste runs to twin sets and garish patterns. She can pull off that look, but it makes me appear as though I should be performing in some circus. Speaking of circus freaks, there's also the real reason I need to go back to my apartment. Why can't I just tell her? It's not as though she'll be surprised. In fact, she's really the only person who knows what's wrong with me. As much as anyone knows about my condition, that is.

"It's no big deal."

"I know. I just feel more comfortable in my own clothes." Why does she have to make this so hard?

"I've got to drive all the way back."

"Do you mind?" I hate that edge in my voice. I want to be respectful to my mother. Deferential, even. Maybe it's enough just to try to love her.

"No," she says. "I guess I don't."

She drives me back up Highway 101 and exits onto Route 217, passing campus. In the daytime it's a series of buildings set against the blue ocean. At night it might as well not even exist.

Nails tosses her credit card across the hotel's sparkling counter, a deliberately casual gesture. "We want a view room," she says. "As close to the ocean as you can get. And room service. You *do* have room service, don't you?"

It's always painful to watch my mother act the fancy lady. Her car, her credit, the bits of duct tape that hold her together— look at them for more than a minute and the whole act goes translucent. She signs the receipt with a steady hand. There it is— that classic, straight-out-of-the-box cursive. I would recognize it anywhere, from ten miles' distance, through a thick winter fog.

Our room has a single queen bed and a mountain view. There's a padded headboard, a thick quilt, and the standard chair-

and-desk set that no one ever uses. It's decorated in Southwestern
pastels, which wins my mother's approval even if she's peeved
about the view.

When I was a child, I would sleep in bed with her when Rooster
went on business trips. I would climb into their big king-size, rest
with my head on her stomach and listen to the gurgles there, move
my head to that space above her breast and feel the ticking of her
heart. There I would fall into a deep, reassuring sleep.

She shrugs into a faded nightgown, opens the window, and
balances herself on her elbows. She stands there like that for
a moment, just breathing, taking the air in and out of herself.
She presses her heels into the thick carpet and spins. I think she
means to face me, but her balance is off and she's looking at the
bland hotel art instead. Her face crumples and opens. Then she
laughs. She comes out with a huge, deep belly laugh that's so
endearing it takes me with it. We laugh together. It feels good.
This could be the shattering I've wanted. It is a sweet shattering,
a crystal symphony.

"Bill," she says. There it is. The thread from lunch. She's
picked it back up. She *wants* to talk about it. My breath catches. I
can't at all predict what she's about to say.

"You know what," she says, her glee slowing to a series of
hiccups, "that loser couldn't find his asshole in a rainstorm."

You know what a dog looks like when it really pays
attention? When the ears go precise and cocked, still as stone?
When the eyes focus and fix, and there's just a single thing in the
world?

Call me Rover.

"Yeah?" I say. It's all I can say. I want her to cut the crap,
get to it. I want her to tell me that she's kicked him out. That our
home, however changed, however damaged, is once again ours.

She says: "I took him to Harry Matier to get business advice, and . . ."

The rest of her words go missing. They fall into a sharp, harmful haze: a tule fog—a thick air mass that forms on clear nights. The kind that comes after the season's first rainfall. You can't see in tule fog. You can't predict its arrival. You can only react, blind, hoping for the best.

She took him to Harry Matier? *Harry Matier?* Tina's *father?*

A Tom Vu infomercial plays on the television. Tom's kicking back on a sailboat, gesturing wildly amidst a gaggle of bikini-clad babes.

"Are you man enough to get off your lazy American ass and go to Vu's seminars?" he asks. "A lot of your friends will tell you, 'Don't come to the seminar. It's a get-rich-quick plan.' Well, tell them, it is a get-rich-quick plan because life is too short to get rich slow."

Bill is this type of skeezy entrepreneur. He's always scheming on ways to make buckets of cash without having to leave his poolside perch. Right before I left for UCSB, the owner of a local restaurant chain died in a plane crash. Bill asked my mother if she thought he'd be able to buy the chain on an installment plan. *What installment plan?* I thought when I heard the story. *I took all his cash!*

"He's got these ideas," she says now. "You wouldn't believe them. They're ridiculous. I took him to Harry because I figured we could *all* use a good laugh."

Harry Matier's in finance. His wife works as the principal of a Catholic school. They're decent people, caring parents. They always treated me kindly when I came to their house. What the hell is my mother doing bringing her whatever-he-is to meet *my* people?

"He wanted Harry to go in with him," she says. "A partnership. Aw, go ahead and laugh. They did. I did. We all did! Except for the schmuck who couldn't figure out the joke. *You're the joke, asshole! You have to laugh, Igles. You really do.*"

She used to call my father The Schmuck. Bill is Schmuck Nouveau. There's a new sheriff in town.

"Don't call me that," I say. The words leak from my mouth. They sound like air slowly hissing from a punctured tire.

She's tapping her slim green cigarette box. All out, no menthols for her.

"I knew you were going to be mad," she says. Her eyes are mostly green right now with just a hint of brown, a playful hazel. "Come on, *Allison*. It's a little funny. Right?"

I'd be charmed if I didn't know better. When the anger comes, it comes as a numbness on the outside of my calves. It comes as a flush of the ears and a tingling of the elbows. All these little things to let me know: *Here comes the cavalry. You want to kick some ass, we're here.*

She's sat with him and ridiculed me. I'm certain. I'd bet everything I have on it.

"A little funny," I say. "A little *funny?*"

I've seen fear, but rarely on my mother's face. I can make someone afraid. I can make my *mother* afraid.

"Well," she says, sitting on the bed, her short legs dangling, "yes." She is wearing leggings and a sweater that says DKNY. My mother is not a Donna Karan woman.

"Do you talk about me with him? Do you?"

A mumble, a vague hand gesture.

"Speak *up*, goddammit. Don't fucking play sign language with me."

"He said you need help. Okay? You happy?"

133

Happy? I'm floored. How ironic is it that he points out to her the need for action?

"Like I need his help? I needed your help and I never got it. And by the way, I'd appreciate it if you stopped shipping him around to my friends' houses. I'm sure Harry Matier would rather watch his van rust than talk to that douche."

"I hate that word," Nails says.

She's clinging to a *word*? "Okay," I say. "Rather than talk to that bum."

"That *bum* grew up with an alcoholic mother. He deals with depression every day."

"I get mistaken for a guy in the grocery store. Where's the sympathy for that?"

She blinks. I try to figure out where that's coming from. Is it surprise? Sadness? Something I can't figure out how to grasp? Her lower lip twitches. She bites it, perhaps trying to keep it still. Inside her nightgown her body is shaking slightly. Do I scare her?

"I have sympathy for you," she says. "I always have."

Nails have sympathy? That's like Jesus eating a bagel and cream cheese. Then again, some claim he did.

"I didn't do the best by you. I know."

How do I react to this Nails? Anger is too over the top, surprise not nuanced enough. I could just hold my arms out for a hug, give and receive comfort all at once. I just sink into an armchair and release the breath I've been holding.

She wants me to say it's all right. I can't say that. She wants me to tell her I love her. The words press against my tongue but will go no farther. I can't speak. I can't move. This is the confession I've waited for since I was ten. Now it is here and I can't dredge up a response.

My mother wants a cigarette so badly. You can tell. She'd smoke the carpet if it would give her a buzz. She chews on her fingertip. Getting that acrylic fixed is going to cost her. But it's okay, I think in a cruel inner voice. She still has one of my father's credit cards.

Does a confession matter when it comes too late?

"Yeah," I say. The word sounds flabby and lazy. It tastes weak. It's all I've got.

"I want to help you now."

"By doing what?"

She reaches for her purse. It's one of those huge monstrosities. She shuffles through it and pulls out her checkbook.

She's going to solve this with money.

I want to say that I'm going to reject it, that I'll tell her I don't want her handful of dimes, that I'll turn on my heel and walk out the door. What happens after that point is up to me.

But I just sit and watch as she writes it out. There it is again: that elegant, familiar penmanship. I don't want to feel anything as I look at it, but the lump in my throat says otherwise.

She hands it to me. It's blank. I could write any amount. It's up to me.

I tuck it in my jeans pocket. It throbs there like a small, flat heart.

"Al," Tina says, using the nickname I hate, "I didn't even know."

"Bullshit. Your parents tell you everything. Why didn't you tell me?"

"Why do you think I didn't?"

"How should I know?" I wrap the telephone cord around my wrist, pull it tight. The flesh goes pale, then flushes. My hand tingles.

"I didn't because I didn't *know*." I picture her in her off-campus apartment in central Texas, a hot flat place with more than its share of dust and coyotes. I've never been there, and my imagination isn't terribly fertile when it comes to figuring it out. I wonder what she sees every day, the accents she hears. I'm curious how her daily life differs from mine. But right now I'm not asking any questions about that. Now I just want to know why. Why, why, why?

She says she didn't know that my mother brought Bill to meet her parents. I don't believe her. I can't. I want to be angry and vindicated, to believe that I'm putting Tina on the spot. I want to be right. For once in my life, I want to be right.

"Al—"

"Don't. Call. Me. That."

"Al*lison*. Better?"

"Much." It's just me at the apartment, and I'm glad. Carol and Sandy went bead shopping. I took a pass.

"Okay. Listen to me, bitch. Okay?"

"I'm listening."

"You sure?"

"Hunky-dory positive."

"Okay. This is the first I've heard about Mr. Pennzoil showing up in my parents' living room. You don't think I'm pissed? You don't think I would've wanted to know? Baby, I'm on your side. Remember that."

I grab a hunk of my hair and hang onto it, pull it until it hurts. Then I run my fingers through its length, feeling the softness. Why is hair acceptable in some places but not others? "I know," I say. "I just . . . I think I wanted . . . I don't know."

I can't explain.

"I get it," Tina says. "But next time, don't call me up being all accusatory, okay?"

She's changed since we went to college. She's less brass, more bravery. Her voice is steadier, less prone to shrieking. She's gaining confidence. She's growing up.

"Okay," I say. I pull at my hair again, feel a few threads spring free at the roots. I run my fingers along my chin. It feels smooth. It's deceptive. If I look in the mirror, I'll see evidence that it's there, lurking under the skin, waiting.

Don't call me Al. Please don't call me Al.

"I should be pissed at my parents," Tina says. "They totally kept this from me."

"Maybe they thought it was best."

"Deception sucks."

Not always, I think. Sometimes it's necessary.

"It just hurts," I say. "You know?"

"Totally. He's already gone after your family. Why should he get access to your friends?"

"Damn," I say. "When did you get so smart?"

I tell Missy about my mother's check during our weekly phone call. We switch off calling each other, sharing the long-distance expense. I picture her up in Berkeley, eating organic salads on Telegraph Avenue, walking past drum circles and tree-sitters on her way to class. Berkeley seems like another world, a smart and creative and offbeat place. "You'd fit in here," she tells me.

"Do you?"

"As much as I fit in anywhere."

Just as college has increased Tina's confidence, it seems to have made Missy even more unsure of herself. "Come on," I say. "You're sharp, you're cute, you're a hell of a friend. Where wouldn't you fit in?"

"Let's not talk about it."

137

"Why?"

"Look," she says, "this isn't a therapy session. I don't want to talk; that's it."

"You know how to stand up to me," I say. "That's a start."

"You're easy. You don't judge me."

"Baby," I say, "everyone judges everyone else."

"Well put. What's going on in your world?"

"You know how my mom was here?"

"Yep."

I'd put my mother's check in my underwear drawer. It seemed to belong there alongside my granny panties and practical white bras. I didn't want to look at it or touch it.

"She gave me money."

"And this is a bad thing why?"

It communicated a siren song of need, of ties and commitment. It's just another piece of paper, I told myself. It's not necessary.

"I don't want her money," I say. The words feel like a lie of convenience, a stab at simplicity. They're so easy to say. It's the feelings that are harder to understand.

"You never did," Missy says.

I think about the credit card she threw at me whenever I sought her attention during that long hot summer before I left for college. *Here. Go buy something.* The unspoken: *Go away and leave me be.* A bribe, a paying-off of sorts. Here it comes again. I want her concern, but I get her cash.

"What's the money for?"

"Books," I say. This time the lie is automatic and deliberate. There's no way I'm going to let Missy give me yet another lecture about needing help.

"Don't your student loans cover that?"

"What is this," I say, "the damn Spanish Inquisition?"

"Don't get defensive."

"Look who's defensive. You're the one who moans about not fitting in anywhere."

"That's not *defensive*. That's just true. Look up 'defensive' in the dictionary. You won't find me."

We're at that point in the fight where it can spiral down, get ugly, or just get resolved. I dig in my heels. "What does it matter what the money's for? The fact is, she's trying to pay me off. Once again."

"Take it. What else has she given you?"

The word rises to my lips before I can stop it. "Bitch," I say.

Why am I being so protective of my mother? Missy's right, of course. But the anger reddens my cheeks and makes my heart pound against my ribcage.

"I'm sorry," she says. The words instantly defuse me. This is Missy, my oldest friend, my most constant protector. She's always known I've needed help, and she's risen to my defense time after time. I repay her by cursing her out?

"No," I say. "I'm the one who should be sorry. I'm just feeling . . . I don't know, like I should defend her."

"Of course. She's your mother."

"That's not enough reason."

"It's blood. That's reason enough."

Damn. When did she get so smart?

"You love her," she says.

"I guess."

"You don't guess. You love her."

Remember what I said about Missy being unsure? That's not always the case.

"Okay," I say. "Yeah?"

139

"You want to protect her. No matter what she's pulled on you."

But perhaps my mother wants to protect me too. Perhaps the check is her version of protection. Perhaps that's what she has to offer.

"Do you still think I need help?" I'm not sure where those words come from. They feel like acid burbling up through my throat, burning my esophagus.

"We all do."

"Don't get all damn philosophical."

"I mean it," she says. Then she pauses and all I hear is crackling. I think about the phone lines that connect us, wires running from Santa Barbara to Berkeley. Six hours by car, an hour by plane. Such is the strange nature of connection. It depends on what method you take.

CHAPTER 9

1994

I'm attending my first *Daily Nexus* editorial board meeting. I've joined the newspaper, underscoring what I told Ms. Stark years ago in high school: I want to write. We meet in a conference room under Storke Tower, the tallest building in Santa Barbara County.

My colleagues are passing around a bottle of Early Times. According to local legend, that was our chancellor's whiskey of choice when she was pulled over for driving drunk on campus. I take a quick swig. It burns and warms me going down. I grimace and pass it on. Our editor-in-chief is talking about the University of California regents. "They raise *our* fees," he says, "then vote *themselves* a pay raise. Now is that fair?"

Fair? I don't even know what that means. Nothing about life seems fair. We're dealt what we're dealt, and it's our job to wrangle with it. That may not be fair, but that's the nature of existence. That said, it sure does piss me off. I'm financing my education through student loans. Most of the time I try not to even think about the debt I'm accruing, but at times like this it looms over my head. That's part of the reason I took the *Nexus* job—the opportunity not only to write but to get paid for it.

I still haven't done anything with my mother's check. Every so often I glance at it. The slip of paper is growing yellow. I should just tear the damn thing up. But I don't. I hang onto it.

"Okay," our editor, Jason, says, "who wants to nail their asses?"

I'm not sure why I raise my hand, but I do.

"This isn't kindergarten," he says, smirking. "Just shout it out."

"Yeah," I say. "Okay. I want to nail their asses."

I'm learning that this is what journalists do, or at least what they want to do: call people out on the truth, drag them into a splash of light where everyone can see. It's a cause I don't mind supporting.

Later, back in the office, I'm poring over a list of sources the editor scribbled down. This is my first big news story. I've written about lightweight things—an unusual chemistry professor, Cesar Chavez's visit to campus—but never anything where I had to dig deep. The fluff questions have always sufficed. This time it's going to be different.

I pick up the phone and call a guy named Glenn Campbell. He's one of the older UC Regents, a former advisor to Nixon, Ford, and Reagan. He's also argumentative.

"You've got to raise fees," he says.

"Why?"

"Because education without funding is like a woman with a beard. It just doesn't make sense."

Of all the metaphors. Of all the damn metaphors.

"Sense," I say. I am but one part of the office, which itself is a tribute to the word *random*. On the walls are a framed picture of Kenny Rogers, a Communist flag, a basketball hoop. On the news desk a rubber duck sits next to a dildo. I hear "The Rainbow Connection" on the record player in the Opinions office. If a series of inside jokes had a physical manifestation, this office would be it.

I am but one part of the office. I am but one part of this world. I am a woman with a beard, and I make no sense.

"I'd go down on you," the guy who's just invited me to an after-party rave says. He's older than me by half a decade and drunker by a beer. "You'd like that, huh?"

We're at our editor's house. He lives within walking distance of my apartment. Then again, all of Isla Vista is within walking distance of my apartment. It's Saturday night, which means a party. I've been told that *Nexus* people know how to party. I'm learning that this is true.

The guy's name is Brent, I think. He doesn't look like the raver type. Then again, neither do I. He has slightly greasy hair the color of a coffee-stained tooth, and it hangs around his face in a way that's a bit too deliberate. He seems the type to pre-plan his life and find himself surprised only by his own freakouts.

"Think about it, Alicia," he says. He pronounces it like a lispy snake hiss: *Ah-lish-ah.* I don't correct him.

The house is a big bucket of rambling chaos. One of his roommates dabs at a stain that will never come out of the white living-room carpet. The other has disappeared into her room with a guy. Whatever she's doing, she'll probably regret it come morning. Jason himself is trying to keep up with his new boyfriend, a boisterous guy we know only as Gregory.

I am wearing a black sweater and a short black-and-white skirt. My legs are warmed by tights, my ankles sore from stack heels. Tonight I looked in the mirror, waiting for the parts to mesh into a whole. Eventually I stopped waiting. I took my keys from their peg and slammed the door.

"I don't know," I say. "The clap and all."

He likes this, guffaws and everything. "Sweetness, I'm clean."

"How do you know I am?"

He likes that too.

We're in Jason's kitchen. It's a hodgepodge of clashing diets and design sensibilities, organic popcorn mixed with bazooka-size canisters of fiber and Ovaltine, a John Lennon poster, lace curtains, a rug from Crate and Barrel—bought on clearance, even I can tell. Brent motions toward the living room, where Gregory is muddying the carpet as fast as Jason's housemate can try to clean it. "Look at that moron," he says. "I'll do you better than someone like him ever could."

"You can try," I say.

Then we're on the porch, on each other, tearing, close to ripping, nearing the pain point from which there is no turning back. My skirt is up to my hips. My sweater is askew, a slice of skin exposed to the night air, puckering up with goosebumps. The front door opens and then quickly closes. Chirps of giggles, gossip, emerge from the cracked windows.

"I'm parked over there," he says. Inside, the stereo has been hijacked by house music. I know without looking that throngs of Isla Vista boys and girls are dancing around Santa Barbara Gregory, and that he will bed one of them tonight, and that one may not be Jason.

Brent has a 1960s-era American car, a classic model that I'll wager is a Corvair. It has wings and chrome and inside is a giant fucking mess. As we slide inside—him opening the door for me first, then slamming it shut and trotting over to the driver's-side door—I picture the place where he lives. It's a loft, I'll bet, one of those empty industrial spaces. Take the H-bomb and drop it, just chuck it down repeatedly. It can only help matters.

His mouth tastes of the tobacco he's rolled and smoked all night, stinging, dirty. He plays rough, tangles his hand in my hair and tugs, tipping my face for better access. My neck feels like a stretched thing, taffy, caramel, a rubber band taken to its limits.

This is the first time I've experienced anything sexual. I am twenty years old, and before tonight I had never been kissed. I'd looked at lovers with the kind of longing that starts in the gut and moves to the throat, burning. I wondered what it was like, this being held, this meeting of the mouths, the hands, the bodies, the connection.

His hand trails along my knee and inner thigh, then moves north and begins to search beneath the short skirt. I am wet but confused. My mind is a natural disaster, swirling. Already his hand has slipped from my hair to my neck, which he's clutching with disturbing force, his thumb dangerously near my throat. Next stop is my shoulders, and from there it's an express train to my bra and what lies beneath.

I'm scared to stop him. I'm scared to let him continue.

This is sex: the frantic, syrupy desire for someone else's touch mixed with the knife-edge of *what-if*.

"Don't freeze up," he murmurs, his breath a warm puff against my ear, pushing.

If only I'd known it was coming. I'd have spent an hour in the shower before the date, preparing, twisting, turning with blade in hand. I'd be prepared. I'd be ready.

"You want me," he says. Those words radiate in this tight, intimate, heated moment. He's not trying to woo me. He's trying to convince me.

"Yes," I say.

We're lying on the bench front seat of his car. It's got a column shifter and roomy, cracked leather seating. He's shoved the newspapers and CDs and paper coffee cups to the back to give us some room.

I watch the top of his head as he moves down my body. I imagine him at one of the raves he claims to love, moving in the kaleidoscope of lights, eyes dilated from an Ecstasy pill. His hands feel strung together by wires. His fingers feel as if they don't know how to relax. He buries his face in my stomach briefly and I'm shot through with an almost maternal pang.

Then he's fulfilling his promise. He uses his tongue and his fingers and finds spots that make me arch and forget, just blank out on anything except the sting of pleasure. I don't feel beautiful or wanted or anything like that. I don't feel like me. I don't feel like anyone. I'm not a person or even a body. I'm just a collection of sensory waves, connected to the same wires that run through Brent's body.

By the time I recover my body and brain, Brent is sitting upright in the driver's seat, my feet in his lap. He smiles. It's tender.

"You have the hairiest ass," he says, still smiling. "A little beard too. And a moustache."

I'm flushing everywhere, everywhere at once.

"Furry bits," he says. He slips my tights off and massages my toes. One by one he slips them into his mouth and I watch, still lying on the leather bench seat, my head propped against the passenger door. When he speaks to me, his voice is not tender. Neither are the jerky motions of his hands. It's his eyes, only those.

Later, he tries to push himself inside me. It doesn't work. I'm tense and dry. He pushes until he goes limp, and then he resumes his place at my feet. He assembles a hand-rolled cigarette and smokes it, and just as I think he's not about to offer me my own, he extends his to share.

The party's across the street, getting chaotic as every party does at two in the morning. A couple argues, the boyfriend shrill, his girlfriend's voice punctuated with that calm reason that comes from being so drunk you think you're sober. A neighbor calls out, pleads, wheedles for quiet. Brent and I have smudged the Corvair's windows, made them smoky, but I think I can make out the outlines of Jason and Gregory, and I can't tell if they're in love or at war, and then I realize there really is no difference.

"When did you first shave?" Brent asks.

I can leave. I can leave now. It may mean that I leave a shoe behind, perhaps even my favorite pair of underwear, but I can escape with my dignity and my secret somewhat intact.

"Tell me," he says. "I'm your friend, Alicia."

"You're not my fucking friend," I say, and I hope the words cut somewhere deep, some pocket inside of him that he can't manage to clean and sanitize. I hope the wound grows bacteria, mold. I hope he develops gangrene of the heart. I hope it infects and kills him.

"I can still taste your pussy," he says, and takes a hit off his cigarette, holds his smoke deep down, and then, right when I hope he's going to die, he lets out a toxic jet stream. "Tell me that doesn't make me your friend."

"You don't even know my name."

He stubs out the cigarette on the dashboard and slides his hand back up my leg to where my thighs meet. He has yet to touch my breasts. *You'll let me lick you,* he said when I refused, *but you won't let me at those?*

I tell him my name.

"Allison," he says, "you're beautiful."

Beautiful. The way Brent uses that word reminds me of the kid I saw the other day at the beach. He was feeding the birds, dipping his hand into a bag and tossing handfuls, and as I came closer I realized he was hurling the food, and that he was yelling, and that the food was not food but rocks.

"Yes," he says. "You are. Your hands. Your voice."

As dawn approaches, he says he wants to come home with me. The last party guests left maybe an hour ago. I wonder if Gregory's sleeping next to someone, his bare back facing the ceiling, and if Jason's the one at his side.

"Or come to my place," he says. He's lying with his head in my lap, looking up, and I'm trying to figure out how to get him to sit up straight before the sun rises and the light reveals that the hair on my chin has grown. Before he stops being sweet and switches to cutting.

"No," I say. I don't give a reason. I don't try to find an excuse. I don't owe this person anything. Even if he went down on me twice tonight.

There's a knock at my bedroom door. "Tina's on the phone," Sandy says.

"Hey," Tina says when I take the receiver, "what's the dirt?"

I motion for Sandy to leave. She does so reluctantly. Nosy busybody. I close the door and return to my position on the bed. "I did it," I say, "almost."

"No shit."

"No shit. He was older too."

"How much?"

"At least twenty-five."

"Damn."

I hear myself speaking in a voice I don't recognize, praising the experience.

"Why didn't you go all the way?"

Because it hurt. Because I was tight. Because I was strung up and drawn up from his criticism, his critique of my body, and I didn't trust him enough to let him in.

"Aw," I say, affecting a jaded attitude, "he just wasn't big enough for me."

We both laugh.

Tina still hasn't lost her virginity. Missy did last year, though. Now she's going steady with the guy and I don't hear from her quite as much. Maybe that's what happens when you get into a relationship: You disappear from the rest of your life. You get shunted into the tunnel of love.

"Al," Tina says, and the forlorn tone of her voice makes me forget that I hate the nickname, "what's it like letting someone else see your body?"

Until this moment I never realized the extent of Tina's insecurities. She's asking me for advice. I haven't the slightest clue what to tell her.

"Amazing," I say.

"Yeah?"

"Yeah. It's . . . magic."

I bite my lips to try to stop the flow of crap coming out my mouth. Magic? I must have one strange definition of that word.

"If it was so magical, why didn't you go all the way?"

"I told you."

"No, you didn't. Not really."

I picture Brent sucking my toes, insulting me. *Furry bits. Little beard and moustache.* "It just wasn't right," I say, and really, I'm telling the truth.

After I get off the phone with Tina, I head into the kitchen to make some lunch. It's one of those slow Sunday afternoons where everything seems to be moving through a thick curtain. I'm on a few hours' sleep and my vision is blurry, though in a pleasant way. Carol and Sandy are playing Scrabble at the kitchen table. "Bah," Carol says. "For twenty-six points. I'm almost caught up to you."

"Good luck," Sandy says, and makes her move.

I can't imagine playing with those little tiles right now. Letters mean nothing to me. I need food. I decide to make some pesto. I grate cheese and chop walnuts, smash garlic, and tear basil leaves. The noise of the food processor is almost more than my head can take, but the result is worth it. I make some damn good pesto.

"Neve," Sandy says. "Beat that."

"What the hell is a neve?" I say.

"Definitions aren't necessary," Sandy says. "You've just got to be able to put words together."

"I can barely put some pasta together right now."

"Not my fault you rolled in at oh-dark-thirty. What were you doing anyway?"

"Reading poetry," I say, and drain the linguine that's been boiling. I mix in the pesto, add some pepper, sprinkle some cheese on top. I like cooking. I like having a set of instructions to follow, a series of measurements.

"Who? Longfellow? Frost?"

"Sandy," Carol says, "don't be so damn naive."

I take my bowl and sit down in our battered recliner. I'm kind of enjoying the attention. "Bukowski, actually," I say.

"That bum?"

"Sandy," Carol says, "it's your damn turn."

Watching them play, eating my homemade pasta concoction, it comes to me: I need to get myself diagnosed. I need to put my

mother's check to use. I need to fix myself. What have I been
waiting for?

In my bedroom, my drawer makes an odd moaning sound as
I pull it open. The furniture in this apartment is not what anyone
would call modern or stylish, but it serves a purpose. Under
a pair of frayed blue panties sits my mother's check. I pull it
out and hold it up to the light. It's been the better part of a year
since she wrote it. There's her classic, flowing cursive against
a background of a beach chair and an azure ocean. I don't get
designer checks. Mine are austere, a white background with a
blue border. Why waste creativity on bills?

I arrange myself cross-legged on my bed, still looking at
the check. I'm not sure what I expect from it. It's just a piece of
paper, a slip really, a scrap with a little bit of familiar writing on
it. But it has its uses.

I start with the phone book. I know no other place to begin. I
don't want to weave my way through the student health insurance
maze, and I'm not even sure that it covers specialists. I know I'll
need to see an endocrinologist. I may as well go straight to the
source.

I page through the list of doctors. How to choose? I have
more experience selecting lollipops than I do a physician. At
least I can differentiate between grape and cherry, strawberry and
rhubarb. Do they even have rhubarb lollipops? I digress.

Running my finger down the list of names, I get a thrill. So
many people from which to choose. So many potential outcomes.
So much hope.

Should I choose a woman or a man? An exotic name or a
pedestrian one? In the end, a cynical voice tells me, they're all
the same. But that can't be true.

Dr. Peter Anderson isn't hot. That surprises me. I'd expected him
to be built like *Cosmopolitan*'s interpretation of a Greek god,
swarthy and muscular. He's cute, thin gold-rimmed glasses, a
dimple in his chin, a likable demeanor. It doesn't put me at ease,
but then again, I'm not sure anything would.

"You were diagnosed as hirsute, but never treated?"

"Yes," I say. I want to have some explanation—my parents
perished in a tragic plane crash on their way back from consulting
with the Mayo Clinic; they died trying to make me hair-free—but
there is none.

"Okay," he says. "Let's see what we can do."

He hands me a cotton hospital gown. I glance at it and notice
there's a pattern: roses. On closer inspection it makes no sense:
The roses are brown. Is there even such a thing as a brown rose?
Have I entered the David Lynch Medical Clinic?

I stand with the soft bundle in my hands. I'm going to have to
undress. I'm going to have to strip down to my underwear—a bra
and panties that don't even match—and cover myself with this
thin piece of cloth.

"Take your time," he says. Then I'm alone. This room is
so white. Color exists only in small pockets: a pink tissue box,
turquoise chairs, black and beige linoleum tiles on the floor
reminiscent of the See's Candy floors I skipped across as a kid.
Don't step on the black. Bad luck. I was a child the last time I
showed my body to another human being. In school locker rooms
I found abandoned corners where I could sponge-bathe after gym
class, then change clothes away from the eyes of others. In the
communal bathrooms of my dorm, I dressed in shower stalls.
Then there was the experience with Brent. I covered myself as
much as possible, but even that wasn't enough.

I talk myself through the process.

152

"Start at the top," I say, and pull my hooded sweatshirt over my head.

"Now the shorts." I unsnap and unzip and push the denim down over my hips. I kick the sneakers from my feet but leave the white socks. Protection.

I fold everything military-style. I stack the shirt atop the shorts. I place both on a chair. I align my shoes perfectly and place them against the wall.

Then I reach for the gown. It's so white in here, such negative space. We use negative space when we lay out the newspaper. Emptiness as a positive element. It works well in the editorial pages. Here it just feels like the tundra.

I pull the gown over my arms. The cotton is soft against my skin. I think about the others who have worn this gown. Were they shaking too? Did sweat lie clammy on the backs of their knees?

There are two sets of ties: one at the neck, the other at the waist. I pull them as tight as possible. It doesn't work. My back and ass are on display. A knock.

"I'm ready," I say.

He starts at the top and works his way down. He looks everywhere. Being seen is like getting a massage from a blowtorch. Being touched is worse.

"When did your hairline start receding?"

When did I become Rooster? Will my combover flap from side to side as I stroll Butterfly Beach? Will I start bringing coupons to every restaurant meal, and when they're caught out as expired, fish a backup out of my wallet?

"Have you tried any other method of hair removal? Just shaving?"

153

I once tried waxing. When I pulled off the sticky strip, it turned my chin red and took not one hair with it. I considered using Nair. I pulled the pink bottle from the drugstore shelf and thought about the spoof ad I'd seen: two monkeys, one with a baby-smooth ass. The ad trumpeted: *So easy anyone can use it!*

I wasn't just anyone. I knew I had problems beyond those of your ordinary simian. I replaced the bottle and walked out the automatic door.

"How about your periods? Regular?"

Strangely, they've reappeared. I took up jogging two months ago and am now buying sanitary napkins for the first time in years.

"Are you sexually active?"

I suppose what I did with Brent was sex, even if it wasn't going all the way. Even if in the end it felt less like intimacy and more like intrusion. I will never see him again. I would rather spend the rest of my life alone, nose pressed to the window looking in at life, than be with him.

He's examining every inch of my body. There is nowhere to hide. He palpates my belly. The muscles in my arms tighten. My fingernails bite into my palms. "Try to relax," he says.

Sure.

There are pictures on his cluttered desk—pink dresses, wide grins. *If it were my daughter*, my pediatrician told my mother years ago, *I'd take care of it as soon as possible.*

Dr. Anderson, do you heal thyself? Do you provide for these dark-eyed little girls? Would you help them when they asked for it?

The doctor puts his clipboard aside and comes to sit close to me. He smells the way I wish Rooster smelled: cologne and something deeper, something smart and trustworthy. How would my life be different if, by some fluke of time and genetics, this were my father? Would I be one of those dark-eyebrowed little girls in the frames, carefree and cared for?

"You're an extreme case," he says.

Extremity. On the outside, the fringes. Something far out, practically unreachable.

"We'll take care of it," he says.

He writes up a lab slip. This time I'm walking straight to the lab, extending my arm, and offering up what's needed.

There is hope. There is a future. The answers from the lab tests could lead to a diagnosis. The diagnosis could lead to medication. Medication could send my body into reverse. The hair could shrink and disappear from my face and body. My hairline may thicken, my waist could slim. Heads could turn for the right reasons.

A year, two years, a decade from now, I will sit in a booth with a paramour, a boyfriend, a husband. He will stroke my smooth chin, play with my bountiful curls. I will smile and cross my slim legs at the knee. My body will be just that—a body, a tool, not an enemy.

Dr. Anderson hands me the lab slip. I feel it wrinkle slightly, crumple under the weight of hope, that palm-slapping drunkard. Then the doctor sits up straight and gets a look of—what? Pity? Empathy? Whatever it is, I don't want it.

"I have to ask you something," he says.

Nothing good starts this way.

He wants me to appear in a textbook. "The pictures wouldn't be of your face," he says, as if that makes it any better. "Just your body."

He says it will help others. There are people in my position, hiding just as I do every day. To expose myself is to help them move out of the shadows.

No. Fucking. Way.

As the lab tech calls my name, I reconsider. Maybe I should. Maybe my pain can be of use to someone else. But I can't. I can't.

I follow her into a white space spotted with Post-it notes and fill-in slips, all inscribed with handwriting I can barely read, let alone understand. I settle into a seat and offer my arm. My eyes fix on a lone teddy bear propped on a counter, its head swaying low, its gaze directed at the floor.

"My name is Layla," the tech says. "I'm an intern. Can I draw your blood?"

Layla, no offense, but an *intern*? Do I really want anyone but a certified professional fucking around with my veins?

"Sure," I say.

She takes a swath of what looks like rubber-band material and ties it around my upper arm. It's tight. It cuts into the skin. I bite the inside of my cheek but say nothing. Sometimes you lack the strength to advocate for yourself. Sometimes you let the world roll over you, wave after wave, mouth closed, eyes open, hoping simply not to drown.

Layla rubs her gloved pointer finger in the crook of my arm. She presses down and makes a clucking sound. "Your veins are *hidden* or something," she says. I bite back the impulse to apologize.

We switch to my left arm and somewhere in there she finds a willing participant. She unwraps the tight rubber band, swabs the puncture site with alcohol, dries it with cotton and tears open a plastic package. "A pinch," she says, and breaks my skin's surface.

The doctor calls with my official diagnosis: congenital adrenal hyperplasia. There are several different types of CAH. I have the most common, 21-hydroxylase deficiency. In the world of CAH, I am normal.

Normal, of course, is relative. My body overproduces hormones, which in my case causes male-pattern hair growth and baldness, irregular periods, infertility, and obesity. The disease can cause height retardation, which may explain why I have trouble reaching the top shelf.

It also causes genetic ambiguity. This manifests differently in each CAH patient. I'm lucky enough to only have a mildly enlarged clitoris and reduced vaginal opening, which makes intercourse difficult.

I got lucky, though. I could've been intersex, a woman with a penis. Try explaining *that* to your new boyfriend.

Having CAH means I've gotten two copies of an abnormal gene. I'm a scratched CD. I'm a videotape that won't fully rewind. I'm a partial, a taste. I am incomplete.

It's hereditary. Rooster's hairy back, Nails' experienced hand when it came to shaving—they handed that down to me. I imagine them meeting at some bargaining table, scrawling their signatures on paperwork, consenting to merge, to create a copy of their combined selves. I picture them finalizing the decision, brisk and businesslike.

Each carried an altered gene. Perhaps they held it like a wedding bouquet, self-conscious and proud. Or maybe they hid it, using the same sort of coping mechanisms I'd later develop and grow to resent. They each lay the gene—that ugly, gnarled thing—down. Then they walked away.

Dr. Anderson puts me on three medications: spironolactone for the excess hair and receding hairline, dexamethasone to battle infertility, and a birth-control pill to continue regulating my periods.

Having a prescription is surreal, a means of battling my own body. I hold the hope of coming out ahead, hugging it lightly in my moist palm, as if grasping it fully might kill it.

I take it onto my tongue as a sacrament. A visible sign of an invisible truth. An outward appearance of inward grace. The melting is bitter, biting. I wash it down with tap water and call it holy.

No guarantees.

A month after I start the pills, he orders another series of labs. He wants to monitor my progress, make sure I'm on the right mixture. I'm more nervous about this time than the last. That was an unknown, a blank slate. I wasn't hoping for anything; I was simply expecting the worst. This time I have hope, and it's sitting on my shoulders like the devil.

I walk in with my heart so far in my throat it feels as though I can taste it. It's not the white, antiseptic parts of the lab that get to me. Those are comforting. It's the human element that jars me—the birthday cards and stray half-inflated balloon; the scraps of paper with scribbles written in cursive, in purple ink; the woman who says, "Hi, I'm Fannie. I'm an intern. Can I draw your blood?"

I wonder what happened to Layla, but I don't ask. I settle myself into the blue pleather seat and offer up my arm. Fannie pokes around and finds a vein. She swabs the spot with alcohol, then pops open the plastic package. I don't know whether to watch or look away, so I observe through slit eyes. When the needle goes in, it feels like a wake-up call.

I can only hope that this medication is working. I can only cross my fingers and pray, pray to whomever, whomever will listen. I watch the blood rush from my arm down a slim tube. Fannie unhooks one vial and pops on the next. Six vials in all.

I want to ask her if that's a lot, more than normal, if *I* am normal, but she stays quiet and thus so do I.

The phone rings three days later. "Your levels took a spectacular fall," Dr. Anderson says. "The medication's doing its job. We just have to have patience."

Patience?

"The hair didn't appear overnight. It won't disappear that way either."

I feel a push of stubborn anger, an outward press from inside my chest. I'm not asking for it to disappear overnight. I just want to see some results.

"We're making progress," he says.

We? My health is a day job to him. Still, his words are my lifeline. Month after month I drive to the clinic where he works. I stand in line at the sunlit pharmacy and exchange my Bank of America card for three small bottles of persistence.

Sometimes I hesitate before walking through the sliding doors. I let all hope go, the efforts at joy drop to the ground and shatter. I allow the weight to sink down my shoulders. I watch the people move in and out of the building, their feet stepping one in front of the other, taking them where they need to go, and I marvel at how happy my sadness makes me feel.

CHAPTER 10

1995

Each year the *Nexus* staff attends the California Intercollegiate Press Association conference. We throw our clothes into bags, our weed into Ziplocs, and ourselves into a clutch of secondhand Hondas and Mazdas.

This year's conference is in San Diego. It's going to cost at least fifty dollars a night to stay at the hotel with the rest of the staff—and that's if I share a room. I don't want to share a room. I don't want to share a bathroom. I don't want my grooming rituals to be exposed, and besides, I can't even afford fifty a night.

That leaves my parents as options. That's like choosing between the rack and Chinese water torture. I start with the rack.

"Allison," my mother says, "you know better than that."

I'm sitting in my living-room recliner. Sandy is knitting on the couch; Carol is beading on the floor. They both glance up at me, then return to their respective crafts.

"It just won't work," Nails says. "I just can't trust you around—you-know-who."

"Say his name," I say.

"You already know it."

"I want you to say it."

Now Sandy and Carol are looking at me in earnest. Carol's eyes are very blue tonight. How does she see *me*?

"Bill," my mother says, almost in a whisper. I wonder who she's hiding from. I picture her tucked away in my former bedroom, door shut, sitting cross-legged on the bed as I often do. My mother looks a little like me sometimes. Have I ever mentioned that?

"Bill," I say. My voice is a foreign thing, raspy and lost. The word's one syllable seems elongated, stretched to its maximum capacity. My eyes water. My throat hurts. Out of nowhere I think about the check she gave me. Did she even realized I cashed it? Did she understand why?

Nails starts to cry.

"What's wrong?" I ask.

"Everything."

"Tell me about it."

My roommates have studiously gone back to their projects. Sandy uses her knitting needles as weapons against the defenseless yarn. Carol stitches as if someone's life depended on it. Maybe it does.

Time for Chinese water torture.

"Been a while," Rooster says. I'm holding the cordless phone so tightly my knuckles ache. My hand shakes. I'm no longer sitting. I'm pacing around the living room, stepping over Sandy and Carol as I circle the small space.

"Yeah," I say. It's all I can say. It's been at least eight months, maybe more, and I'd forgotten how much he scares me.

"What's going on?"

"You know. School. And stuff."

"Stuff?"

"I'm coming down to San Diego next week."

"Yeah?"

"And I was wondering if—"

"Yes."

I blink.

"You need a place to stay. Right?"

"Uh-huh."

"And you can't stay at your mother's."

"Uh-uh."

"Real winner she's got living with her."

I already knew that he knows, but for some reason remembering twists my stomach. Maybe he spies on my mother from the safety of his car. When you say anything's possible, the phrase defines my father.

"Uh," I say.

"I know you're not going to say one way or the other. I just want you to know that I know."

"Okay."

Fear is a constant clench to the gut. It's a dread, a dry mouth, an emotion that transcends the simple four-letter word. It's a stain, an indelible one. You can scrub, but you can never entirely remove it.

Rooster's house sits on San Diego's suburban outskirts. It has a small, cautious ocean view that becomes evident if you stand on tiptoe by the west-facing bedroom window. There's paperwork stacked on his dining-room table. The kitchen's center island is home to ketchup packets, toothpicks, and a single Hungry-Man dinner coupon.

"I need to clean up," he says, offering me a can of lemon-lime soda. "I just haven't had the time. The travel, you know."

I do know. He travels all the time for work. I grew up hearing about disparate places: Cedar Rapids and London, Alamogordo and Adelaide. I never quite knew what he did on those trips. Paperwork, probably.

"You can stay in Jonathan's bedroom," he says. He takes my luggage and carries it up the staircase, which has folded loads of laundry stacked on it. I pick one up and follow him. The clothes are the same ones I used to wash when we all lived in the same house. Laundry was my chore, a way of getting to know my family through the items they donned that day.

Jonathan's bedroom is by far the cleanest in the house. The bed is made, the carpet vacuumed. He's ten years old and the best housekeeper of all of us. This room feels different than the rest: relaxed, orderly, lived-in. It feels like my younger brother, and it makes me wish I could spend more time with him. Sometimes I wish I could take him away from the struggle between my parents, the weekdays with my mother and Bill, the weekends with my father. It's not just that he's too young to deal with it. He shouldn't have to.

Today Rooster is in a good mood. You can always tell when he's in an up cycle. His voice grows strangely joyous, animated. He gestures and grins. He does things like carry my luggage up the stairs and offer to do my laundry for me.

"That's okay," I say. "I don't mind doing it."

"Kind of like at home. Right?"

Home? Where is that? There is a room that is no longer mine, a house that is off-limits to me. There is an apartment that holds my possessions, but not necessarily my heart. There is this place of familiar furniture and strange emotion, a painful brew in which I can never entirely get comfortable.

"Right," I say.

Then the silence strikes. He watches me, eyes going from brown to black and back again. I sense he has something to say but can't force the words from his tongue, can't muster the courage. I want to reach out and shake him, tell him to *Just say it!* But what good would that do? What good would anything do?

I just stand there. Sometimes that's how you deal with emotions that are out of your realm, sadness and wishes you can't quite fathom. Fact is, I don't know my father. We just share the same wicked DNA.

"We'll do it together," he says. He takes the plastic shopping bag filled with clothes and carries it back down the stairs. It feels almost intimate, close enough to burn. Following behind him, I realize that his hair is going gray. My father is getting old, older. There is no preventing this.

In the laundry room we stand side by side. His affection is both repulsive and touching. As I watch him carefully add detergent and start the machine, I realize I prefer his old rattlesnake self. A snake can shed its skin, but does anything different lie underneath?

"Now," he says, "let's go get some lunch."

The phone rings on our way out. His answering machine picks up. It says *We can't come to the phone right now.* He's the only one there.

It's *Nexus* tradition to cross-dress for the conference's closing banquet, skewing the suit jackets and high heels worn by most attendees. Pictures of banquets past litter the office walls, wigs crooked on male heads, button-downs and khakis slightly loose on female forms. I've always known my time to attend would come. I'm dreading it.

Cross-dressing feels like a cat's cradle into which I don't care to tumble. Of course there are women who want the world to recognize them as men. They're called transsexuals.

I am not a transsexual.

Tonight, though, we are all transvestites. Rooster rifles through his dresser drawers and finds a tie with tiny golfers facing off against a green background. He sits on a chair and I stand before him. His touch is tentative, probably as unsure as when he first held me. He places the tie around my neck and I flinch. I haven't let him this close in years.

"It doesn't hurt," he says. "It's just a tie."

He straightens the ends until they are even.

"They call it the half-Windsor," he says. "I just call it a knot."

He narrates each step: Start with the wide end, then cross over the narrow end. Wrap the wide end around and behind the narrow end, then bring the wide end up. Pull the wide end through the loop, then back down.

"Then," he says, "you tighten."

Tightening. Yes. All my muscles are on ultra-lock mode. Will he look at the hair on my face and make a comment? He's never said anything before. It always fell to my mother to manage.

I almost want him to say something. Maybe the secret feels worse as a secret. Maybe it's best to push it out into the air between us, make us address it.

"And that's it." He gives the tie a final tug and looks over his handiwork. In that moment the tension changes, turns tender. He's not looking to criticize. He's looking to help.

I think about help as I get into my aged, beloved Toyota. Help always felt like another country, too humid in climate, too touchy-feely in culture. Help required too many visas and vaccines. To go would mean never to be safe.

Turning the key brings forth the engine's throaty cough. Toto is on the radio, singing about places a world away: *I bless the rains down in Africa/Gonna take some time to do the things we never had.* There is a slight rain and it mists my windshield, blurs my sight. It takes a minute to realize that it's tears.

Things are so much easier as black and white. More palatable, easier to digest. Victims and villains, heroes and pirates. But no one fits those confines, do they? The world is a blur, one line after another getting crossed.

I shift into reverse and back down the driveway past my father's fledgling grass and strangely alive flower bed. He was never able to bring anything to life in our family's garden, but here he's managed to give daisies an existence.

He lives on a cul-de-sac, that creation of the suburbs, a dead end with only one way in. The houses themselves are creatures of white stucco and red roofs, the visual symphony of northern San Diego. They are surrounded by accents of green: lawns, hedges that block backyards from view. No need to wonder what lies back there; it is the stuff of my upbringing. A pool and patio furniture, a barbecue and perhaps a friendly dog. Nothing to fear here.

A series of turns leads me past the community center and through the entry gate, which is never locked. As I wind my way out of Rooster's neighborhood, the rain begins to patter down harder. My wipers work hard to keep up. I hate driving in the rain, and I cling to the wheel. Again, I am thinking of help. Could somebody help me in this situation? Sure, they could offer to drive, but could they ever teach me to be unafraid?

I am on the freeway, Southern California's backbone. It is the spine along which all life flows. I'm driving south on Interstate 15, headed toward Hotel Circle, where the conference is taking place. I keep expecting the tie to feel as if it's choking me, but I barely notice it. The exit names are blurry in the rain, foreign yet familiar with their Spanish words: La Costa Avenue, Encinitas Boulevard, Via de la Valle. To keep myself calm, I translate their meanings. By the time I hit San Diego proper, there are no longer foreign words, just names like Grand Avenue and Sea World Drive.

As I take the Interstate 8 exit ramp, the car fishtails slightly. I am alone, beyond help. Assistance will come only after the accident has occurred. Pink Floyd is on the radio now: *So you think you can tell heaven from hell, blue skies from pain.* I almost want this to be the end, but it is not. It is one moment of one day, a pointed slice of time to be sure, but just one. It is not my time. This is not my moment.

I pull into the hotel parking lot. It is a swath of concrete, nothing more. It is vast and blameless. Above me the sky is muddy. The rain is steady, more irritant than intrusion. I am a woman dressed as a man. I brought myself to this place, but if you asked me, I couldn't tell you how I got here.

The good news is that they look as ridiculous as I feel. Hairy legs poke out from loud floral dresses. Sport coats sag on slim feminine shoulders. Everyone is awkward, and no one entirely owns their body in this moment. This comforts me. They feel the way I so often feel. I want to see what we're doing as a gender spoof, to believe that we're turning the concept of male and female on its ear. I'd like to think somehow we're making a strike for people like me, girls who sometimes get called *sir*, boys whose voices make them sound more like a *ma'am*.

But we aren't spoofing anything. We make no stand. We seek attention, and we get what we're seeking.

"I like your shoes," one guy tells our sports editor. There is much to like. They're an impressive pair of heels that match his red dress.

"Nice moustache," another guy says to our news editor. Thank God he didn't say it to me.

"Cool tie," a girl tells me.

"Golfers," I say.

"Vintage," she responds.

We also win awards: Best arts coverage, best editorial piece, best news story. I don't realize that they're talking about me until I feel a nudge. "Go up there," our editor says. "It's yours."

The story about the Regents. Glenn Campbell. Woman with a beard. I hadn't even realized they'd submitted it for consideration. I find my footing and climb onto the stage. In my hand the award feels like a welcome weight. A point of pride. A badge of honor.

Ned appears to me as an outline, a set of sketches, unfilled and incomplete. He approaches me at the banquet's after-party. The girls are loosening their neckwear, the guys yanking at their clip-on earrings. The room smells like cheap beer and potent pot.

"Why don't you *shave?*" he says. "You're disgusting."

He doesn't wait for an answer. He just turns and walks away in search of another Keystone.

I almost admire his honesty. I also think he's a dick and that this party is over. Keith intercepts me on the way to the door. He's the *Nexus* arts editor. He has sincere brown eyes and looks a little like Kermit the Frog.

"I'm sorry," he says.

My eyes are burning. Can I just *go?*

Keith motions as if to touch me on the shoulder but doesn't. I don't blame him. I must look radioactive, not safe for prolonged exposure. "Do you want to talk about it?"

No one's ever asked me that before.

If I were to talk about it, what would I say? How do you find the words for something you've spent a lifetime trying to ignore?

"No," I say.

I give him a brief hug. Hugs offer comfort and closeness, connection. You're supposed to like hugs. Hugging Keith feels like I'm pushing against a series of internal walls. The walls push back, and it feels like a very old ache.

"Thank you," I say.

I grip the wheel the entire way back to Rooster's. It's only after I pull into his driveway that I realize I've been biting my lip. The taste of blood fills my mouth. I long for a toothbrush, a swig of mouthwash, a sip of Diet Coke to wash this night from my senses. I would even take a taste of my father's horrible lemon-lime soda, anything.

I ring the doorbell. I don't get a key when I stay at my father's house. "You'll forget it," he says. "I'll never get it back."

He comes to the door wearing torn Jockeys and nothing else. He's tired and yawning. He scratches his armpits like a monkey. Hair everywhere on my father's body: chest, arms, legs, back.

"How was being a man?" he asks.

"I'll stick with being me."

I loosen the knot around my neck and slip the tie over my head.

"They like it?"

"Yeah," I say. "Actually, they did."

I hand him the tie and he smiles at me. It's the indulgent smile of a proud father. Why now, with the damage already done?

"Well," he says, "good night."

He shuffles up the stairs past the laundry and stacks of newspapers. I go to the kitchen and pour myself a glass of water. The liquid feels smooth going down my throat, necessary. I listen to myself breathe: the rise of intake, the fall of exhale. I chip at my nail polish with my teeth. Outside the rain has slowed to barely a whisper.

I think about my family's kitchen, its granite countertops and built-in breadbox, its Dutch door and a view of the winery. It was different there, not this place stacked with emptiness. There is something about the presence of people that makes a room human. Our kitchen had that. We weren't always—or even often—happy, but we were there. Sometimes that's enough.

CHAPTER 11

1996

Life picks up steam my senior year. I'm bearing down on
graduation, facing the prospect of a life without classes and student-
loan checks. My roommates are busy too. Sandy is concentrating
on her art and Carol on her upcoming wedding. She and Dave
are getting married after graduation. I don't know whether to be
envious or dismissive. The idea of having a partner for life sounds
wonderful, but having him as a partner seems far less so.

My favorite class this year is Physical Anthropology. I like
learning about how our bodies have developed and changed over
the years, how time and turbulence shape who we are. I also like
the professor, an Indiana Jones type who appeals to most girls in
his classes. But it's not his looks that get me. It's his knowledge.
And maybe his blue eyes, but just a little.

The beginnings of spring are evident as I walk to class:
jasmine and eucalyptus that much stronger in the air, birds that
seem cheerier than normal. I am wearing a UCSB T-shirt and
shorts, just like most of the other people in the classrooms and
bike paths. Today I feel bullish on the future, excited about what
is to come, though I don't have much idea what that is. In this
moment the details don't seem to matter.

I reach Buchanan Hall with five minutes to spare. Buchanan
is yet another discordant note in the mishmash that is campus

architecture. It's not simply nondescript, it's angular in an almost offensive way. UCSB seems to specialize in these oddball buildings, things of clashing characteristics set against a backdrop of mountains and ocean. Maybe homeliness and beauty can coexist after all.

The lecture hall is only half full when I walk in. It's that point in the quarter when people start to slack off—that time of year when sand appeals far more than study. I take a seat and wait for Professor Symons to appear. When he does, he announces that this morning we're going to be talking about the evolution of hair.

I don't know whether to be intrigued or scared.

Turns out hair dates to our ancestors. Some say it evolved from scales. I picture myself as a dinosaur, a quadruped clutching a BIC in my mouth. *Evolution*, I write in my notebook.

It evolved to retain body heat. It also served as a skin protectant, a reflector of sunlight, and an attraction to potential mates. I start to write in my notebook, but I drop the pen. Prehumans had an affinity for hirsutism. They *wanted* mates with fur, the thicker the better. What happened? What changed? I want Professor Symons to talk about that, but he describes the different kinds of hair: fur or vellus, straight, curly, or kinky. I tug at my own hair, which I'm wearing in a short brunette bob these days. Curly. Middle of the road. Then I run my finger along the underside of my chin. Too sparse to be fur, too apparent to be vellus. Vellus covers almost our entire bodies. It's so fine as to not be noticed. I examine the backs of my hands. If the hair is there, I don't see it. Presence and absence in one patch of skin.

I pick up my pen. *I don't get it,* I write. Right now, evolution seems more idiosyncratic than anything, a whim of whoever created us. In kindergarten we drew stick figures. We could make them fat or skinny, male or female. We had the power. Years later,

I see how much significance that carries.

Maybe evolution is nothing more than that: the drawing and redrawing of stick figures, the rejiggering of characteristics to make it all fit. Be it whim or will, my stick figure is shaggy.

After class I find a patch of lawn and stretch out in the sun. There are so many beautiful girls on this campus, so many lithe bodies all covered in vellus. Wanting to be them is too easy. What I want is to have it all: my interior, their exterior. Is there some sort of transplant for that?

Behind me two students are discussing today's opinion piece in the *Nexus*. "What a crock of shit," one says. The other disagrees, anger in his voice. I smile. I wrote that piece.

June blows hot breath on my graduation day. Rooster, Tina, and Missy have all descended for the big event. My phone rings as I'm walking out the door to head over to campus. Through the closing door I hear my voice on our answering machine: *You've reached sisters Allison, Carol, and Sandy. We've taken a vow of silence, but leave a message and pray that we call you back.*

"Sister Allison, this is the Mother Superior. Pick up the phone."

Oh, hell. I let myself back in and grab the receiver.

"I blew a tire on the 405," she says. "I'm not going to make it."

I twist my tassel around my finger. In two hours I will move it from the right side to the left. The shift signifies change, achievement, progress. It means I've done something right.

"How are you getting home?"

"Triple A's going to come put on the spare."

I picture her on the slab of concrete that is a Los Angeles freeway, pulled over to the side of the road, talking on her car phone. The top is down and her scarf is blowing in the wind. I am sure of these two facts.

"And then you're going home."

"It's a baby spare. I'll barely limp back to San Diego on it. Look, I'm sorry." I expect her to start crying, but she doesn't, at least not from what I can hear. "I wanted to come. I did."

I almost say *I wanted you there*. And if I think about it, that's the truth.

After the ceremony I stand on a patch of grass and watch Rooster, Missy, and Tina approach. My mouth is dry, my jaw trembling slightly, my heart making odd motions inside my chest. I am the poster girl for mixed emotions.

Rooster kisses me on the cheek. Missy and Tina hug me. So do Sandy and Carol. These embraces, these good wishes. All around me are balloons and flowers, cheers and whoops of joy. What do these celebrants really feel inside?

"Well," Rooster says, "you're grown up."

"Not really. I still need a step stool to reach the top shelf."

He rubs a blade of grass with his foot. "Now what?"

"Lunch," I say. "Everything else can get figured out after that."

We go to Aldo's, which my father pronounces *Ahl-dos*. Missy and Tina have gone back to their shared hotel room to take a nap. I've taken off my cap and gown and left them in the car. It's too damn hot to keep them on this long. The manager greets us at the table and congratulates me on my degree. How did he know?

"That," my father says, and points to the rolled-up paper diploma I received at the ceremony. I'll get the real one midsummer. I've already bought the right frame, made room on the wall. Graduating means I've started something and finished it. It means I'm capable of forward motion.

"What's your plan?"

"I think I'll order the veal Parmesan."

"You think everything's a joke, don't you?"

I'm brought back to being eight years old, a moment outside a suburban pizza parlor. The weather changes quickly in my father's head. Dress in layers. Bring protective gear.

"Most things are," I say.

"Even when it comes to earning a living?"

That's the biggest joke there is as far as I'm concerned. I'm dreading entering the world of work, the 9-to-5 grind with two days off so you can reflect on just how much you hate your job. I don't want to punch a time clock, answer to a boss. I want to direct my own destiny, whatever the hell that means.

"I'll find my way," I say.

"How?"

"Do we have to talk about this now?"

I don't want to admit that I'm not sure what I'm doing. I have enough student-loan money to get me through the next few months, but then the well will be dry. I've been concentrating on schoolwork, putting off applying to jobs. Now the time has come, and I'm not ready.

"No," he says. The waitress arrives and we order. I butter a piece of bread and eat it slowly, feeling each piece pass through my throat into my esophagus. They say today is the first day of the rest of your life, and on this occasion they're right.

"The problem," I tell Missy and Tina later that night, "is that I don't want to do what it takes to earn a living."

"That's called lazy," Tina says. She and I are sitting Indian-style on the floor of my bedroom. Missy is above us on my desk chair. She spins around, and I wonder if the motion is making her as sick as it's making me just watching it. We're finishing up the remains of some Woodstock's pizza. I like Woodstock's because they stuff the crust with sauce. Clever.

"Maybe not," Missy says. She stops spinning and looks at us with her watery blue eyes.

Tina smirks back. "How's that?"

Missy says, "It's not lazy. It's human."

"If it's so human," Tina says, "then why do people work?"

The blue eyes squint in thought. "Not everybody works."

"Like who?" I ask.

"Your mother."

She's got a point.

"Why wasn't she there today anyway?" Tina asks.

I feel a piece of pepperoni go down my throat the wrong way. I swallow hard. "She blew a tire."

"She could've made it if she wanted to."

"*Tina*," Missy says.

"But she didn't," I say. "Can we get back to what we were talking about?"

"Why don't you want to talk about it?"

"*Tina*."

"There's nothing to say. She didn't show up. End of story."

"But she's your—"

"*Tina—*"

"No." Tina's pissed and she's on a tear. "This is just the latest way in which she's fucked you over."

"Well," I say, "that may be true, but it's not my first concern at the moment."

Through the closed door I hear Sandy come in with her family. I should go outside, say hello, be polite. I reach for another slice. My relationship with my mother is an ongoing thing. It's the long-distance run. The job is the sprint. Right now, I need to sprint.

"I hear you," Tina says. "It's not like I've got a job lined up."

"But your parents help you out."

"Not forever. Only until I get on my feet."

"How's that working out for you?"

She waves her bare soles at me. "That's how."

Next week, Missy starts a job as a veterinarian's assistant. She and her boyfriend are making plans to move in together. If I've gotten a bachelor's degree in forward motion, she's already mastered in it.

"You're going to be a writer," she says to me. "You *are* a writer. Remember all the shit you gave Ms. Stark?"

The career counselor. It took me a moment to remember. "I did," I say.

"That was for a reason. Writing for the newspaper these last four years—that was for a reason too. You're meant to use this, Allison. You're meant to do something with it."

"Like what?"

Missy yawns and doesn't bother to cover her mouth. Other than the occasional curse word, it's about as rude as she gets. "That's for you to figure out," she says.

Journalist. The word sounds weird when you break it down, like someone scribbling their deepest thoughts into a locked notebook rather than digging for information to reveal publicly. But that's what I've been doing for the past four years. Why hadn't I understood earlier that it was a career path?

Because I never really wanted to be a journalist. I wanted to be a writer. Those are two very different things. One looks outward; the other goes deep inside. But going deep isn't going to pay the bills, so I start looking for journalism jobs. On a whim I send résumés to places where I can't imagine living: Oklahoma, Idaho, Indiana. These states don't feel quite real, and neither do the jobs in them. I don't take the process quite seriously. I brag about my cookie baking in my cover letters. It's not enough to simply advertise my editing prowess. I want them to know I'm Martha Stewart with an *AP Style Guide* stuffed in a tea cozy.

I get a call from an editor. I catch his last name but not his first. It's Burkhart.

"I've never been to North Dakota," I say.

"Neither have I," he says. "We're in Nebraska."

I wasn't aware there was a difference.

"Tell me about those chocolate chip cookies," Burkhart says.

"Extra vanilla," I say. "And a sprinkle of cinnamon. That's the secret."

The paper is called the *North Platte Telegraph*. I'm picturing stories about Rotary Clubs carved on stone tablets, ferried by horse-riding couriers. Exactly how much breaking news is there about corn?

"Think about it," he says.

After we hang up I rub my eyes hard, harder. I rub so hard that I see patterns and spots, my own personal laser show. I sit cross-legged on my bed and try to meditate. I concentrate on my breathing, focus on the candle in my mind. But my worries blow the candle out, and I decide to do dishes.

I turn the water to hot, nearly scalding. Nebraska? This should be an easy decision, a *thanks-but-no*. I run a caked, greasy pot under the stream: chili. We made it last night, Carol and Sandy and I, dicing onions and shredding cheese. It was one of those cool roommate moments that makes you remember that living with others can sometimes be enjoyable. But our home is about to come apart: Carol is moving in with her fiancé and Sandy is eyeing places downtown. That leaves me holding the bag on our apartment if I choose to stay. But I'm not choosing to stay. I want to leave Santa Barbara. It's time.

Scrubbing the tines of a fork, I think about the medication that I take every morning, would-be magic pills at the tip of my tongue. They tamed my numbers but not what really matters. How would a bearded lady play in the Midwest?

Then I drop the fork into the soapy water. I'm irritated with myself. Why does it always have to come down to this? But I understand myself too. Life comes down to the pinpoint of what consumes you most. We all see life through the lens of our own worries.

Nebraska. I walk away from the sink, wiping my hands on my jeans, and study the U.S. map that Sandy's pinned to the kitchen wall. Nebraska is shaped like a square teapot, its handle pointing west. It has neither the length nor the size of California. It is straight and angular. It looks like a place that makes sense.

"But it's *Nebraska*," Tina says when I call her. "It *snows*."

"It does?"

"You didn't know that?"

"It's called sarcasm."

I'm holding a hand mirror. I alternately frown and smile into it. Then I grimace. It's an exaggerated motion, a pulling-back of the corners of my mouth. There are my eyes, my nose, my cheeks and mouth. There are my ears. There is the hair. One of these things just doesn't belong.

"Do you actually want to live there?"

I look around my room. Controlled, just like my dorm room. Step inside and you're in a world of symmetry, tightly tucked sheets, alphabetized textbooks. I can either hide inside this place or start my journey into the outside world. "I don't know," I say.

"You're telling me there are no journalism jobs in California?"

"Nope. Not a one."

"There's that sarcasm again."

"Tina," I say, "maybe I want to shake it up a little bit."

"There's shaking it up and then there's shattering it."

I picture my life in small, sharp pieces flung across the floor. Tiny enough to overlook, painful enough to sting.

I take the job.

My first meal in Nebraska is a runza. It's a rectangular sandwich pocket with meat, sauerkraut, and onions. I eat it in a fast-food joint of the same name, a place where employees wear green-and-yellow uniforms and seem genuinely happy to be there. It comes with crinkly fries and a soft drink of your choice. I pick Mountain Dew, which seems a lot more popular here than at home. The caffeine jolts my bones and pumps its way to my heart.

I have *done* this. I packed up my room in Santa Barbara and spent the last bit of my student-loan money on a U-Haul. I went out and bought a heavy winter coat. I broke the news to my parents, and they were not impressed.

"It's *Nebraska*," Nails said. "You fly over it, you don't live there."

"You can come visit if you want."

"Your *aunt* lived in Omaha. She broke her *toe* running away from a tornado. I think I'll pass."

Rooster laughed when I called with the news.

"You have to go through this phase?" he asked. "You couldn't just become a Buddhist like other kids your age?"

"Meditation bores me."

"Yeah," he said. "Me too."

I am the *North Platte Telegraph*'s wire editor. We're a 12,000-circulation daily covering twenty counties. Rumor has it that in one of those counties, you can call Information, ask for Buck, and get connected without having to give a last name. I start work next week. Right now I'm just getting settled. I'm staying at the Hampton Inn near the interstate, house-hunting by circling classified ads in the *Telegraph* itself. Today I will open a local bank account, get some snow tires on my car. I will build my life here one step at a time.

After lunch I meet Burkhart for coffee. He takes it black, straight up, no chaser. He's a no-bullshit kind of guy, one of these hardass old-school journalists. He tells me he's interviewed Magic Johnson, that he's good friends with Ted Turner. "But I came to this shithole for the same reason you did," he says. "I wanted a challenge."

I sip my apple cider. "Is this a shithole?"

"Look around, kid. This is not L.A."

"I'm not from L.A."

"You're from California. It's *all* L.A."

Burkhart lights a cigarette and gives me a look. It's one of those looks that could mean anything. This guy isn't easy to read. "Tell me something," he says.

My heart starts to pound. I hate being addressed like this, especially when there's so much I don't want to tell.

"Why are you here?"

"I like backward, redneck shitholes."

His laugh is big, all-encompassing, head-turning.

"You really want to know?"

"I asked, didn't I?"

"I'm here for the same reason anyone goes anywhere else. There wasn't enough to keep me where I was."

A silence falls between us. I glance at the chalkboard menu, the pictures of Paris on the walls. What would it be like to dream of the Seine in this place of flat land, big sky, dramatic sunsets?

"Yeah," he says. "Me too."

Burkhart leaves my second week. I find out when I walk into the newsroom and everyone's talking about how he's gone. No one knows whether he walked out the door or was pushed, only that he is gone and I'm left to make sense of what I've found here off Interstate 80.

A small city with a cobblestone downtown. An airport that closes for lunch. A bar called Doris's Tavern that features pictures of hometown soldier boys and takes checks for its two-dollar drinks. We rush there after putting the paper to bed each night, skidding on icy roads past farms and churches.

"He betrayed us," Wendy says. Wendy's one of the two copy editors I supervise. She has blonde hair, blue eyes, and a Wisconsin license plate on the back of her Chevy.

"He got out," John says. John's from Kentucky. He's been trying to teach me how to play "Driver 8" on the guitar. Thus far, the lessons haven't taken. "You'd get out too."

"Maybe I will," she says.

My cheeks are flaming red. I feel abandoned and I'm not sure why. It's not as though Burkhart was my best friend. We barely knew each other. But he'd convinced me to come to this place, and now he's leaving. The newsroom feels no different, but I do. This is my first pang of regret.

Once homesickness sets in, it spreads. A week after the editor left, Wendy tells me to go to Lake McConaughy, Nebraska's biggest body of water. "When you see it, you won't miss California," she says. "Squint and you won't see the other side. It's no different than the Pacific Ocean."

Turns out I could be blind and still see the other side. There's also another difference between an ocean in California and a lake in Nebraska.

"It was frozen," I tell her. I'd driven a two-hour round-trip to look at a big chunk of ice.

"Well, Toto," she says, "you're a long way from home."

I think about that as I sit in my recliner watching "The Farm Report" at five o'clock in the morning. I came here almost as a lark, a fuck-you to my California life. Now I'm failing to see the wisdom of that decision. I'm no different here than I was at home. I'm here and I'm me, and I still need medication. In fact, I need a refill on one of my prescriptions. When the sun rises, I call a local pharmacist.

"This is for your husband?" he asks.

"No," I say. "For me."

"It reverses *hair loss*."

"Look. I have a prescription."

I'm clutching my black cordless phone in my hand, gripping it a little too tightly. I never thought I'd hold it the way I'm holding it right now, less tool and more weapon.

"Okay," he says. "Bring it in. I'll fill it."

I picture the pill bottles, a trio of good soldiers sitting, awaiting me in that pharmacy across town. I think about how they feel in my hands: smooth, sturdy. They are assurance, a promise waiting to be kept.

Nine months I've been taking them. And—nothing.

I can be at the pharmacy in the time it takes to listen to three Sheryl Crow songs. I like her. She's strong. She's sexy. She sings about loss and Las Vegas.

I can get there in ten minutes, fifteen tops. But why? Why spend more money that I don't have on medication that isn't working? When I last talked to the doctor, he counseled patience again. It's a bitter drug, so easy to prescribe when you're not the one having to choke it down.

Better to tie yourself to the blackness of the inevitable. More truthful to prop your fists against that wall, to press your cheek to the plaster and to feel that ice.

Best to drop a fight you can't win.

"No," I say. "It's fine."

Then I hang up before he can question me further.

No more refills. No more money thrown into that body of water called hope. There is no view of the opposite side, no means of paddling through high tide. There is a lonely coastline and a chill wind and me. Just me.

CHAPTER 12

1997

The sky does not fall. The waters of the frozen lake do not part. Nothing changes after I stop taking my medications, because I never saw anything change in the first place.

I get a different divine sign.

It's January. According to the bank I passed on my way home from work, it's minus 3 degrees. Now I'm turning onto my street. It's a place of small one-story homes, broad porches, clapboard windows. It's Mayberry sold at a discount.

My house is nothing you would ever find in California: a brick split-level. It's the best part of being here. It's got carpet in the bathroom and sponge-painted apples on the kitchen cabinets. I love it the way a child loves her favorite teddy bear as it grows worn and used, as it loses an eye and gains battle scars. I'm standing at the living-room window watching the snow fall. This hasn't lost its novelty. I'm holding a mug of hot chocolate, my nose pressed against the glass. I am five years old again. The world is new.

Then a crash.

"What the—" I mutter thoughtfully and go to inspect the damage.

My garage door is hanging by a bolt. By. A. Bolt. It must have gotten ripped off by the wind. Unless God started working out and flexed *his* muscle on my poor house, there is no other excuse.

It may be time to polish up my résumé.

"Already?" Missy says when I call her.

"What took so long?" Tina says a half hour later.

"What's snow like?" Sandy wants to know.

All these familiar voices. They make my stomach ache. I'm realizing how alone I am here. Every so often John and I go to Perkins for some chicken-fried steak, or Wendy and I go to the mall—which is called *The Mall*—for some recreational shoe shopping, but I spend most of my time alone. Too much time. Too much space to think. Not enough input. No distractions.

I'm still talking to Sandy when the power goes out. The phone goes dead in my hand. I'm alone in the dark. "Well," I say to myself, "isn't this symbolic." Then I fumble for any source of light I can find. The flashlight on my nightstand has dead batteries. The matches come with no corresponding candle. I wind up grabbing an old hand-held Tetris game and turning on the display just for some illumination.

"Well," I say again, "*how* symbolic."

Sometimes the symbolism is so neat that it's irritating. No one would write it that way, because it would just be so damn perfect. When the lights flicker back on, I don't know whether to cheer or groan. My eyes fix on a flashing clock radio: 12:00. 12:00. 12:01. It's marking time from an arbitrary beginning, but then again, aren't all beginnings arbitrary?

The next day at work, John says: "Hey, Allison. Where's Fairfield?"

Connecticut?

"No. In California."

I look at a map. I squint for a moment, then spot it—halfway between Sacramento and San Francisco.

"There's a copy editor gig there."

Huh. I look up the job listing. It's at the *Fairfield Daily Republic*, a newspaper slightly bigger than the *Telegraph*. They want editing and headline-writing skills, knowledge of AP style, an understanding of desktop publishing. The basics.

Before I can read any further, our news editor approaches me. Like Burkhart, she is no-nonsense. Unlike Burkhart, she's a native Nebraskan and comfortable in North Platte. It's hard to relate to her. I close the job listing and put on an *I'm-working* face.

"Did you do the obits last night?" she asks. Her name is Joanne and she is tall and thin.

Obituaries are a big part of any paper. So is "Dear Abby."

"I wanted to show you this," she says, and puts down a folded copy of the paper on my desk. Circled in red is an obituary for a woman—with a man's mugshot embedded in the story. "That's upsetting to the readers, and it's upsetting to me. Don't let it happen again."

Then she walks away. I watch her go. She wears practical pants and a shag haircut. She is right, but I bristle at the criticism. Criticism is a big part of journalism. Everything runs through editors. Editors nitpick for a living.

I hope they airbrush my photo when I die. I don't want to be mistaken for a man even after death.

I'm in the shower when the call comes.

"This is Bill Buchanan," the voice on the other end says as I stand dripping on my blue carpet. "I'm with the *Daily Republic* newspaper in California."

I'd sent in my résumé a month ago and promptly forgotten about it. It was a lark, nothing more.

"Oh," I say. "Hello!"

Things go fast after that point. I'm naked and shivering under my thin towel, but the shaking comes from excitement. We agree to have another phone interview tomorrow. After we hang up I get dressed and blow-dry my hair, which I've finally learned to do so I don't show up to work with ice crystals hanging from the roots. I warm up my car, and it sits running in the garage with no door. I drive the streets of North Platte, passing a sheaf of fast-food restaurants, over the Buffalo Bill viaduct near Bailey Yard, the world's largest rail classification yard.

I've been here all of three months, and now I'm preparing to leave? What happened to commitment, to challenge, to adventure?

Carol once told me that adventure is a good thing only after it's been lived. Maybe she was right. Still, I feel guilty as I drive through town. Could I not stick it out for more than three months? Am I that weak? Or is it okay to give up on something that's not working?

Look at Nails and Rooster. How long did it take them to give up on the marriage? And how much ground was gained by stubbornly staying in it?

Two days later I give notice.

"You came and went," Joanne says. "It's like you're just blowing through town."

"I'm sorry," I say.

"No," she says. "You're not."

But as I stand in my cheap, cozy house with the sponge-painted fruit on the cabinets, packing up everything that hasn't remained in boxes the entire time I've been here, I do feel sorry.

I'm sorry that I couldn't start something and stick with it. I'm sorry I couldn't step beyond my comfort zone. I'm sorry I couldn't go on a leap of faith and trust that things would be okay.

I rip up copies of the *Telegraph* and roll mugs in Dear Abby columns. Each move seems to highlight my own inability to make something stick. Not a job, not a medical regimen. I want to throw one of the ceramic chunks across the room out of frustration, but I just keep packing. I've got the oldies on the radio.

Hello, I love you.

I stack the mugs one atop another.

Call on me, darling, and I'll come to you.

I close the box and seal it shut.

Any time at all.

Such welcoming lyrics. Were they sung by lonely people? Did they too feel thwarted by their own failings? Did they bludgeon themselves with what could have been done, or was done but could have been done better, or what never should have been done in the first place?

Outside the sky opens to a universe of universes. Here you can see stars. Their shine is more vivid than I've ever seen before. Of course I wonder what's out there. Don't you?

I arrive late on a rainy night. Berkeley at first glance isn't exactly what I expected: a grimy main road leading from the freeway, a clutch of sari shops, convenience stores with their doors thrown open to the storm. It looks run-down and dirty. Where was the Berkeley of my dreams, the porches alive with hanging crystals, polygamists relaxing over espresso? Where are the psychic shops, the cafes? I press my disappointment aside and pull into the Travelodge parking lot.

Inside, there is a bearded lady.

My God. The faded Thai restaurants and copy shops of University Avenue are forgotten. I hadn't even dared to hope that I would find something like this.

An actual live bearded lady. It isn't just stubble either. It's a full beard that covers her chin and carries on down to her neck. It's blonde hair, so it's not as obvious as it might be, but still. She's unshaven. How exciting. How brave!

For a moment I forget why I'm here. I am captivated. I can't stop staring, even though I, of all people, realize just how rude that is. Then she gives a polite cough and I blink.

"Sorry," I say. "Long trip."

"What's your final destination?"

"Here."

"Welcome home, then."

Home. I've come to Berkeley hoping it would be exactly that. I see this woman as some sort of sign, a bit of encouraging symbolism. People like me do exist, and they exist here.

Up in my room the euphoria fades a bit. Of course there are people like me. I've always known I wasn't the only one with hair on my face and body. My problem isn't that I'm alone. It's that I don't want to be like those people. I don't want anything in common with the woman downstairs, regardless of how brave I think she is.

I flip on the television. There. That's what I want to be: thin, smooth. I'm not sure if it's because society told me that or I told myself.

Does it matter?

"Of course it matters," I mutter to myself. "It makes a difference."

I go to the window and look outside onto University Avenue. It looks no different than when I drove down the street twenty minutes ago, but somehow I can see it as home. I lean on my elbows and lower my face into my cupped palms like a child.

Of course it matters.

I don't want to believe my self-image comes from billboards and brochures. But I can never be entirely sure that I haven't subscribed to society's ideas about hairy women. It's not as if I had to. The woman downstairs hasn't. She's gutsy enough to stand on her own as what she is.

I want to be like her.

I want to stop trying to hide what I can never fully conceal.

I want to be what I am.

The exhaustion hits like a tsunami, pulling back at first to allow me to feel all my energy at once, then moving in as a solid, single wave. It pulls me from shore and drowns me in sleep.

I wake at 5:30 in the morning, feeling as if there were no pause between the time I dropped into unconsciousness and the moment I came to. For a moment I'm uncertain of where I am. Then I remember. I stagger from bed and sit on the toilet, blinking down at my freckled thighs. I pee for what feels like forever. The flush sounds like a roar. As I'm washing my hands, I watch the girl in the mirror. She frowns at me, then smiles.

Back in bed I run my hands over my face. The stubble seems somehow less pronounced. Have my hormones somehow righted themselves overnight? I slide my hands under the faded UCSB T-shirt I wear to bed. My chest is not smooth. Nor are my arms and legs.

I've never thought to accept it, to stride into the world with everything unshaven. I've never considered throwing away the razors letting it grow, putting aside concerns about what others think.

Confidence. Enviable concept. Assurance, freedom from doubt. The ability to move through the world in harmony with oneself without stumbling. I'm not entirely lacking in it. I have confidence in my writing, my friendships. I believe I'm smart, sassy, aware. I'm twenty-two years old, and I'm excited about my future.

Yet the woman downstairs has something I don't. She moves in harmony not only with her mind but her body. She may wake up and worry, but not about the follicles on her face. She lets them grow with abandon, and for all I know she smiles in the mirror at her own reflection. I hope she does.

I move to Sutter Street. It's a big pink house in a leafy neighborhood. From the living room you can see a slice of the Bay Bridge. Marty and Peggy are my landlords. They live upstairs. They run a costume shop in the basement and breed Pomeranians upstairs.

David is the other tenant. He's a Lenny Kravitz look-alike who tosses verbal barbs. He's a graduate student studying computer animation, formulas that look like scrawled ancient Greek when I peer over his shoulder. He's observant, too observant. I find myself afraid of the perceptive vision he so often masks with dark glasses.

I grow familiar with the home he and I share. I learn the squeak of the floorboards as I walk from kitchen to bedroom, the feel of the dull kitchen knife in my hand, the pop and click of the toaster. Sometimes I'll clean the mold off the single white chair in Marty and Peggy's overgrown backyard and sit in it, turning my face toward the sun. *It will tan your face evenly*, my mother says in my memory. Maybe there's still a chance.

I get accustomed to the bathroom. I learn the tricks of the light, the exact angle at which to hold my chin while looking in the mirror, the ways to fool myself into thinking the hair doesn't show. I figure out the pulse of the shower head, the sting of the water as it beats on my back. *You don't hate your body*, I tell myself, running the razor along my skin, wincing as the blade catches and blood begins to flow. *You just haven't figured it out yet.*

My new workplace looks like Cookie Monster's asshole. Blue cubicles, blue walls, carpet the shade of sky. Maureen, a stocky blonde with bangs who is now my boss, leads me through the maze on my first day. Behind every cubicle is a face. I evaluate each and know they are doing the same. I want to believe that journalists, those involved in the world of words, are different, that they judge from the inside out, that they look at the eyes and evaluate the soul.

Bullshit. They discriminate on looks just like everyone else.

Maureen leads me to the copy desk. It's a place where people sit together all day and don't get up. "This is where she'll be" she says, gesturing to a cockeyed blue chair that looks like it'll fall over in a stiff wind. It doesn't matter that she's referring to me in the third person as if I'm not actually standing right here. I am a *she*!

"Now," she says, "the paperwork."

I fill out all the necessary information: date of birth, address, Social Security number. I write as clearly and legibly as possible on the cramped white lines, picturing the folder into which this will be inserted. This will go down on your permanent record. Everything does.

Copy editors work at night, wrangling with other peoples' words. When the reporters leave at six and rush to the bar, we're just

195

beginning to mull what to do on our dinner break.

We're meant to be invisible. When we do our best work, no one ever realizes we were there. I want more.

More happens quickly. Two weeks after I start at the *Daily Republic*, Maggie Honey gets pregnant. The last time this happened she miscarried, and now she's taking no risks. She'll be gone for four months on extended maternity leave. Someone's got to fill in for her spot on the Features desk.

I want it to be me. I want to profile the official Fairfield poker team. I want to write the weekly senior-center column. More than anything, I want to leave the office at six and head to Grizzly Bay Brewing Company with the rest of the reporters.

I go over to Maggie's desk. She's a sweet woman with puppy eyes and an ever-present candy dish. Sometimes I can hear her laugh across the room, and it's like an odd ray of light breaking through fog. I start to open my mouth and she puts a hand on my arm.

"You know," she says, "the job's probably yours if you want it."

And how!

After I get the job, I arrive in the office at eight in the morning and work until ten at night. I interview breast cancer survivors and aging prom queens. I spend a day on San Francisco's Haight Street and another winery-hopping. I fly in a small plane piloted by a tough woman and squeal when she flips upside down.

I've hit my stride. Yet sometimes I feel as though I'm stumbling.

"We've got to send a message," the woman on the couch says, her slender body splayed across the leopard-skin print. She is a dark punctuation mark, a hyphen that occasionally stretches into an em dash.

She's the publicist for a local hip-hop band. She is easily twice
the band members' age, and she confounds them. They adore her.
They are confused by her. And I'll be damned if they don't go
home and jerk off after each meeting she holds with them.

Her apartment is a sly sex chamber. It's dolled up with
lighting and scarves, design elements that wink and flutter
knowingly. Magazines that smell like perfume samples are
stacked on glass end tables. Scented candles make my nose
twitch.

"We got to get the word out," she says in sultry, assured
tones.

She's perfect for PR. She's got image down to a hot little
pinpoint. She's studied how to join the five senses, build a silken
cage of experience, a sensual trap that gently but firmly sucks
away all other memory. She is all you know, what you remember,
the sum of what you want.

In an odd sidelong way, she reminds me of myself. I know
how to draw attention away from my failings and toward my
positive qualities. I've developed an extroverted personality that
far outstrips my inner self. I am forceful. I control my image as
best as possible.

"These boys have something to say," she tells me.

I've been here a half hour and still don't have a clue as
to their message. I do know that I need to pee. She gives me
directions: down the hall, left at the glass curio; please don't
bump into it, there's valuable stuff in there. I smirk to myself and
traverse the thick carpet.

Then I'm in the bathroom. I lean against the window and
collect myself. The hardest part of my job is talking to people,
parrying their words, collating my notes, making sense of what
they have to say. Sometimes I feel drained by their energy, their

need for recognition, for acknowledgment. If I can't always do that for myself, what makes them think I can do it for them?

I sit on the toilet. I wonder if she's on the other side of the door, listening, taking notes. She seems like that kind of woman, fragrant and fragile on the exterior. Inside, I bet she's got the heart of Hitler and the moral compunction of Michael Milken. When I talked to her band members on the phone, they sounded like little hip-hop hypnotics: *She fly. She kick ass.* I'm supposed to quote them on this?

I wash my hands. Her soap smells like jasmine and cloves—one part air, the rest fire. I meet my eyes in the mirror, and for once I can look at my entire self. There I am, reflected. I am a person. I am fatally flawed, just like everyone else who walks this earth.

I poke into her medicine cabinet. It opens with the slightest creak, designed only to be heard by the guilty. I look around. What do I expect to see? There's no accusing finger wagging in my direction, just lots of Body Shop potions and gilded mirrors.

Initially I'm disappointed: a stack of Crabtree & Evelyn Botanical Beauty bars, Body Time face cream, and something called hydrating serum. Fancy finds, but hardly surprising.

Then I push aside the Honey Dream Hand Cream, and everything hits.

Celexa.

Lexapro.

Valium.

Huh.

Other people need things. Beautiful, lithe people who dress up their cookie-cutter apartments like Egyptian sex dens. They too have holes to be plugged by pharmacology. I already knew this, but I'm not opposed to being reminded from time to time.

Why does she pop all these pills? Does she crave that injection of happy transmitters? Are you even supposed to mix all this? I wonder if she ever considered doing what I've done: giving it all up, going au naturel. I doubt it.

Nestled next to the pills are yet more pills: Imodium, Pepcid, stool softener. Couldn't you just push some body butter up your ass and be done with it?

I flush the empty toilet again. Better she thinks I've done something obscene in there, something requiring the blush-worthy double flush, than suspect I've found her age elixirs and rectal potions.

Where to wear one's flaws? On your face, where they can never be concealed? Or inside a mirrored bathroom cabinet, where they grow more shameful with each hidden moment? Where to handle those flaws—in the light of day or in the gauzy dimness of a feminine bathroom? What to do with the burden of being human?

By the time I get back to the newsroom, some shit's hit the fan. A kid got killed in a car crash and one of our reporters wrote it up. There's a problem, though. When someone dies, you're supposed to confirm their identity with the Coroner's Office. Our guy didn't bother to do that. Big mistake. Turns out that the kid who died was some thug in Oakland who had the same name as a local kid—and he'd reported that it was the local kid who died. That local kid was once one of Fairfield's star student athletes and is now a member of the military.

"The guy's *mother* read it in the paper," whispers my friend Judith, bug-eyed and excited, "and had a *heart attack.*"

Well, now. This is certainly going to overshadow the fact that I got in late today and took a long lunch.

"Where's Matt?" I ask. Matt's the culprit, a frat boy with a cleft chin and not much else to recommend him.

"Downstairs with Bill," Judith says. "They're in a meeting. Looks like the guy walked in *alive* with his commanding officer."

Oh boy. What I would give to be a spider on the wall for that one.

Matt is a burr in my butt. He's the only other Jew in the newsroom, so we fight over working Christmas and reaping the subsequent overtime. I can't figure out why he cares, since rumor has it that he lets his paychecks pile up. Doesn't bother to collect them for weeks. I, on the other hand, *run* my ass to the bank on payday, hoping the money will get credited in time for my rent check to clear.

The guy likes to saunter up to my cube, drape an arm over the blue wall as if he had the right, and say: "Landa. What's up?" in that chummy, obnoxious way. Christ. Take your game of beer pong somewhere else, chump.

"*Some*-body's getting fired today," I tell Judith.

"Not so fast," she says.

"Come *on*, dude. The DR's on the hook for a freaking *huge* bunch of flowers for the mom at least, if not a big fat lawsuit."

"He's cute," she says—as if that explains it all.

I don't buy it. The whole beautiful-people-have-it-better thing seems like a cop-out, an excuse. *I didn't get the job because she crossed her legs! He got an A and I didn't . . . because he's got a six-pack.* It always seems like bullshit.

Matt's getting kicked to the curb. That'll be the last time he fails to call the county coroner to make sure he's telling the town that the right kid croaked.

And I'll be proven right.

"They *what?*"

"Don't make a thing out of it," James says. "It's not like it's going to help matters."

James works on the copy desk. He's a heartfelt guy, sometimes fiery, given to popping off at the mouth and then taking it back twenty minutes later. He's short, stout, with dark stubble much like my own.

I like James. I feel comfortable with him. And what he just told me pisses me off.

"You got a talking-to because you didn't place the correction on Matt's story prominently enough? Meanwhile, he got off without even a warning?"

James pops a handful of trail mix into his mouth and offers me the bag. I pick out a handful of almonds and some blue M&Ms, no raisins. He shrugs.

"That's the way it is," he says.

The way it is?

"James," I say, "I've seen you kick holes in the wall because you fucked up on a *Jeopardy* question. You're telling me you're going to stand for this?"

"No," he says, "I'm sitting."

How easy to hate people like Matt, the ones who cash in on their advantage by flashing a big blue-eyed smile and melting some hearts. How liberating to hate the beautiful, while at the same time plotting how to become them.

If only I felt the fury I'm trying to instill in James. I just feel sad.

Matt's downstairs sweating under his Abercrombie shirt. The dark punctuation mark in Suisun is fingering her multiple bottles. We can aspire to move into the leagues of the gorgeous, but in the end this changes nothing. They are human. Like us.

CHAPTER 13

1998

"I love that about you," he says. "Your vitriol."

"Fuck *you*," I say, and toast him with my Wyder's hard cider.

Matt and I. Friends. Who would've guessed at that one?

It started after I left the *Daily Republic* to freelance. Even the joy of writing features couldn't blind me to the fact that office life felt like a cage, the type where you can neither sit nor stand nor lie comfortably. All you can do is continually rearrange yourself and, in the end, realize anew that you're existing in a trap.

He started calling me after I'd quit. "Let's go drinking, Landa," he'd say. *Christ.* The guy didn't give up. Finally, I said: "Sure." I knew the perfect place: The Pub. A place for conversations and the occasional drunken revelation. It's nothing you'll ever see in ads. You just need to discover it.

We're sitting at a scarred wooden table, our drinks sweating into thick cardboard coasters. No more smoking in bars, but you can still smell tobacco from the Reagan era. Johnny Cash plays on a boom box, and the bearded, bespectacled guy behind the bar tallies the day's take on a notepad, writing in pencil. No cash register here.

He's brought a bag of goodies: a *Harper's* magazine, a column clipped from the newspaper, a book called *Going to Pieces without Falling Apart.* "Check this out," he says. "You'd never have bought it for yourself, so I got it for you. Do you meditate?"

I don't think so. What good does it do to close your eyes and *breathe* while some flickering candle threatens to burn down your apartment?

"I'm open to it," I say.

Matt is the reason I know looks matter. But it's a Friday night, and he's sitting here drinking with me, giving me gifts. If looks mattered that much, would he be here?

I can't let myself be fooled. This could be one of those little tricks life likes to play on you every so often, the way it yanks the chair out from under you as you sit down so that you sprawl on your ass and everyone laughs, and the best thing you can do is laugh with them, even as the tears sting your eyes.

"You wouldn't believe what went on today," he says. "Not everyone's lucky like you and got the hell out."

"Most people make their own luck," I say. "Not everyone's born with a silver trust fund in their mouth."

He smirks at the jibe and continues. "I walked over to the printer and Cat was waiting."

Cat is my former boss. The name's accurate. She's feline to the point of practically scratching the furniture and peeing in a box.

"She was already holding my printout, and when I went to grab it, she said: 'Your mother doesn't work here, you know.' I guess it had been sitting there a while. Then she handed it to me, and then—"

I'm smirking too. I see what's coming next.

"Then she reached out and slapped my cheek. All light and flirty-like."

Okay, I hadn't seen that coming. Maybe a little lecture, sure. But nothing like a come-on. Women like Cat don't come on to guys like Matt. Or if they do, they get ridiculed around drinks with the guys after work.

Does Matt consider me one of the guys?

"Well, hell," I say. "I would've hauled off and belted her."

"What good would that do? Hitting her is like hitting Godzilla's punching bag."

He's got a point.

"She likes you," I say, and feel my cheeks grow warm.

There's a reason they call it a crush. It feels as if your heart is pinioned between your ribs, too trapped to beat, too full to remain still. It's a dry mouth and sweaty palms. It's a canker sore you bite constantly because it's too bloated to ignore. Sure, there's pain, but what can you do?

There are different stripes of crushes. There's the fun kind, where the pain is that of sport. A burning of a muscle, the stretching of a ligament. Temporary. Optional. Stop when you want; pick it up whenever it pleases you.

Then there's what I'm feeling. This is the anti-fun. It's muddled, murky and unclear. There are no straight lines or definitive answers. And since I'm not about to come out and ask him if he reciprocates my feelings, there is also none of what they call closure. It's just an awkward struggle, something that's sitting on my mind whether I want it there or not.

"Slip something in his drink," David says. We're making cookies at three in the morning. "Then rip his Dockers off."

I'm sifting flour, baking soda, and salt with a fork. It mixes better that way. "I feel like I'm in high school."

"It's worse than high school," he says. "It's life."

He cracks eggs into a bowl and reaches for a wooden spoon. "Use a whisk," I say.

"You're a real honky, aren't you?"

"What does that have to do with utensils?"

"Not much. I just thought I'd say it."

The kitchen is the cleanest part of the house. It's a small space hung with the typical culinary-themed pictures: tomatoes, chaffs of wheat, wine bottles. What sets it apart is the dead stuffed squirrel hanging along the curtain rod. Its dead eyes seem to ponder the situation and say, *This ain't working, guys*.

Our landlords have a soft spot for dead animals. The living room features Native American-style dream catchers with bird corpses in the middle. They've framed a mouse brought home by the cat and hung it on the dining-room wall. How did I not notice the quiet carnage when I first signed the rental agreement?

"Maybe I don't want that," I say.

"Then you're a liar. Everyone wants that."

Don't be so sure, I think but don't say. The idea of being naked with Matt puts my whole body on insta-freeze. I have no desire to take my clothes off in front of him, to have him rub his hands along my skin. The crush may not be platonic, but it is PG-rated.

David sprawls in a chair and mixes chocolate chips into the batter. I watch his arm moving in a rhythmic motion, the grip of his fingers. He is an attractive guy, but I couldn't be sexual with him even if it were in the cards. The night with Brent is still too real. The observation. The ridicule.

I throw a spatula at the squirrel. "What are *you* looking at?"

David's lips twitch. "Someone's on edge."

"Someone's tired of the dead outnumbering the living around here."

"Move."

"You think if I had the money, I wouldn't?"

We drop the cookies in little balls on the baking sheet and slide them into the oven.

"About this guy," he says.

"Yeah?"

"Sounds like a douche."

"Hey," Matt says when I answer the phone a few days later. "What are you up to tonight?"

"Blowing Prince Charles. He's been depressed since Diana died."

"So, The Pub? Six?"

He sees my stubble. He must. Yet he's never commented, never stared. If anything, I feel *attractive* around him. I'm not going to go so far as to say he accepts me, but I feel it could be possible.

I arrive before him and take a seat in one of the comfortable chairs near the fireplace. When he shows up, he's wearing a battered leather jacket. "Pulled it out of my closet, last-minute," he says. "Looks kind of yuppie but fits well."

I want to believe I don't care about his looks, that I can see through them the way you see through the words of an excellent novel, the way they become a portal to something more, transporting you to a story.

But damn, he is so cute.

"Rich-boy chic," I say, and want to punch myself. I'd pulled down a metal gate to hide the rush of affection, and it turned out to be electrified.

A line appears between his dark eyebrows. "Always got to go there, huh?"

I'm sorry. Please don't be angry.

"Cry me a goddamned river, Little Lord Fauntleroy-berg."

And just like that, we both laugh.

Somehow we end up in his car, drunk, too drunk. He recently traded up to a hand-me-down Toyota Camry from his parents. A doctor and lawyer in Marin. Does it get better than that? I'll bet if *he* were a girl with a beard, they could not only cure it but could sue God for damages.

I glance at the cut of his jaw. His head lies against the steering wheel. "Don't you dare drive."

"No shit."

We don't drink for the act itself. Orange juice, Diet Coke, bottled water—they're all in a different category than alcohol. Minute Maid doesn't offer that rush of looseness and freedom, that sense of possibility like walking off a cliff.

We drink to make our lives something they're not.

"I masturbate twice a day," he says out of nowhere. "Three times on weekends. I can't believe I'm telling you this."

What if I shared my secrets?

"Matt, check it out. It's not like I'm a guy or anything, but I've got mass testosterone just slamming through my veins. Dare me to grow out my beard until I can braid it? I can do that, you know, because even though I was taking medication, it didn't stop the hair. My *levels* were awesome, Matt, but you know what? It didn't change a thing. Now I'm not on medication and I don't bother with the doctor. I can't *believe* I'm telling you this."

What if I took that risk? We're drunk. It's the perfect time. Just get it out there. It's not as if I don't know things about him besides his masturbatory habits. I know about his long-distance college girlfriend and how she dumped him, leaving his head spinning on the plane back home. I know he likes his mother but is intimidated by his father. I know about the time he got drunk at a jam session when he was twenty years old and left his drum kit at some dude's house. It took him a week to go back for it, and at that point the thing was long sold.

He can talk to me. Why can't I talk to him?

We head to Ashkenaz, a rambling barn of a world-music community center down on San Pablo. I've had my car break down outside there a few times, but I've never actually gone in. *What the hell*, I think with my newly loose, open mind. *This is the kind of place you go to get in touch with your feelings, your inner self. You leave a different person, your hair flowing loose, your feet bare against the magical sidewalk concrete. You may even walk out Cuban or Jamaican.*

We walk in, and the dream dissipates. There's a cavernous dance floor and a lot of loose skirts twirling across it, those Indian-style wraps sold in every secondhand shop on Telegraph Avenue. I can't wear clothing like that, the ambiguous cotton. I want to know my clothes are securely fastened and bolted, separating me from everything else.

We fumble in a dark punctuated only by small twinkling bulbs and stage lights. He goes to buy drinks. I'm alone, not knowing where to put my hands or eyes.

How do the dancers do it? Are they drunk as well? High? Did someone whisper the secret of life into their multiple-pierced ears? Did that come free with the price of admission?

He comes back with two frosty, sweating pints. The simple act makes my throat burn. I blink back the tears and am thankful, so thankful for the dark.

The singer takes the stage. She's from Cape Verde. I have no idea where that is. It's one of those places where I imagine you can make a career out of drinking mai tais and saying slowly, languidly: *Eduardo, I love you, but I must be free.*

Her name is Fantcha. It's one of those one-name names, like Sade or Kleenex. Inside her clothes her body is lithe and nimble, her hair a black outpouring like heartbreak. Matt watches her white skirt drift around her ankles and leans to whisper to me.

"I fall in love twenty times a day," he says.

"Bullshit," I say. I don't know where the word comes from, only that it falls from my lips. I don't regret it either. Twenty times a day, huh? Give me a goddamned break.

Fantcha is singing something that sounds like the aural version of a mojito. Girls with flowers in their hair and boys in paisley get up to dance. We stay seated.

"Dude," I say, "falling in love is not like fast food. You don't just order it up every time you get a hard-on. You know?"

"No," he says. "Tell me."

I can't read his expression, and I'm not sure I'd be able to even if the lights were on full. I can't figure out the tone of his voice, the little wrinkles of nuance. I need some fresh air.

"I'll be back," I say, and leave before he can object. Outside is cool bliss, relative quiet, the intermittent *beek!* of the handicapped "Walk" signal on a traffic light. I find an alcove, a recess within the building's wall, and I tuck myself inside it.

Twenty times a day. Hyperbole, sure, but to what extent? What exactly is his definition of love?

Something materializes out of the dark. "You're beautiful," it says. "Perfect. Love to come in there and make sweet love to you."

I groan, grit my teeth, push past the apparition. I walk past the smoking hippies and lean against a wall, hoping not to be found. Not by Matt, not by the voice, not by anybody. I'm tired of walking this tightrope, reading into every small gesture and throwaway statement. Why not cut the rope and face the gauntlet?

The voice is gone. What would being with him be like? If he ignored my stubble, could I have ignored his stench?

I walk back inside. Fantcha's still onstage, crooning. The music sounds like a puree of everything I don't know and can't understand. Cut the rope. Face the gauntlet.

I throw myself down into the seat next to him and take a swig of my drink. "I was thinking," I say—and stop. I was thinking—*what*? My mouth seizes up. My tongue goes dry. My hands grow clammy around my glass. I really need to pee.

Then drink rides in on his jocular, fat-bellied horse.

"I was thinking maybe I'd move," I say.

When I was a kid, I used to write book reviews on fabricated novels. When my teacher called me out and asked me why, I said: "It's easier than doing the work."

My tongue somehow overcomes the dryness and continues to flap.

"I listen to this music, this . . . *inspiring* music"—dear God— "and I think maybe it's time, you know? Maybe I just need to go somewhere and throw off all my . . . *American-ness*."

Holy shit. This is not coming out of my mouth. But yes, ma'am, you betcha, sir, it is.

Oh, I'm not really thinking of going anywhere. Where would I go? I only speak English and—

"Spanish," I say, my cheeks flushed, my heart racing. I am transported, taken out of my own body. For once I'm not thinking about the hair, my weight, my receding hairline, my symptoms, my diagnosis, or my disease. "I've always wanted to go to Barcelona. Teach English. Live overseas for a year. Come back and be a different person. A better one."

He's stroking the cleft in his chin. He doesn't say anything.

"I know. It's a crazy idea. But what's keeping me here?"

When I wrote those false book reports, I always snuck in a moment of discovery if the teacher chose to recognize it. I would muddle details, insert just that bit of sloppiness for the thrill of potentially getting caught. That hook, that bait. They never took it.

A line appears between his dark eyebrows. My god. Is this working?

I'm not as sober as I thought. I drop my keys while trying to open the front door. I'm still at the home on Sutter Street, but I'm looking to move. I want an apartment, a life on my own. I stab at the lock with my car key. I manage to open the damn thing on the third try, but not without enough giggling and cursing to elicit an angry *honey-shhh!* from my landlord's wife.

I need orange juice and ramen, *stat*. I have both. Could life *be* any better?

Matt dropped me off at the car and cut the engine. "You've given me a lot to think about," he said. Then he pointed his hand-me-down car in the direction of the city and I hiccupped, triumphant.

A lot to think about, huh? *Now* let's see who falls in love twenty times a day.

"I know," I say to David when he finds me with my bowl of Chicken Creamy Pesto Maruchan. The things we do after alcohol. "You think I'm going over the top. I probably am."

He grunts and roots in the refrigerator.

"I mean, I don't know. I just put it out there, you know?"

He pulls out three packets of string cheese and some ketchup.

"Isn't that what you do?" I say. "Put it out there and see how the universe receives it?"

He peels the wrapper off the first packet and dots the cheese with ketchup. Then he shoves the entire thing in his mouth.

"Yeah," I say. "I know it's bullshit too."

Then it's morning. I'm not sure how I got from the kitchen to bed, but somehow I found my way. I'm half-dressed, bra on but shirt off, jeans wrinkled around my legs. Mornings are always hardest for me. Break through the deep pool of sleep, push toward the light at the surface. Break through and gasp: It's there, everything that must be done to meet the day, the wrangling with the structure that traps me.

I start with some Folgers and email.

Email is like the Christmas stocking that turns up stale Tootsie Rolls, socks personalized with your mom's picture, and a dream catcher with a real-life dead bird in the center. Every so often, though, you shake out a diamond ring.

Among the forwards and spam is a message from Matt.

I couldn't sleep last night. I stayed up and thought instead.

My heart is slamming against my ribcage and I'm on the verge of spilling my crappy coffee. I try to steady my hand, to scroll down.

What you said about throwing off the American-ness, changing yourself. It hit me somewhere. I've been thinking about it for a while, a way to break open my world. And I'm going to do this.

Do what?

I'm moving to Barcelona to teach English. I don't expect to write the Great American Novel or find the love of my life, but you never know, right?

Nope. You never do.

I think about the book he gave me. How do you go to pieces without falling apart? Right now, I can't tell the difference.

CHAPTER 14

1999

Going to Europe is one of those decisions I know to be stupid from the start. Stupid, and I'm determined to follow through for reasons I don't understand. No rationale or reason. Just an unremitting *I-want*. That's not necessarily true. What I want has smoky eyes and curly hair that frames his face just perfectly. Yes.

It helps that Rooster's big on travel. It's one of life's priorities, so much so that he's willing to finance it with a frequent-flyer ticket. He's an easy sell when I call.

"Open-jaw," he says, sounding very pleased with himself. "Fly into Venice and out of Barcelona. I'll even take care of the taxes."

He doesn't question my motives. Good thing, because I couldn't even name them. Best I can describe it is that it feels like one part retribution, one part jealousy, and a dash of *this is the kind of thing you should want to do.*

"Go to Paris," Rooster says. "Best city in the world. Your mother and I went there on our honeymoon. It's not like things didn't go to shit down the road, but yeah, we had Paris."

I'm spinning around in my desk chair. I stop, but the world continues to turn. Some tiny, winged thing flutters in through the open door. It buzzes over to the floor, stumbling over the carpet until it runs across the floor heater. It drops with a thud, and the sound gives me dull pleasure.

"No traveler's checks," Rooster says. "Don't bother. You'll get the best exchange rate going to the ATM. Trust me."

Moments like this he scares me the most. It's one thing when my father is sullen, accusatory. I can handle when the line develops between his black eyes. I can't take the turns of kindness, the unexpected paternal instinct. They evoke in me a wordless feeling I experience in every sense. It tastes like mud, smells like a forest fire. It sounds like a sweet song played off-key, looks like a poorly photoshopped picture. It feels like a razor running along the skin, smooth and slick, dangerous.

It would be easier if he turned me down.

But the gatekeepers of my life seem determined to let me go. "Why not?" Philip says. Philip runs a real-estate news website, and I churn out multiple versions of the same story for him. Market's red-hot, get while the getting's good. It's going up 1000 percent this year. Haven't you heard?

"You don't need me?"

"Someone else can sub in for a month. That's why you're a freelancer, right? Take some time for yourself?"

That's not what he was supposed to say. He was supposed to cough, clear his throat, then tell me sorry, wish we could give you the time off, but we need you, maybe some time later this year. I find myself irrationally angry at him. What kind of boss *is* he?

The doors are opening fast, too fast. I feel too scared to pass through. I'm waiting for something to stop me. My plans have wrapped themselves around my throat, and I can't back out now. They're calling the shots. I'm just watching, fist held to my mouth in fear.

How to make myself normal?

Laser hair removal. It has a zing and a zap to it, a sharpness at
the consonants. There is a precision to its flow, a painful angry
coherence. I like how it sounds.

I sit at my outdated desktop with its fourteen-inch monitor
and do research. The self-help books would say this is a step on
the right path: Confront your troubles, approach them head-on
and with your chin held high.

I never lift my chin.

"It is an affordable, intelligent option," I read aloud in a
Martha-Stewart-bakes-shortbread-and-knits-a-toaster-cozy voice.
"Change your life forever."

Change your life forever. Change yourself.

Who am I without the hair?

I look up the phrase *bearded lady*. It's the name of a lesbian
bookstore somewhere in the South. The subject of several fetish
websites. And an online photo gallery.

It's dedicated to Brenda, the Bearded Lady of Guildford.
Brenda is sixty-four years old. She is British. Snow-colored hair
flows from her head and chin. She does not shave or even shape
her beard. It is ragged and curly, and it touches her collar in
pictures where she is slumped on park benches.

Everywhere she is accompanied by the camera's eye. Here
she hunches her way down some cobblestone street, a bag
under one arm, another clenched in a fist. Hauling a wire basket
through the Christmastime red-and-white aisles of a grocery
store. Tucked into a plastic booth at a fast-food joint, glowering
over a burger.

Leaving a mall, a plastic bag hanging from each hand, in the
background two trash cans emblazoned with the Burger King
insignia and something that makes my ears red with recognition: two
teen boys, a pair of blue hooded sweatshirts and jeans with blurry

faces, heads turned in Brenda's direction, fingers pointing. I know what they're saying, the tone in which the words are spoken.

Then come the fan photos. Young people, boys and girls with lithe bodies and easy smiles, posing. Sometimes they're with Brenda, flanking her with dual thumbs-up, white chicks throwing gang signs. In other moments they're in the foreground, Brenda in back, their obscene freshness a counterpoint to her bearded countenance. She looks surprised, almost pleased with the attention.

Whose creation is this? Whose fascination with Brenda grew so strong that they would create a—what can I even call this? Tribute? Torment? Who would need their digital finger pointed squarely at Brenda the Bearded Lady so that the whole world— me included—could experience for themselves, twenty-four hours a day, the depth of her absurdity?

I want to believe it's a means of torturing this woman. I can't entirely convince myself of that fact. There's a respect in these photos, a twisted admiration even, the same sort of oddball respect you might throw a snake charmer at a county fair. *I don't want to be you, but you fascinate me.*

Is this what lies behind the glances and looks, the stares and even the ridicule? Some small element of recognition, of regard? Do these boys value Brenda? Is that why they've turned to gawk, to call out her presence, to let the world know a freak is nearby?

Brenda, I want to know if the throngs explode as you pass them on the street. Tell me if your toes grow warm, if they scratch at the inside of your shoes. You can confide to me that you bite the inside of your lip and pierce your palms with your fingernails. I won't judge you for fleeing the scene.

Perhaps you've met the same people I have: the boys shoving one of their own toward you, the victim protesting: *She's not my girlfriend, not!* The well-intentioned older women who slide uninvited alongside you at cafes: *I have to talk to you. It's about your health.* Kids who don't know any better, looking up at you, whether it's San Diego or the United Kingdom, different accents, same question: *Are you a man or a lady?*

Brenda, sit with me for a while. Make yourself at home on my battered, comfortable couch. Prop your feet on my coffee table. I got it for free, off the street. Someone didn't want it. I took it in and made it a part of me.

I'm about as scientific in choosing a laser-hair removal place as I was in choosing a doctor: I pluck a name from the Yellow Pages. The name I've picked is The Clinic. It sounds simple, accessible. It sounds like a place I can trust.

But instead of calling, I sit slack-jawed on the couch, tapping the phone against my knee. Every so often I hit my reflex spot and startle myself. Then I go back to *tap-tap-tap.*

My other hand curls around the remote control. The television flickers into life, and suddenly I'm watching Maury Povich. Joe is making his third appearance on the show. He's fat and tearful and confessional. He kneels in front of his wife and begs forgiveness. "Shelly," he says, "I been cheating on you with twenty-five other women."

"Jesus," I say to the ceiling. "Who would fuck *either* of them?"

Now it's time for Shelly to reveal her secret. She has a baby face and a pudgy double chin that waggles when Joe is caught on tape with a sexy decoy.

"You've been keeping a secret from him for a long time!" Maury says. He's wearing a baby-blue shirt, and he looks delighted. His mouth moves quickly, animated. His eyes open wide.

"Yes," Shelly says. She has beautiful long hair, straight and blonde. Does she know that? Does she value herself? She's wearing a maroon button-down shirt and matching pants, the big-girl special. I judge on looks. Who doesn't?

"What's your secret?" Maury asks. I break out into goosebumps. I sit up straight, my attention riveted. It's three o'clock. I've hit—and missed—my daily deadline for Philip. He's my main client, and I need to keep him happy. But somehow, I can't drag myself back to my computer. I can't make myself stop watching this.

Shelly snuffles. It all seems so fake. Is she an actress? Are they making this up?

Once she confesses, I'll call. I'll make an appointment, and I'll write it in my Salvador Dali calendar. Then I'll switch on my computer and file my story. It shouldn't take more than a half hour. I may come in a few minutes over deadline, but it's real-estate news. No one's going to lose a limb over the fact that they need to wait a little longer for their daily dose of mortgage fodder.

Shelly takes one more deep breath. "*I* cheated," she says. This pleases the audience. They pump their fists and holler. Shelly's thick lips twitch. She looks in the direction of her shoes until the shouting stops.

She's been with two guys. They're romantic. *Joe's* not romantic.

"Can I tell you something, Shelly?" Maury asks. He's looking at her with such eager empathy that you know it's all bullshit.

"Shelly," he says, "I don't care what Joe says or what he does. It's not your fault."

"Yeah," I say to the wall. "It's not my fault."

Would life be better if I were a Shelly and I had a Joe? There would at least be someone. Granted, that someone would be a schlump who was apparently boffing half the population of the Eastern Seaboard, but we all make sacrifices.

The first time I call, I hang up before anyone answers. The shaking of my hands is steady and seamless, consistent. My palms are dry. Is it possible to be both confident and nervous? I look at my computer with its blank Word document, untitled, unsaved. It's nothing but a flashing cursor, a waiting thing. I haven't just missed my deadline. I've blown it.

When I call again—if I call again—who will be on the other end of the line? It's too easy to expect that it will be someone gorgeous, an intimidating sex bomb. For all I know, Shelly works as a receptionist at The Clinic. Who's to say?

This time the phone rings three and one-half times.

The voice that answers is—normal. She sounds like the kind of girl who went to college at a state school, lettered in softball maybe.

And the confidence dissipates, leaving nerves in its wake.

I could've handled a voice that was off-the-charts feminine, a bird with eye makeup, something small and squeaky. That would've given me something to condescend to: *What a bimbo.* Or the other end of the spectrum: an uncertain Shelly-voice, raspy with its own nerves. That might've made me feel more confident, brassier, as if I weren't the only one with shaking hands.

But this middle ground is a different story.

My lungs shut down. My mouth opens and closes. I feel like something lured by bait and captured on a hook.

"Hello," the cool-girl voice says. "Hello, The Clinic, may I help you?"

My throat makes a clicking sound.

"Ma'am? Sir? Hello?"

And in that instant I find my voice. I am *not* a sir. I've been mistaken for one for the last time—on the phone or in person, it doesn't matter. I am a woman. I want to look like one.

"Hello," I say.

Four minutes later I'm opening my Dali calendar and writing with a half-empty pen. At first I think the ink is going to fail me, but at the last minute it comes through.

"We'll see you on the third," Cool Girl says.

"Eleven o'clock?"

"You got it."

"That's it?"

"That's it."

When I hang up my hand is still shaking, but this time it's with triumph. I'm booked. They're doing the consultation and treatment on the same day. It's going to be a little intense. Cool Girl had asked if I had anyone to drive me home.

"You might not feel like focusing on anything afterward," she said.

My body tingled all over at that thought. It wasn't a good tingle. "Sure," I said. "I can ask someone."

Who?

Who could I trust with the knowledge of what I'm planning to do? Who can I look in the eye and ask for help?

No one. I'm telling no one. I'll drive myself home, but Miss Letter Sweater doesn't need to know that.

It's the day before the appointment. I'm walking the aisles of Piedmont Grocery. The place is such a throwback. The cashiers are full of backtalk and lip, a refreshing departure from the zombies at Safeway. They hum old college fight songs and banter back and forth between registers. The butchers wink and flirt, no matter what you look like. Come at the right time and you can spend half an hour sampling at the cheese aisle.

I'm sticking a toothpick in my third cube of Havarti with dill when the thought hits: *Am I crazy?*

I swallow hard and reach for a fourth sample.

I must be, because I'm going through with this. All of it.

I browse over to the bread. Seeded sourdough baguettes, country levains, a single asiago pugliese. For a moment I lose myself in the shapes and textures. *Could I be reincarnated as a loaf? Toast me, spread some butter on my skin, and I'm done.*

Later I'm with that poorest of companions, the computer. It pulls me in, riles me up. I start thinking. Thought is the enemy of sleep. I shift in my desk chair, low on patience, waiting for the machine to yawn its way out of hibernation. I dig my fingernails into the soft nap of my desk chair, my teeth into my lower lip.

Less than twelve hours and I'll be there.

I haven't told anyone about the appointment. Telling tastes like a rip in a sensitive piece of flesh, the inner part of your lip between the two front teeth, perhaps, the one you can't stop tonguing even when it stings.

My computer wakes up and the desktop appears. Once I connect to the internet, my instant-messaging program automatically pops up. This always bothers me, but I haven't bothered to change the settings.

My mother is online.

Oh. God.

Whenever she sees that I'm on, she tries to get me to talk. When that happens, I feel a wall rise inside of me. It makes breathing difficult, but it also protects my heart.

She starts in before I can shut the program off. *Hiya, what are you up to this late at night, is everything all right?*

Fine, I respond. *Just fine.*

How's work?

Great.

What's been going on?

And here's where I should tell her everything. Right? This is the moment of reconciliation, the pixelated version of a hug. And it does feel like a hug. A cold, overwhelming bear hug.

Nothing, I write. *A whole lot of nothing.*

It's that wall. Once built, you can't reason it out of existence. You need something huge and heavy to knock it asunder.

There's no sitting still and nowhere to go. I click a ballpoint pen open and closed, flip the television on and then silence it, pour a glass of water and forget to drink it. I check the door to make sure it's locked, the windows too. I turn the stove off and on just to be sure. Then I sit on the toilet and look at the light freckles on my thighs.

I notice a slight blemish. I brush it with my fingertip. The motion is light at first, a tracing touch. Then I touch my finger to the skin. I press to the point of pain. Somehow I begin to pick. I'm surprised to find myself doing this. It's like kissing an acquaintance you don't much like, his mouth pressing on yours like an open wound.

Then my vision clears. There's blood, a puffy welt that seems to rise while I watch it. I gasp. Only then do I realize I've been holding my breath.

Morning, and I'm making my way down the path that leads to The Clinic's front door. I'm walking through a rock garden, past beds of flowers, little miniature waterfalls whose tinkling makes me want to pee.

I feel like I'm walking down a hallway, and the damn thing keeps getting longer and longer. I've seen horror films like this.

Just when you think you've reached the end, you find that the
end is out of your reach.

Just when I start thinking it's a sign, there it is: the front door.
Damn. Two fewer steps in the fog and I could've given up, left,
called when I got home: *Sorry, couldn't find it; will call back to
reschedule.* I could've never rescheduled. I could've never had to
face the voice on the phone, that sweet down-to-earth tone that
belongs to—

"Hi," the woman says. "My name is Jessica."

She's not what I expected: pudgy with braces, heavy
eyebrows, a little roll of fat bulging beneath her shirt, which says
"Oil of Olay," spelled out in little rhinestones.

The front lobby is comfortable. That sucks. I'd wanted it to
feel sterile to the point of hostility, stripped down and yet at the
same time hatefully design-savvy. Leather couches and subtly
lit mirrors, a smoke machine maybe. A medical-spa version
of a disco, a bachelor pad in shades of black, white, and gray.
Metrosexual and clinical. It looks like the kind of place where
you'd want to house-sit. Warm, soft tones, an olive-colored rug
on the floor, a glass-topped coffee table with copies of *Rolling
Stone* and *Harper's*. A large, cushy-looking couch striped in
olive and beige with tons of pillows faces off against a flat-screen
television set.

"Is this where you do the face stapling?" I ask Jessica.

"Nope," she says, and leads me into a private room. This is
what I expected: white-on-white, not even a Thomas Kinkade
knockoff to liven things up. Excellent.

"Have a seat," she says, and I perch on the exam table. I
picture myself prone on this thing, eyes shut, nails digging into
palms. She offers me a drink. Jim Beam perhaps? I opt for a Diet
Coke and roll the cold can between my moist palms. The air in

here smells like nothing, nothing at all. It's as if they deep-clean the oxygen between appointments. For all I know, they do.

She pulls out a drawer, a clipboard, a piece of paper, and a valentine-colored pen. She uncaps the pen and I notice the short, unpainted nails on her stubby fingers. There's something endearing about her hands, something natural and undiminished. She marks a diagram, drawing with red ink on the blank, expressionless example. She's a lefty.

"Full face," she says, tapping the paper with the pen's tip. It's still uncapped. She's giving the paper diagram freckles, acne. "Upper lip, chin, cheeks. The whole pickle."

I bite my lip hard enough to draw blood—not from nerves, but to reassure myself that I'm here, I'm alive, I'm doing this.

Jessica puts down the clipboard and fixes me with a metallic smile. They make invisible braces, why didn't she go that route? Then I flush, angry with myself. *You're judging her?*

"Six sessions," she says. "At least."

Six sessions at three hundred a session. If I go for the package, it's fifteen hundred total, one free treatment. A laser hair removal Value Meal.

"Jessica," I say, "I've been to two doctors. Neither of them could fix me. If I pay you fifteen hundred dollars, can you make me look like a girl?"

She says: "Let me tell you how it works."

The technician uses a hand-held laser instrument. It sends a light beam through the skin. The beam seeks melanin, a pigment found in hair and particularly in dark, coarse hair like mine. It hits and destroys the hair follicle. Cooling gel protects the skin. Topical cream and aspirin minimize pain.

The laser light works best for people with dark hair and fair skin.

Dark hair and fair skin. *That's me!*

That's Jessica too. She tells me how her hairy arms made her feel like something out of a freak show. "No more," she says, rolling up her sleeves. Now there's just smooth, freckled skin.

Her eyes are warm. *Trust me*, they say. "I'm very happy," she says. "So are my clients."

Clients, not patients. Client means choice. It means you're the boss.

"We're on," I say.

She shows me a video.

The background music is something you'd expect to hear from a violinist at a wedding, self-conscious and self-important. A brunette in a tank top walks in, smiling. Smiling! She sits in a high-backed chair, crosses her legs, and leafs through a magazine.

Smash cut: a white-coated technician smirking into the camera. "When you've got unwanted hair," she says, "you're not living your life to the fullest."

I feel like I know what's going to happen next: The brunette lies prone on an exam table. She's grimacing, crying beneath the dark goggles that prevent her from being blinded by the laser. She digs her nails into her thin thighs, begs the technician to stop. But the laser keeps flashing.

I turn the video off before it can hit that surreal moment.

In the exam room, Jessica hands me a Popsicle stick with cooling gel. I swipe it across every problem area. My pupils are dilated with worry, my left eyelid twitching.

"Hop up," she says, patting the exam table. I do this with a motion that is nothing like hopping. It is more like the walk to the guillotine.

"Lie back," she says, and I lower my head until it is level with my feet.

"Hold these," she tells me, and places a cotton ball on each of my eyes. She pins them with the goggles, and in this moment I learn that I am claustrophobic. Blinded, I feel trapped, boxed. I gasp for air, but I try to do it quietly.

"When I activate the laser, I'll say *pulse*," Jessica says. "That way you know what's coming."

Behind me the machine hums into life. The sound is background to the pulse that beats in my chest, wrists, and temples.

"You ready?" Jessica asks.

I think about the plane that will take me to Europe. What if a wave of claustrophobia rolls over me in that second before the doors shut? Will I make for the exit before my lungs shut down entirely?

"Make it quick," I say.

It is not quick. It takes an hour, and that is made bearable only by a break halfway through. My hands dig into the crinkly white paper beneath me. I feel one of my fingernails pierce the surface and it's almost like permission to scream. I moan instead.

"How you doing?" Jessica asks.

It feels like someone scraped my face with the blunt, rusty side of an ax, then sprayed it with lemon juice.

"Fine," I say.

I'd trawled the internet to find out just how much this was going to hurt. *Like a rubber band snapping,* said one message board. Another warned of *a little stinging, a little swelling.* One laser clinic's website advised that patients might feel a *slight prickling or burning sensation.*

Let me post on those message boards. I'll give a rebuttal to that clinic. *It feels like someone's going fishing in my face,* I'd write. *And Captain Ahab is as sadistic as they come.*

The laser feels like a roving hook. Each time it bites into my face, I hear a *beep-beep-beep.* That's the beam seeking the follicle. Once found, it goes *zap.* That's the hair frying. Not only can I feel it, I can also smell it.

"Jessica," I say, "talk to me. Tell me anything. I don't care what you tell me, as long as you can distract me."

"Well," she says, "a few weeks ago my boyfriend and I went to a sex club."

They had to wait in line. There were rules. No cameras. No drugs. No giggling.

"Downstairs, there was this dude. He was all strapped into a sling. Naked as a jay . . . *pulse* . . . except for his hipster glasses."

The guy's clothes lay under the sling, folded military-style, all corners matching. He had his dick in his hand, half-hard, not so much jerking it as playing with it, reassuring himself that it was still there.

"Looked like he'd just come from some start-up job. *Pulse. Pulse.* Phil called him the Dot-Cummer."

I picture Jessica and her boy floating around the Power Exchange. I'm jealous.

"We didn't screw there," she says. "If you're wondering."

I'm not. What I do wonder is whether he tucked his arm around her waist, played with her black curls, kissed her lips. I'm wondering if he loved and accepted her even before she lased off the fuzz that decorated her arms.

"Just about there," Jessica says. "You okay?"

Outside this clinic, lovers are having late-morning breakfasts. Bikers and joggers huff past. Tennis partners square off. Drivers pump gas at the Chevron. Mothers squat in front of strollers and shake fingers.

What I wouldn't do to be any one of them.

"Hurry," I say.

"Four more," she says. "I'll count them down."

Pulse.

I bite my lip, curl my toes, remind myself why I'm doing this.

Pulse.

No more razors in the morning, pulling my skin this way and that to get the closest cut. No more second shave of the day, the hair so thick and persistent it grows back even as it's shorn.

Pulse.

No more stubble, no more shadow.

Pulse.

No more walking in a room and wondering: Are they looking at me?

Done.

"Jesus," I say.

I pull off the goggles. Light, beautiful, blessed. I struggle to sit up. My tailbone is tentative, unsure if it's able to hold me. My head is runny, my brain muddled. My face is a balloon expanded with too much air.

"Hand me a mirror," I say to Jessica. All my politesse, my good-girl training, has vaporized in the moment. I need to see what's been done to me.

"You don't look that bad."

"Hand me the damn thing."

She hands it over.

There I am, my eyes red and wet above my inflamed skin. The singed hairs are everywhere, some already falling out. I brush at them in triumph.

I look great.

CHAPTER 15

1999

The blisters emerge within hours: huge, hot, painful. Under my hand my skin feels volcanic, capable of eruption. I run my finger along the ridges and cringe away from my own touch.

This wasn't supposed to happen. Jessica didn't say anything about breaking out. There was no warning on the message board. It's nearly six. I pick up the phone to call The Clinic and it rings in my hand.

"Landa," Matt says. "What's up?"

Isn't it the middle of the night there?

"I'm drunk," he says.

I realize I haven't even thought about him over the last day or two. I've been so consumed with my travel plans that I've forgotten why I'm even doing this.

"Yeah," I say. "Me too."

Talking is starting to hurt. The skin around my mouth is swollen, and my lips themselves feel freakishly small. The blisters are worst where the hair grows with most vigor—edges of my chin, corners of my mouth.

"Bullshit," he says. "You ready for your trip?"

My face is a roasting pigskin, tight and crinkling.

"No," I say.

"Better hurry up. Aren't you leaving tomorrow?"

"Yeah. What's up?"

The connection is clear. It doesn't sound like he's calling from halfway around the world.

"I don't know," he says. "I guess I just wanted to hear your voice."

I bite my tongue. Hard.

"And I'm drunk."

The teeth marks feel like pinpricks, small and stinging. "You mentioned that."

I try to picture his surroundings. I can't do it. All I can imagine are off-white walls stained by nicotine. My childhood bathroom. That's what I'm picturing. But he doesn't live there. He lives in a rented room in some apartment.

"I feel like there's something I want to say." His voice is higher than I recall, nervous-sounding. "But I'm not sure what."

"Well," I say, "when I get my membership to the Psychic Friends Network, I'll be sure to help you out."

"I miss you," he says.

I rub my eyes so hard that one of my contact lenses slips, lodges under the eyelid. "Damn it," I say.

"Yeah, I know. It would be cool to have you here."

"It hurts," I say. Everything does. My tongue, my face, my eyes, my heart. All the portals to who I am.

"Wait'll you see this place. It's like New York in the 1980s, crazy like that. Huge buildings that cast shadows on the alleys. Damn, I'm talking like a writer. I guess I am. Fuck, I'm drunk. And dude, Landa, the women—they're incredible."

The pain is spreading. My throat, my shoulders, the backs of my knees. It's a monster wave after the earth shakes, a raging tide come to destroy everything it meets at landfall. It's not jealousy.

It isn't longing. It's the desire to put an end to these mixed messages.

"You should go," I say. "I can't imagine how much this call is costing."

"What's wrong?"

The idea of telling him about the laser hair removal feels like a rip in soft skin, a pain that's neither stinging nor burning but born of friction, a result of contact and tension, a giving-in. "I guess I'm just nervous about the flight."

In a way that's true. Planes push you together with a crew of strangers, everyone trying to figure out where to put their eyes and hands and feet. I don't want anyone's eyes to land on me. I don't want to field any questions.

"I hear you," he says. "It's always something, you know? There's always something. It can't ever be perfect. I want it to be, you want it to be, but it's not."

"I don't want perfect," I say. "I want manageable."

After we hang up I sit down at my computer. I find out that there is a name for what's happening to me. It's called folliculitis. Folliculitis is an inflammation of the hair follicles. It causes small crops of pustules and a reddening of the skin. It itches. And boy does it hurt.

You might say it's the start of a chain reaction. A tumbling of dominoes, a collapse set in motion by a single soft breath.

"It was impulse," I tell Missy. We're on the phone. I wish I could see her in person, but she no longer lives in Berkeley. She left shortly before I arrived and is now in veterinary school at Davis. Her voice on the phone has a calming effect, a comforting tone that makes me want to confess everything I've done to myself. I can't, though. I can't tell anyone.

"Impulse," she says. I imagine her watery blue eyes, clear and alight with understanding. She's a good person, Missy. I'm lucky to have her.

"Yeah. It wasn't exactly something I thought out."

"You're visiting this guy?"

"I'm also going to see Tina. You know she's living in France, right?"

"Yeah. Teaching English, right?"

"Yep. Making peanuts."

"But loving it."

"She's Tina. She can make something good out of just about anything."

It's ten o'clock at night. I've just come back from the drugstore, where I bought bags of frozen vegetables to press against my face, a logic-puzzle magazine for the plane, and some fresh razors. The razors give me a chill. How am I supposed to shave with this Jabba the Hutt case of acne? It's like dragging a blade across a minefield.

"When you see this guy, what are you going to do?"

"Drop to my knees."

"Get real."

"I don't know. I just want to go out there and see if I have the courage to—"

"To what?"

"To tell him."

I rest my chin against some frozen peas. It helps.

"Are you in love with him?"

An old song lyric floats through my head: *What is love? Baby, don't hurt me.* "I wouldn't go that far."

"But you like him."

"I'd say so, yes."

"Would you marry him?"

Marriage. My parents. A tumultuous union, an acrimonious parting. Why would I want something like that?

"We're not even dating."

"Why are you going over there?"

Oh, that's the question. Is it for love? A crush? Or is it just a war I want to win?

"Missy," I say, "Do the words *I don't know* mean anything to you?"

"Sure. I just never thought I'd hear them from you."

Maybe I'm really that determined, that definitive. As with everything else, it's always easier to see from the outside. Inside, I so often feel tentative, as if I think I know what to do but don't have the path to quite get there.

I feel a weird flush of pride. I'm not finding a path, I'm making one. Step by nervous step, I'm going somewhere.

"Okay," Missy says, "impulse."

"Yes," I say. I ice my face and ruminate. *Impulse:* in psychology, a sudden urge; in classical mechanics, a change in momentum. Combined, the two look much like a collision course.

My first glimpse of Venice takes place at Marco Polo Airport. A lot of people with luggage and policemen with guns, and the trick is not bumping into either. I dip my ATM card into a machine and come away with a fistful of odd-looking bills.

I wheel my bag outside and realize just how different this place is. There's more water than land, more seagulls than people. Their cries mix with the lap of waves, and the joyous cacophony makes me forget about myself for a moment.

Now I know why people travel.

Under my feet the dock sways, and everyone waits for the water taxi that will take us to shore. They all seem so nonchalant. I feel like the only tourist here. Next to me a woman is texting, fingers expertly working the keys. Her glow tells me she's talking to a lover. No one else can make someone look quite that way.

I'm reminded of the times Matt and I talked about meditation, of being in the present. "It's about being where you are," he said over beers. "Whether it's calm or not, whether it's good or it sucks. It's being with what is."

It's the same Berkeley bumper-sticker message that's drawn my derision over the years: *Be here now.* I hate to admit this, but there's some wisdom to it. I've tried paying attention during the most mundane of times: standing in line at the bank, idling at a red light, scrubbing the sink. And you know what? It works.

Why haven't I done it when it counts? Would mindfulness have helped the pain of saying goodbye to Matt? Of feeling the laser light strike my face again and again?

"You know what's weird?" he once asked, his eyes glowing blue. "They say pain is an aid to mindfulness. It keeps you focused."

Standing on this swaying dock, I access that pain. I connect with the pain of my skin and the ache in my heart. And you know what? He was right.

My hotel room in Venice is a cluster of dark objects: ceiling, furniture, floor. A shower with no curtain, a small chair perched in a cramped entryway, and a window that lets in weak light. I pull back the curtain, and there lies a lagoon. From here I could jump into it.

I have nothing to fight the swelling. I can't bear to seek out an ice machine. I turn the sink to cold, let it run. I soak a washcloth and press it to each of my red, angry cheeks.

In the movies, this would be where I catch my own eyes in the mirror and see something that changes me, or devastates me, or has some other fundamental and dramatic effect.

But I'm just really ticked off.

"God*damn* it," I say, my favorite expression. God*damn* it just covers so much. I say it a few times. Then I rinse my face once more and do what I must to face this strange new continent.

At the front desk sits my confirmation that I'm in Italy. He's equal parts Frank Sinatra, Don Corleone, and Super Mario.

"Beautiful!" he says. "How are you?"

"Beautiful!" he says again. "You sleep well?"

I'm thinking of the word *effusion*. In chemistry, that the process where individual molecules flow through a hole without impediment. In literature, it's an opening of the emotional floodgates.

I want to learn the wordless, sensual experience of effusion. Perhaps it can begin with this man.

He's about sixty, dark, with a crumpled countenance courtesy of each smile, each burst of colorful verbiage, each multisyllabic curse word, another bit of skin folded over to mark the occasion.

His world has marked his face. I can relate.

"*Bella*," he says, "what is your name?"

I tell him.

"You like to practice the English?"

Why not?

We craft a patchwork of conversation. Every so often he apologizes for his lack of English skill and I reassure him that his English is far better than my Italian. He teaches me the basics: *mille grazie, molto bene, mangi.*

"You remind me of . . . how you say, my wife?" he says. "No, my daughter."

237

Yeah?

"Yeeeah," He adopts my slang. "She a crazy girl, fire in the eye. *Pazzeca*, my Carolina. All day sleep, all night out. She make me see the green mice."

She what?

"This is expression in Italian. Make me see the green mice. She—" He puts his hands together, pulls them apart, wrenches them throughout the air. I see another fold mark his face, an indelible reminder of our time together. "Make me . . . *sono pazzeco*."

Insane?

"Yeeeah."

Beyond the open hotel door lies a gate. Beyond runs a small road, and beyond that the Venetian Lagoon. Emboldened, I feel ready to explore.

If I get looks or stares or curious glances, I don't see them. Maybe that's because I'm busy looking and staring myself. Maybe it's because I'm distracted by the angles, the pathways, the color and light and scent. Or maybe it's because I'm damn cold—Venice in December, all that water; you do the math. I'm wearing an overcoat and a hat jammed over my ears. My hands are stuffed in my pockets, my chin tucked down against the chill.

What strikes me most about Venice is its sound: the often-interchangeable jumble of word and song, the boats coming and going, the water lapping, the seagulls screaming, the gondoliers paddling for visitors' pleasure. I don't buy anything, and I don't stop to rest.

I just walk.

I walk and watch.

I walk and listen.

I walk until I hit the narrow passageways, walls on either side, pressing in, pressing down, choking the life from my lungs. A black pair of goggles blinding me. An assault of the senses: feeling of flame, scent of fire. No way around. I can only pass through.

Awakening is not a voluntary thing. It's explosion, disorientation. I'm not even sure how I made it back to the hotel, but somehow I'm here, fully clothed atop the bedcovers. I hadn't even bothered to get under the sheets.

My first thought is that I have arrived in hell. I look in the mirror and know it's true.

It would be easier not to recognize myself. Had I simply become the modern-day Elephant Woman, I could separate from what I see before me. That's not the case. I recognize my eyes, the jut of my chin, the curve and bow of my ears.

I recognize myself in pain and fear.

I reach for my calling card. I reach for the phone. Two-thirty in the morning in Venice, five-thirty in the evening at home. Are they still open? It's worth a try.

I dial from memory.

"Good afternoon," a voice says. It's not Brenda. It's smooth but not quite sweet, as if there are glass shards under the tongue. "Thank you for calling The Clinic."

"Hi," I say—and can go no further. My tongue feels like a melting thing, something whose molecules are forcing a change from solid to liquid.

"Good *afternoon*," the voice says again. "How may I help you?"

I can't speak. *I can't speak.*

"Hello?" the voice says. "Ma'am?"

At least she called me ma'am. This makes me happy enough to loosen my vocal cords. "Hello," I say.

"Hel*lo*."

"I'm a patient. I've been having some problems."

"Okay, ma'am," the voice says. "Tell me what's going on."

"First of all, my name is Allison."

"Okay, Allison, what's up?"

"I had laser hair removal on my face the other day. I've had an awful reaction. I've—"

The tears. Oh shit. The tears.

"Ma'am? Allison? Are you there?"

They're full force, a winter rainstorm. I can't remember ever feeling this alone, vulnerable, scared. I know the name of what's happening to me, but not how to combat it. I'm a world away from home, and I'm walking around as a *frigging female Frankenstein*.

"Allison," the voice says. "Take a deep breath."

I do.

"Now another."

Okay.

"One more."

Done.

"Now tell me what's going on."

I spill my story: laser, full face, Jessica of the formerly hairy arms promising me a happy ending.

"And I'm in Venice," I say.

"In Los Angeles?"

"In Italy."

A pause. "Oh," The voice finally says. She seems at a loss. "Is it . . . uh . . . cold there?"

"With my face on fire, it's quite pleasant."

The anger is magnificent. I love it. It's the type of enjoyment you get from a canker sore. It hurts. You want to get rid of it. But

240

hell if you can't stop tonguing it.

"What's your name?" I ask her. For some reason, I need to know.

"Miriam."

Miriam. That sounds like a down-to-earth, easygoing name. It's a woman with an apron and a relaxed halo of hair. Not like *Jessica*, a slut name, a crack whore on the corner presenting herself to anything that walks by.

"Okay, Miriam, here's the deal, okay? I got lasered by you guys and I broke out big-time, and your technician, *Jessica*, okay, acted like everything would be fine and guess what, Miriam, I'm in Venice, that's like *half a world away*, and I need you guys to fix it."

Matt's voice flashes into my mind: *Pain can help you focus. Pain can aid mindfulness. Harness the pain,* his voice says. *Use it, Landa. Focus.*

"Don't panic," Miriam says.

My breath begins to rattle as if on cue. I chew on a fingernail, cutting it down to the quick. I watch the blood well up and I slide the finger into my mouth, sucking it. Regression. Focus on *that*, Matt.

"I've seen this before," she says.

I hiccup. "You have?"

"Yep. And I can help you, Allison."

"You can?"

"Listen," she says. "You're on vacation. Don't cry."

One percent hydrocortisone. That's the weapon against folliculitis.

Unfortunately, I don't know how to say it in Italian. I go to my friend at the front desk. If he notices that my face is continuing to morph into a series of pustules, he doesn't let on. He draws a map and shoots me a grin. "Farmacia Ponci," he says. "Oldest pharmacy in Venice. They no have what you need, you no need it."

I take the water taxi and follow his directions. It's on the Strada Nova, which my guidebook tells me is one of the city's widest streets. I pass hotels and wine bars before spotting it across from a church. Inside, it is all ornate carved wood, fancy vases, a display of porcelain jars that look like they date back to Napoleon's era.

It's beyond well-preserved. It's been restored with a loving hand. Fellow tourists coo and aim their cameras in every direction. Before stepping to the counter, I do the same.

And the drama is done. Sometimes it happens just like that. I smooth it on and it works within a day. Five o'clock shadow still scars my face, but at least I can shave without losing half the blood in my body. I'm back to where I started, but somehow that feels like a victory.

I go to the front counter. Time to check out. My friend isn't working today. I leave him a note with a single word: *Grazie*. He'll know who wrote it.

CHAPTER 16

1999

Tina picks me up at the Toulouse train station. She's wearing baggy jeans and a T-shirt that says MY DOG CAN LICK ANYONE. "You bitch," I say, hugging her.

Three countries in the last week: Italy, Austria, and Germany. Riding trains, walking cobblestone streets, sleeping on narrow beds in faceless hotels. Pictures, postcards, and emails, incessant scribbles in my journal. *Adventure*, I wrote on the train from Munich to here, *is better after it's been lived. It can really suck while you're going through it.*

I've been lonely. Days are easier than nights. When the sun sinks and the neon comes out to play, you really feel that weight. So often I've wanted to turn to someone and say, "Look at that!"—and no one was there.

In those moments I thought of Matt. Matt, whose name makes my stomach churn these days. Matt, the mystery. Matt, the mirage who may be more symbol than substance. But I'm going for it anyway.

"You'll love this place," Tina says. "Totally your speed. Cafes everywhere, bars and bookstores, surprises around every corner. You're never going to want to leave."

I doubt that. I've fought homesickness the entire time I've been on this continent. Even after my face healed, I felt out of place and bent out of shape, longing for the known, the familiar. Still, as we walk through the quiet streets listening to the *clack-clack-clack* of my bag rolling along the sidewalk, I feel something I haven't yet felt during this trip: fascination. The buildings are framed by pink brick and punctuated with pitched roofs. Cats climb out onto black wrought-iron balconies, stretching and yawning in a happily bored way. The scent of cigarette smoke trails out of open windows. The whole thing feels like something out of film noir, the kind of scene you might imagine existing only on-screen.

"Here's home," Tina says, and turns into a crumbling courtyard. It's that artistic kind of crumbling, the sexy kind. She helps me carry my backpack up the four flights to her apartment. By the time we reach the final landing, I'm huffing and sweating. "Le 24-Hour Fitness," I say.

"Fuck that," she says, and lights a cigarette.

"Since when do you smoke?"

She fumbles for a key and fits it to the front-door lock. "My visa depends on it."

Inside is a wide hallway, a wash of color and starlight. The hall gives way to a single room. Tina, in typical Tina style, turned it palatial with the strategic use of something like six scarves. She flops down on an unmade futon. "Place is yours," she says. "Welcome to your Toulouse home. Now get in the kitchen and make me a snack."

"Fuck you," I say, and root around in the small refrigerator. Atop an only slightly smudged tray I place plates of cheese, foie gras, three different types of crackers. I twist a corkscrew into a wine bottle and lift. Tina lights a second cigarette off hers and waggles it at me.

"What," I say, "you want me to wind up like my mother?"

"Let me tell you something. When I first met you, I thought you were already a pack-a-day smoker."

"Why? Because my mother drove me to school while she was chain-smoking like you?"

"It's not chain-smoking. I'm handing it to you. And yes, you always smelled like smoke. I made my assumptions. Sue me."

I look at the burning thing in her hand. It looks different than those my mother has toted around for as long as I've lived. These are short and stumpy and seemingly without a filter. "Gauloises," Tina says. "I've acclimated."

I'm standing at an awkward angle to her. From her position on the futon, she has a straight shot to the underside of my chin. And she's looking right at it.

"Sure," I say, trying to distract her. "Hand it over."

She does, but her mind isn't on it. Her eyes are narrowing just slightly enough to make me aware of the fact that she's thinking, noticing, taking mental notes. I bring the cigarette to my lips. It feels like I'm betraying someone or something, but I have no idea why. I inhale and do what I hoped I wouldn't: cough madly.

"Suppress the cough," Tina says with the baritone intonations of One Who Knows. "Eventually, your body will get the message."

"Tell that to my lungs," I say among gasps. I sit down next to her on the futon and continue to hack.

"Are you okay?" Tina asks.

"I'll live."

"I'm not talking about the coughing."

My teeth find my lip and bite down. I need the pain. I want it.

"What did you do to yourself?"

"Nothing," I say in a very small voice. The cigarette continues to burn between my fingers. I take another puff. I suppress the cough. Tina was right. It goes away with enough effort.

"You have scabs all over your chin."

"Tina," I say, "shit happens." I spot an ashtray shaped like Mickey Mouse's head. I ash into his skull and then stub out the cigarette. I can't take the burn of the tobacco, the heat of the cylinder in my hand. It smells like an accusation. It feels like the gates of hell.

"That didn't just happen."

I think about how far I've come from home. I'm 6,000 miles from my apartment, my car, nearly everything I own except for what I've stuffed in a rolling bag and a backpack. Somehow I got myself here. Somehow I made it through.

"You're right," I say, "but I don't want to talk about it."

The refusal feels like a chunk of concrete in my stomach, a barrier, a wall. I want to spill. I want to tell. I want to share the load, but I can't face handing it off to someone else. I refused Missy's help years ago. After a while she got the picture. I thought Tina had too. I was wrong.

My need to confide in someone wells like tears. I stay dry-eyed.

Tina takes my hand. Her fingers feel like a memory, a bygone home. "I had an abortion last month," she says.

"I didn't even know you were dating anybody."

"I'm not. That's why I did it."

Tina, alone and scared on an exam table a world away from home. A picture of vulnerability, a portrait of pain. I admire her for being able to share her secret. I envy her confidence in doing it. And, shamefully, part of me resents her for having someone to touch her body, even if it was a stranger.

"I had to tell someone," she says.

I squeeze her fingers. "I know," I say. "I know."

To break the tension, I check my email. Matt writes: Barcelona for New Year's? He'd travel from Madrid and Tina and I from Toulouse, him by train and us by car.

"I actually get to meet Romeo?" Tina asks.

I look up from her laptop. "That's Romeo-berg to you."

"Jesus."

I'm already trying to figure out how to hide the scars. I hadn't realized how bad they were until Tina called me out on them. She got the message, I think, and hasn't mentioned it since. Still, I make sure not to stand over her, not to give her a direct view. Better to conceal, to hope she'll forget. I wonder if she hopes I'll forget her confession. I wonder if she offered it out of need or strategy: You show me yours, I'll show you mine.

I try to push those thoughts aside and concentrate on responding: *Sure,* I write. I leave it at that. I'm wary these days. I worry that one slip of the keyboard will reveal everything I've gone through to get here, the whole painful process. He feels like a stranger in an unknown land, an ambition held but not understood.

My fear, I realize, is simple and stark: *I will never be loved.*

A lifetime locked apart from existence, nose pressed against that glass, watching. This isn't just missing out on the positives: holding hands over dinner, embracing in a hotel room, laughing together. It's also the screaming matches, the awkward silences, the pockets of boredom. Any of it, all of it.

It's missing out on the brawling and the banal, the commitment that lies light one moment, stifling the next. It's remaining frigid, frozen. It's the life of the forgotten.

Barcelona feels like glass, scattered and shattered along a wave-licked coastline, seductive and perilous. Tina and I check into a hotel on Calle Ferran, a ritzy, narrow street still canopied by Christmas decorations strung lightpost to lightpost. The place is undergoing an extensive remodel. The lobby is a vast swath of half-stuccoed walls, hanging plastic sheets, and a continual din of banging, drilling, and what sounds like a cacophony of Spanish swear words.

"Funny," Tina muses, "it looked a little different on the website."

"You mean like somewhere habitable?"

"Yeah, but we've got no choice. Unless we want to sleep in an ATM enclosure, we're hauling our crap up to the room and liking it."

The room in question reeks. It's a corpse-like stench originating from an alley filled with overflowing trash cans, an essence of sour milk and decomposing potato peelings. We flop on our separate beds.

"I guess I should call him," I say.

"Kick yourself in the head," she says, flopping on her bed and lighting a cigarette while lying on her back. "From the sound of your voice, it'll be more pleasant for you."

I gesture toward the cigarette. She hands it to me, I take a puff, suppress the cough, and hand it back. Then I realize she's looking up at me. I sit down on my narrow bed. What would she have named her child? Does she have regrets? Who doesn't?

"No," I say. "Might as well get it over with."

It feels like the walls of the room are pressing in on me, crushing my internal organs. My vision blurs. Why these emotions, this trip across the world?

It's not love. It's something entirely different. It's seeing someone as a vessel, a container to be filled with one's own hopes and fantasies. Chase the vessel and you chase a mirage. Cross that desert and drink from an empty golden cup.

"Suit yourself," Tina says, and flips on the television. On-screen, Bart Simpson widens his eyes and exclaims: "*Ay! Caramba!*"

My whole body feels like a sigh, like I'm chasing something that's outpacing me. I think about my father with his paperwork, my mother with Bill. My father still buries himself in his taxes months before the actual due date, and Bill still lives with my mother. They keep me at arm's length, but if I think about it, I return the favor.

That's not love either. Not my definition at least.

I pull a piece of paper from my pocket. I've scribbled Matt's phone number there. Enough digits to choke a damn donkey. How many numbers do people here need to dial to reach each other?

"*Digame,*" he says.

Talk to me. That's how the Spanish answer the phone. I heard it in the hotel lobby, in the cafes and restaurants where we stopped on the drive here. It's said now in a familiar voice, a statement awaiting a response.

"Hello," I say.

I don't know when we stopped identifying ourselves on the phone. Somewhere along the way, we just learned each other's voices.

"Hey," he says, clipped and cautious, but also familiar.

"*Que pasa?*" I might as well try to speak his new language.

"Um, I'm on the beach," he says. "I'm with a Spanish friend."

A concrete-block blow hits me full in the face, then pulls me back and slams me sidelong. I close my eyes. My hands quiver.

"Friend," I say. "Beach."

"How's your trip going?"

Of course he's seeing someone. What's stopping him?

"Haven't been thrown off the continent yet," I say.

"Give it time."

"Fuck you."

Our banter finds its regular, reliable beat. Is this what I've come all this way for—our conversation?

"So," I say, and there are no other words. Things are changing quickly, too quickly. I can't keep up. I'm huffing, out of breath. Soon I will stop and lean against a wall, and then I will be left behind.

"Are we meeting up tonight?"

"Tonight."

"New Year's Eve?"

Tina sighs and turns on her side. I can feel her watching me through the back of her head as she smokes.

We arrange a time and place: We'll meet in the hotel lobby at 9 p.m.

"One more thing," he says, and his voice goes lower, confidential. "Is your room nice?"

"It's okay," I say, "if you like design inspired by Kosovo."

"Is it . . ." and he pauses, as if he too is unsure of his words, as if maybe in the months he's spent abroad he's already shed half his English . . . "big? Roomy?"

Suddenly I am aware of every ounce of pain I've carried throughout this journey. It comes in a wave with a single realization: He's looking for a place to crash.

"Why did you tell him yes?" Tina asks after I hung up.

"I didn't say yes."

"You didn't say no."

"I didn't say anything." I sit down on my bed and start cracking my knuckles one by one.

"Stop that. It's disgusting."

"It's what a shrink would call a nervous habit."

"It's what I call nasty. Cut it out."

I bite my lip and feel the flesh swell beneath my teeth. I bite hard, harder. I can't bring forth enough pain. Each sensation feels like a phantom, something sitting just on the other side of the wall from reality.

"Look," she says. "The car sleeps one. Let him go sack out in there."

"He has a girlfriend," I say, and stupidly begin to cry.

"Oh shit," Tina says. Her face is set in lines of empathy, her eyes soft. Yet at the same time there is a hardness. I recognize that the anger is directed at him, not me. How come I can't feel it too?

She reaches out a hand to me and I stand up, move away. I feel radioactive, something not to be touched. "I'm going for a walk," I say.

Calle Ferran leads me cobblestone by cobblestone toward Las Ramblas, the weaving spine of central Barcelona. Where Ferran is a narrow street, a glorified alley really, the Ramblas are the city's wide, dense grab bag.

I pass tourist shops, tapas joints, and the Erotic Museum. I have no interest in any of this. Take San Francisco's Market Street, give it a Spanish accent and a few more pickpockets, and I could've saved the plane fare.

A wide median in the middle of the street beckons with flower stalls, street performers, and crowds. I cross the street to reach it, cutting off small cars whose honking horns sound like the distant cry of seagulls, and find myself face-to-face with a caged rooster.

Its eyes are nothing like my father's. They're scared, alert, searching. It opens its mouth and the sound emerges as a moan. It is a feminine keening, the fractured cry of heartbreak.

Soon this bird will be sold. It will change hands and leave its cramped quarters for another home. It will be held captive and then consumed. Its fate is written.

And ours?

All of Barcelona seems to freeze around me in the moment. Even the heavens hesitate, the clouds pausing in their sweep across the sky.

If our fate is written, could it be in our own handwriting?

"You're not coming," he says. It's half question, half statement.

"No," I say. Across the hotel room, Tina's lips quirk in a grin.

"Any particular reason?"

Because I mutilated myself for you. Because I traveled half a world away. Because I loved you—yes, I did—and you abandoned me in every way possible. It would be one thing if I were alone here, thinking the familiar could comfort me. But it's the familiar that's drawing and quartering my heart.

"No," I say.

"Bullshit, Landa. You have something you want to tell me?"

Yeah. I feel both envy and empathy for you. Your phone calls made me both happy and scared. You touched something inside of me, took it, and now I want it back.

"Our fate is not written," I say.

"Are you high?"

"We can choose where we go and what we do. You know?"

"I do know. You're definitely high."

"And I'm choosing to say, 'Fuck you.'"

Again, that freeze. Tina sits motionless on the bed. The silence stretches at the other end of the phone line. Even the room's stench takes a momentary breather.

"Fuck you?"

"Yeah. Fuck you."

"Am I missing something?"

All I want right now is a boy to rub my neck. I want his fingers right where I keep all my tension, at that nape. I want him to look at me with something like a mixture of love and curiosity. I need him to know me, to accept what I am even if it's not a neatly wrapped package. Especially because it's not.

"Landa," he says, "look. I've seen every side of you. You know that? Every fucking side."

Every side?

He's seen me gossiping at work, giggling and drunk at The Pub. He's seen me thoughtful while discussing Bukowski and the Beatles, furious as I am in this moment. He's even glimpsed a slice of that good-girl core, the one who says *please* and *thank you* in restaurants and bars.

But every side?

"You know what," I say. "Maybe I've been high for a long time. Maybe I'm just now sobering up."

The connection goes dead. I'm the one who cut it off.

CHAPTER 17

2000

They're taking down the New Year's banners in Plaza Reial. Tina and I sit in a cafe and watch them climb ladders, stretch their torsos, reach to capture and tug. A flock of birds circles the cloudy sky, diving and flirting.

She picks at her croissant. Everything here is smaller, more modest. "Of course I'll take you to the airport," she says without being asked.

We spent New Year's Eve in an Australian bar, listening to the Spainards chant *bebida, bebida, bebida*. We followed orders and drank. The lights were low and the music high, pumping out hits that I recorded on my cassette player in the 1980s. Elton John and Kiki Dee, Billy Idol, Eddie Murphy. "They're always behind the times," Tina said as I sipped my Guinness with a raspberry float. "A few weeks ago my students asked me where the *Dallas* was. It took me a minute to realize they were talking about the TV show."

Now I say: "You don't have to." That's our way, the American way, protesting. No, don't reach for the check, but really, please do.

"I know," she says.

I rest my chin in my hand and think about how the birds see us. Those squawking, flapping creatures circling above probably make more sense of us than we think they do. They see Tina, squat and curvy, wearing a droopy Annie Hall hat and a leopard-skin jacket with a furry collar, and they smell a mix of diva and depression. They spy me, squat and not so curvy, trying to look sophisticated in a hoodie and jeans. Do they think I'm a man, or do they know better?

"What are you thinking about?" Tina asks.

"Moving forward," I say.

"And?"

"I can't get past the fact that I can barely afford this month's rent."

To finance this trip, I broke into the retirement account I'd carried over from the *Daily Republic*. It seemed like a good idea at the time. Now, having not worked for a month, it seems like a bit more questionable move. I can't even take a cash advance on my credit card—I maxed it out paying for the damn laser procedure.

"What are you going to do?"

"Get a job, I guess."

A job. As a freelancer; it's a concept that makes my teeth clench. An assigned cubicle, a standard-issue desk. Set hours and a standard paycheck. In by morning and out by evening and, come the next day, it happens all over again. I'm not saying I'm too good for it. On the contrary, *I'm* not good enough to be able to handle it.

The birds shriek and dive.

"Doing what?"

"Dragging down banners for a living. Holiday pay will probably last throughout the year."

I'm still watching the men on the ladders. They move with ease, using their bodies as tools, agile, facile. They chatter easily as they work. The birds ignore them. I guess we're more interesting.

Out of nowhere I flash on an image of Tina on the abortion table. Eyes closed, screwed shut, no one to hold her hand. That feeling of blind pain and panic, the dread of always being as alone as in this moment. Under my fingers my chin is scruffy as always. We carry scars. We bear life's war wounds.

I think about Matt. His is a taste of triumph and bitterness, a sweet-and-sour mix. I know there are lessons to be taken from knowing him, from the eventual rejection. I just can't formulate them right now. But I will.

"You're smiling," Tina says.

I am.

"Honey," my landlord says, "it's the seventh."

"I know, Peggy," I say, rolling my backpack toward my room. "I owe you."

"You okay? Your aura is a really deep purple."

Sure enough, I'm back in Berkeley. "It's okay," I say. "I'm just color-coordinating with my underwear."

Then I go to my room and shut the door. In here is everything I own: a bed and dresser, clothes, shoes, books. A few pictures: Tina, Missy, and I at high-school graduation, my family at my brother's bar mitzvah, a shot of San Diego's La Jolla Shores. I remember taking that picture, my finger hard on the camera's shutter button, the waves breaking, ripping themselves to pieces.

I sit down on the bed and wait for the tears. They don't come.

PharmaCorp looks like Auschwitz brought to the Bay Area. Smoke spews from atop jagged manufacturing buildings.

Motorized parts seem strewn across the place, as if a factory blew up from the inside out. People walk the paths, hapless and helpless, badges clipped to their belts.

I'm getting paid fifteen dollars an hour to be here.

I meet Adam on my second day. "Hey," he says, smiling, "you've decided to come back."

Dear God, I think to myself. Master of mediocrity. Jukebox of clichés. He wears a button-down shirt tucked into khakis. I judge him to be about my age, but he seems so much older.

"Yeah," I say. Our department operates out of a trailer, and you can hear every noise not just as backdrop, but as if it were occurring right next to you. Coffee percolates. Someone sneezes. A toilet flushes and I reflexively flinch as if I were about to get sprayed with grungy water.

"Mondays suck," he says, still smiling.

"Sure," I say, "but it's Wednesday."

I'm not smiling.

He seems to embody everything that scares me about being here: structure, stagnation, forced humor. Most of all, he seems *okay* with it.

"Then it's almost the weekend. Let's celebrate by getting a bagel."

And it hits me: The guy talks like a girl. I don't know how I didn't realize this until right now. It's beyond obvious. If I were on the phone with him, I wouldn't think it was a *him* at all. I would call him—

Oh, Jesus.

I would call him ma'am.

I'm sitting here facing my inverse. And he's wearing a rumpled dress shirt and an ill-fitting pair of Dockers.

He talks like a girl. Could be mistaken for one on the phone. And let me repeat: He seems *okay* with it.

"You know what?" I say. "I'm not a morning person." Then I turn away and begin to type. Soon I'm drifting away from formatting documents and begin composing emails.

I'm not sorry, I write to Tina. *I don't regret anything.* Then I hit the Delete key and erase all the bravado.

Of course I have regrets. And yeah, there are times I think about him and wonder what he's up to. But you know, I never think about what we could have been. There really was never an Us. You know?

I write to Missy. *You know I'm happy for you. David's a good guy. And I'm just grateful you're not asking me to be a bridesmaid. If you saddled me with one of those potato-sack dresses I would have to shoot you on general principle. And yes, I did rip that off from Tarantino.*

I even write to my mother. *Came back a week and a half ago. Got a temp job. Don't send forwards to this address, though. They don't like that.*

At 12:01 I hear a girly voice at my back. "Are you an afternoon person?" it says, smiling.

"Here," I say to my landlord. She's headed out to walk one of the Pomeranians. I hate those dogs. Drop a laundry bag on them and make them disappear. The bag could only be half full, but it would do the job.

She glances at the check. "I know it's only partial," I say, "but I'll have the rest for you next week."

"Weren't you just in Europe? If you have enough money to gallivant around for a month, why don't you have the money to pay your rent in full?"

259

Her dog focuses its pop eyes on me and bares its tiny teeth.

"You know what," I say, "you're right. It won't happen again."

Then I go and knock on David's door. He's sitting on his pink carpet with a bong and his laptop.

"Want some?" he asks.

Pot is the social currency of Berkeley. It's the local equivalent of offering a cup of tea. "Yeah," I say. "I do." He steadies the contraption while I breathe in, focusing on getting the water to bubble. When I start to cough, he pulls it away.

"Ignore the cough."

"Tell me how," I say between hacks.

"Hell if I know. Use the Force."

He tells me about the project he's working on. It's an animation called *Spook in God's House*, starring a black cartoon dude trying to enter a monastery.

"The guy bangs on the door, yelling, 'Whaddya mean y'all ain't got no malt liquor up in here? Whaddya mean y' ain't got no hos?'"

"Who's it for?"

"Kodak. They're making a campus visit."

"Swell."

I lie on the Pepto-Bismol-colored floor. My thoughts fold in on themselves, weaving and pancaking. I widen my eyes and contemplate the ceiling.

"You know," he says, "you look like a drag queen." There is no malice. Only truth, something that in this moment feels as familiar as my own heartbeat.

"I do know."

"You should do something about it."

"Who says I haven't?"

260

"Did it work?"

"Does it look like it worked?"

He yawns so loudly and long that it's almost embarrassing. Then he goes to press the mute button and bring the television volume to life.

"No," I say. "I want to talk about this."

Wanting to talk about it feels different than ever before. I am buzzing, alive. My cheeks are red, my ears burning. My toes curl and I feel *great*.

"Yeah, I look like a drag queen," I say. "I look like a man. I have stubble. I can't get rid of it, and I can't seem to cover it up. You want to hand me a solution? Use that computer of yours and figure out what I should do?"

He lights a Marlboro, takes a puff, and flicks the ashes into a coffee cup. For a moment I'm reminded of my mother, a painful memory that tastes sour and sharp.

"Make a choice," he says. "Make a choice and stick with it. It almost doesn't matter what you choose."

I walk out of his room feeling stoned in more ways than one. In the kitchen I pull a Diet Coke from the fridge, give it a few seconds of thought, and follow it with a chaser of potato chips. I take my stash to the bedroom and close the door quietly behind me. I kick off my shoes and put Britney Spears on the stereo. I'm not afraid to admit I have her album. I'm not afraid to make a choice, make a change.

But what is it I'm trying to do?

I pick up my checkbook and a BIC pen, place them on my lap desk. I take out my contact lenses and replace them with the glasses I never wear except when alone, shuck my clothes, and slide the T-shirt in which I sleep over my head. Might as well balance my budget. I run my finger down the list of figures that

261

I can't reconcile. Withdrawals from ATM machines in Italy and France. A bar bill in Spain. And three hundred dollars to The Clinic, that sham shack that turned my face into hamburger meat.

I push my glasses atop my head and rub my eyes. The room doesn't entirely stop spinning, but it helps. Then I catch a glimpse of myself in the full-length mirror—and I look exactly like Nails.

Nails, who was doing bills when she threw me out of the house years ago. Slippers on her feet, calculator by her knee. How did that moment taste to her? Was she scared? Could there possibly be any explanation for what she does, who she is?

I drop my pen and don't bother to retrieve it. The lessons of most of life's moments are not clear, but this one is: My choice is about relationships.

I pop the Diet Coke, pull open the bag of chips. I drink and I eat until everything is gone. Then I slide under the covers and fall asleep with the lights on.

"Strawberry cream cheese?" Adam's frowning down at my plate. "What next, vomit-flavored spread?"

"If it was solid, not whipped, I would go for it," I say. "Think of it as the spirit of adventure."

It's nine o'clock in the morning and we're at Cafe 64, PharmaCorp's corporate cafeteria. I'm still not a morning person, but somehow I've developed a taste for bagels in the hours before the fog burns off the bay. If Adam wants to join me, let him.

We sit at a round Formica table. "You think I'm disgusting?" I say. "What about that sludge in front of you?"

"You mean this thing called coffee?"

"Is that what the kids are calling it these days? To me it just looks like something the dog left behind."

He cackles. "You don't hold back, do you?"

"You have no idea," I say, instantly regretting the words.

He doesn't do anything obvious like lean forward or raise an eyebrow. He takes a sip of coffee and sprays it out of his nose. His face reddens and he starts to cough. People look over and don't bother to swallow their smiles.

I pound him on the back, and finally his hacking settles down. It is, I realize, the first time I have ever touched him. Under my fist he feels solid, something strangely familiar.

"Was it something I said?"

"I just do that sometimes." He grins at the people who are watching, and I watch their smiles change from slight derision to openness.

"You're not embarrassed," I say. It's not a question; it's a statement.

He shrugs. "Too much effort."

Too much effort. I never thought about that. It always seemed an effort *not* to care.

Back at my desk I write to Missy: *I didn't even like him when I first met him. But we've been hanging out for a few weeks. He's growing on me a little bit. Like mold.*

A voice calls over the cubicle wall: "You must be writing a personal email," it says. It belongs to Sue, whose breast cancer still hasn't given her perspective in life.

"Oh yeah? How can you tell?"

"Your typing gets really enthusiastic."

Enthusiastic typing. Now I've heard it all.

Lately I've been—

I backspace, delete the words. I don't know what I've been. *I'm confused.*

I'm not comfortable with that feeling. I like solidity, specifics. I want to know what, when, and how. It feels like an ocean. I like lakes.

CHAPTER 18

2000

"You're moving?" David's usual bored countenance is replaced by a look of bored disbelief. "Who's going to drive me to Taco Bell at two in the morning?"

"Take a cab," I say. "Walk. Fly on your broom."

"You're not going to be so far away. Oakland's close. I'll just call you."

"At two in the morning? When I have to work at eight?"

"That never stopped you before."

We're making cookies and it is, in fact, two in the morning. I combine flour, baking powder, and salt with a fork, then whip together sugar and butter. David hands me the vanilla, and I pour in a liberal amount.

"I'm a little scared," I say. "It's more than I've ever paid in rent before."

"But it's your own place. And you have a Jew father to help you out if you need money."

"Aw, stuff it." I considered asking Rooster for help. Then I discarded the idea, pulled together my pennies, and signed the lease agreement.

While the cookies rise we watch late-night television, a mélange of Lifetime movies and infomercials. "You know," he says over the blare of the tube, "I'll give you credit. You made a choice."

I turn to look at him, blinking with surprise. David is never sincere and never-*ever* complimentary.

"That's all," he says, and turns back toward the screen.

In my bedroom I stuff a cookie in my mouth and survey the territory. I've got to pack up all my belongings, and for some reason that seems like a lot of work. "Well," I say to myself out loud, "start at the beginning."

Start at the beginning. Easy to say, but what the fuck does it mean? I picture the beginning as the starting line at a race, shorts-clad runners jockeying for space and waiting, nerves twinging, for the gun to go off. But there are no fingers on triggers here, no flags waiting to be waved. There is only me, and it is now nearly three in the morning. I should go to bed, worry about this tomorrow. But what if the beginning is now?

I think about my new apartment. It's a one-bedroom in a garden courtyard complex a half block off Piedmont Avenue, a cutesy pedestrian strip. I'll be living across the street from Piedmont Grocery, the place of fantastic free cheese samples, two blocks from the best cafe in the East Bay, and in the middle of just about everything.

Circus act, a voice whispers in my mind. *Bearded Lady. Freak.*

I roll my eyes and reach for a packing box. It's pretty much the same shit that so often floats through my head. If I went to slit my wrists every time it happened, I'd be spending an awful lot of time in the emergency room. I roll picture frames in newspapers, place them carefully one atop the other.

Then I run across my brother's bar mitzvah photo, the one I took from my mother's office the day she threw me out of the house. My mother's Ipana smile, my father's mustached face, my own stubble. Jonathan in his little blue bow tie; Middle, the bar mitzvah boy, looking stunned over the sacred scroll.

I want to be closer with my family.

The surprise of that thought makes my mouth twitch. For years I've wanted nothing less than to outrun them, not just my parents but my brothers as well. I've wanted to forget that at one point I was subject to the wills and whims of Nails and Rooster, that I may have had a voice but could only use it under sanctioned circumstances.

I've wanted to forget Bill too, the rise and fall of a baseball bat, the crack of ceramic. He still lives with my mother. Nothing's changed. Why should it?

And yet hers is the voice I want to hear. It would be so easy: Pick up the receiver, dial a series of ten digits. Intake of breath as she picks up, then speak.

It could've been so easy.

"I'm going to L.A. this weekend," Adam says, pouring himself a cup of black coffee. We're in the little room that passes for an office kitchen in this trailer. It's nothing more than a little niche in the wall, a tight space carved out for relaxation. Good luck with that.

"What's down there?"

"My family. My ex."

"Is he cute?" The words plow out from my mouth before I can stop myself. *Damn it, Landa. Control yourself.*

He smirks. "She's pretty hot, actually."

I picture him holding a woman, bringing his lips to hers. I expect derision and instead feel . . . *jealous?* "I'm sorry," I say.

"For what? Questioning my manliness? Like you're the first

one to do that?" The words come fast and fluid but without anger. Out of nowhere the earth shifts. Dizziness makes me grip the table. I don't feel as if I can move. "You okay?"

"Fine. Really."

"Sit down."

He pulls out the chair and guides me into it. "What happened?"

"I don't know," I say. It's all I can say. How do I explain that he's the first person who has opened my eyes to a possibility I'd never imagined?

He doesn't care what others think. It's a genuine thing, seemingly effortless in that way you know took years of work. I feel my perception of him changing, shifting in the way that . . .

That . . .

"You sure you're okay?"

That I experienced with Matt.

"Allison?"

It's that shift that comes when someone pulls back a curtain, shows you something you hadn't previously imagined. Call it a magic trick, call it alchemy, call it what you will. It's that moment when your vision of someone doesn't so much change as deepen, when your understanding of them expands.

Some might say it's the beginning of love.

Oh, *hell* no.

"I'm okay," I say. "I, uh, got stoned last night."

"Party girl."

"That's me," I say. I stand up, and he helps steady me on my feet.

"You've got to take care of yourself," he says.

"Sometimes I think I don't know how."

"*Maybe* you need help."

His eyes are so blue. How have I not realized that?

"We need to get back," I say.

I feel the bottom of something falling out, a glass ceiling shattering. Like Matt and yet so different. Sure, I'd felt derision toward Matt, but it never quite matured into genuine comfort. I always worried about what he thought when he looked at me.

With this guy, I don't even think about it.

"We need to get back," I say again.

"Why are you in such a rush?"

There is no world around me, no one watching this scene. There is no one here except for him and me, and that intimacy both sears and surprises me.

"Because," I say, and make for the door.

Later I walk over to his desk. He's left for the day without saying goodbye. What's unusual is not the action itself but my reaction to it. I find myself stung. *He doesn't owe you anything*, I tell myself, but I have trouble believing it.

Here's where I wish I could go to my parents for advice. I would love to be able to call up Nails or Rooster and say, "There's this boy . . ." I've never done that. I couldn't see myself doing that. How do you place your confessions in the hands of people you can't . . .

Trust?

I look at Adam's desk. It's a friendly mess, stacks of papers and Post-it notes. No pictures, nothing to personalize it, but I can picture him there all the same.

"Trust," I say to myself, quietly, and walk back to my desk.

On Saturday morning I drive up to Davis. It's a straight shot along Interstate 80. Along the way the jagged, colorful landscape of the inner East Bay gives way to something different, more rolling and lackadaisical. When I worked in Fairfield I ran this route every day, passing San Pablo Bay, crossing the Carquinez Bridge with the C&H sugar refinery winking in the sun below.

Missy's getting married. She's going to have a ring on her finger and a different last name on her driver's license. I can't quite pull together my feelings about that. I'm jealous and not jealous, melancholy and happy. Part of me says that at twenty-six she's too young to make the commitment, but I know better. Missy was always the mature one, the one older than her time. If anyone can take marriage and run with it, it's she. She'll kick the ass of marriage. She'll make marriage stand up to her and show some damn respect.

I blink and the road before me swims. I'm not crying. There's just something in my eye.

I slow down to take the exit ramp. She's getting married on campus among the eucalyptus trees that also decorated UCSB. Davis is so different from Berkeley: compact where Berkeley is sprawling, orderly where Berkeley is untamed. I always feel in control when I'm here. I feel focused, organized, as if everything is in its rightful place. It's a perfect place for Missy, her quiet intellect and watery blue eyes. It's a place that just makes you feel calm.

I find a parking spot, switch off the ignition, and just sit in the car for a minute watching the student bicyclists pedal by. Across the country is the Bronx Jewish Community Center, where my parents wed in 1971. Did they have hope? Did their hearts beat nervously inside their finery? Did they bludgeon that hope, or did it simply die?

I get out of the car. I'm wearing a black dress, and in this heat it feels like an unfortunate choice. The sweat is already gathering at my temples and under my arms. Of course there's going to be a photographer to capture me in all my perspiring glory. I hope they'll find some way to airbrush out the hair. I don't want to look like a man at Missy's wedding.

Damn it, a voice inside my head says, *when will you stop obsessing?*

I want to be rid of it. I want to walk into a room and not worry about how people see me. I want to be able to go to the dentist, the hair salon, and not be concerned about someone coming close to my face, noticing, commenting.

I want to move past this.

I want something else to be the focus of my life.

Some epiphanies hit you hard, a wall of water forceful enough to relocate buildings. Others just come when you're stepping onto campus.

I walk along the tree-lined paths toward the flower garden where the wedding is slated to take place. I don't feel any different, and yet I know a change has taken place. It's kind of like how you feel on your birthday when someone asks if you feel older. You say no, right? But you know that you are.

Tina spots me as I approach. She squeals and runs toward me. I think about the losses we've both experienced and grab her in a tight hug. "You look great," she says.

"Yeah. In my thrift-store dress and the heels that are killing me."

"Your face," she says, and I automatically tense. Even a compliment means that someone's paying attention. Someone's noticing something. Someone's looking, and I don't want to be observed.

"You're glowing," she says.

"Yeah. It's the 800-degree heat."

"No," she says. "You look like you're in love."

The words drift back to me as I watch Missy come down the

aisle, that walk so often memorialized and lionized, the journey of the bride. She is flanked by her parents, each holding one of her hands. *Love. In love.* Do I share Missy's radiance?

Do I too have love?

"She cried," I tell Adam on Monday. "Me too."

We're walking to Tomate for lunch. It's one of the better of Berkeley's sprouts-and-weeds cafes. Cheap too, which is good, because I blew my budget at the bar at the wedding.

"I can't imagine you crying."

"Well, I had to pinch myself to do it, but it was for a good cause."

It's raining. Around us West Berkeley is a strange morass of Victorians and industrial buildings. Adam's wearing a soft blue sweater and jeans. He looks boyish, seventeen at the most despite the goatee and close-cropped hair. He looks comfortable inside his clothes, in his skin. I bet he wouldn't have to have three Long Island Iced Teas to get up the courage to go out on the dance floor.

"I bet you looked cute," he says.

West Berkeley stops around me. I'm stock-still, shaking a little even. *It's just a compliment*, I tell myself. I've gotten them before. But rarely on my looks. And even more rarely with such easygoing honesty.

"As long as I didn't look like Jabba the Hutt," I say, "I'm happy."

Now we're both standing still on the sidewalk, though oddly not facing each other. "You know," he says, "I've noticed something about you."

The pulse in my wrists begins to race. Oh God. Here it comes. The pitch of concern, the I'm-just-trying-to-help.

"It's really hard for you to be sincere," he says.

Now that's one I've never heard before. "Sincere?" I say, as if I had never heard the word.

"Maybe that's the wrong way to put it. I'm not saying you're a liar or you're not a real person. You're totally down to earth. I like that about you. But you just have a hard time talking without being all quippy."

"Huh," I say. Great rejoinder there, but in fact I don't have one.

"Are you actually speechless?"

"Yeah," I say after a pause. "I guess I am."

Then we laugh. I'm not even sure what we're laughing about, but we laugh and it feels good. "I meant it," he says after the giggles die down to hiccups and we begin walking again. "No one's ever told you you're cute before?"

Has anyone?

I'm twenty-six years old. In that lifetime I must have run into someone else who called me cute, considered me attractive. I think about Brent and his charming, damning words; Matt and how he fell in love twenty times a day. I think about the people who have crossed my path. What have they said to me? In this moment, I can't even remember.

"I don't know," I say in a small voice. It's not the voice I use with the outside world. It's the inner voice that counsels and sometimes criticizes me. It's nothing I share with anyone else.

We reach Tomate. Adam turns to me and grins. "You know now," he says.

There's no one else in the restaurant. Maybe we're early for the lunch rush; maybe everyone else is out trying to get someone to tell them they're cute. "Listen," he says, "you want to get a drink?"

"Right now?"

"Yeah," he says. "Right now."

"It's not even noon."

"It's not like you're a stranger to alcohol."

"I really don't drink that much."

"I'm not asking you to. One drink."

"Liquid lunch?"

"Can you see any reason why not?"

I can't, so we go to the Missouri Lounge. It's darker in here than outside. We approach the bar, and he slides his wallet from his back pocket. "I've got it," he says.

"Can I at least leave the tip?"

"No." I put my wallet back and he grins again. I'm starting to feel something low in my stomach, something tight and excited. I'm not sure I know Adam well enough to love him, but I'm starting to understand that I want him. I want to press my cheek to his—damn the torpedoes, damn the stubble. I want to run my hand through his short hair, teasingly tell him I want him to grow it out. *Be my Samson*, I think, and internally roll my eyes at myself.

The bartender materializes. He's wearing a T-shirt that says RELAX, I'M HILARIOUS. "Are you really?" I ask.

"No," he says.

Adam turns to me, and I realize I have no idea what I want to order. I drank a little at Missy's wedding, sure, but mostly I stick to Diet Cokes. Less calories, no hangover, nice shot of caffeine and carbonation. "Order what you think I should have," I say. It seems to be the right thing to say in the situation.

"Okay," he says, and orders me something called a Liquid Panty Remover: melon and raspberry liqueur, peach schnapps, 7UP.

"Very subtle," I say. My jaw feels tight in a pleasurable sense. My toes are twitching. I am starting to sweat, just slightly, more of a sheen, a glow. I'm glowing.

He orders a gin and tonic and we sit on an aged couch. "Are we going to get into trouble?" I ask.

"Don't you like trouble?"

"Yeah," I say, "but I also like paying my rent." I sip my drink. It's sweet and strong. I take another sip and put it down on the table with a clang.

"Don't worry about it."

"Easy for you to say."

"How's that?"

"They love you around the office. You're like the popular boy."

He laughs.

"What?"

"Popular boy? You've got to be kidding. I've *never* been the popular boy."

And he says it with such easy conviction.

"Bullshit," I say. "Everyone likes you."

"You know how many fights I got into in middle school?"

"Why?" But I already know. He's had to learn to live with it, this voice of his. I'm not sure if he sees it as blessing or curse. I think he just takes it for what it is. And in getting to know him, so have I.

There may be a lesson in there somewhere.

We drink in silence for a moment. I think about Matt, our trips to The Pub. Alcohol just makes conversation easier. It loosens you up. On the few occasions when I drink, I can almost forget who and what I am. It's a liquid eraser of sorts, a means of time travel back to a clean slate.

"Anyway," he says. "It's not me who's the cool one. It's you."

"Me?"

"Yeah. You're the world traveler."

"I've been to Europe once and, let me tell you, it was no picnic."

He laughs. "You poor thing."

I flash back to Barcelona, to Las Ramblas and the caged rooster. How can I explain that everything I went through wasn't worth a few postcard moments? I think about saying *You're right, it was fantastic, I screwed Guido in Italy and Philippe in France.*

Then it comes back to me, what he said earlier: *It's hard for you to be sincere.*

"Actually," I say, "it really sucked."

"Why?"

I glance around the bar. A few old blowhards taking up space by the pool table, a guy in a suit sipping a Cosmo on a barstool. The hilarious bartender is nowhere to be seen. Maybe he's scaring up a sense of humor.

Then I look Adam in his blue eyes.

"I got my heart broken."

It's the first time I've put it like that, the first time I've acknowledged out loud how much everything with Matt hurt. And it did. Oh, it did.

He doesn't say anything.

"That's it," I say.

"That can't be it."

"Why not?"

"Because there was some asshole who you loved. And that asshole broke your heart. And there's a story there, and you don't want to tell it. And that's fine, but just admit that you don't want to talk about it."

A story. Yes, a story.

"I wouldn't say I loved him."

"A crush. Okay, same thing."

"It's not the same thing. Love is love. A crush you can have twenty times a day."

276

"I think you loved him."

"Yeah?"

"Yeah. You don't fly halfway across the world for a crush."

Did I love Matt? Or did I love the idea of him?

I finish my drink. "We've got to get back."

Does he realize how close his hand is to mine? "It's okay," he says.

I'm in a bar in the middle of the day, drinking with a cute boy who likes me. I have a choice: I can stay here and see where it goes or head back to the office job that feels more stultifying by the minute. "We should head back," I say.

Damn it, Landa. Grow a pair!

"Tell you what," he says. "I'm getting another drink. If you head back now, you can say hi to everyone for me."

"Another Panty Remover, please."

His grin is wide and real. He motions for me to stay on the couch and goes to the bar. When he brings back the two sweating drinks, I could swear he sits closer than before. His is a clean scent, fresh and boyish. It reminds me of the redwoods, that hopeful perfume of pine.

I feel at the edge of some precipice. I don't know whether to cling or to fall, or to run away without a second glance. I take a sip.

"Okay," he says. "This story."

"Shit. I thought you'd forgotten."

"You don't want to tell me about it, do you?"

"No, it's . . ." I don't know how to finish that sentence. To tell would mean telling the whole story, and telling the whole story means saying things I don't want to say. I guess that means I don't want to tell him.

"No," I say. "I will."

What is it about this guy that makes me keep reversing course?

"You went to Europe to see this asshole."

"Yes. I went to see some asshole."

"And?"

"That's it," I say. "End of story."

Some concrete wall in me doesn't want to let the story spill. It's less that I don't want to talk about it and more that I can't.

"That happened to me once," he says.

"You went to Europe to get rejected by some asshole?"

"Not really. I went to Boston for the same purpose."

The look that crosses his face is familiar. Not because I've seen it on him, but because I've felt it on myself. It's the twitch of memory, that pinch of remembrance.

"She was a family friend," he says. "She lived on the East Coast, I lived in L.A. My family went out to Boston one year and we started dating. Then I went back home and was shitty about not writing to her. By the time I made it back to Boston, she was done with me. We met up and she told me she started dating someone else."

No kidding. "You didn't know until you showed up there?"

"No. She surprised me with it."

"Okay," I say. "Maybe I can tell you the story."

The time when we can go back to work unnoticed has long passed. I have no idea what the clock says, only that the light that dimly filters in under the door has grown weaker. I have switched from Panty Removers to Sex on the Beach, and Adam has his hand on my leg. My every cell is alive and my vision is blurry.

"He's a fucking idiot," Adam says. "Hands down."

"You're just saying that."

"You love it."

"Well, yeah."

"And by the way, I mean it. Not because I'm hitting on you, which I am. But because he was a shitty friend to you. He could have told you the truth before you took a damn flight to Europe, which he knew you were doing because you wanted to see him. He should have told you the truth. He should have saved you the pain."

My mouth is dry, my eyes watering. "There's more," I say.

He doesn't say anything. He just watches me. I've been observed in many ways, some flattering, some not, but never like this. It's as if he already knows what I'm about to say, as if nothing could shock or disgust him.

"I can't look at you while I tell you," I say.

"Okay," he says, and turns to face the bar. In profile he has the nose of Dustin Hoffman, that sort of bird's beak. *The map of Israel,* my mother would say.

"Look," I say, "I've never told anyone this. You've got to promise not to say anything. No questions, no comments. Okay?"

"Okay," he says, still not looking at me.

I spill. I crack far and wide. I shift on the couch and feel it shift with me.

I tell him about my condition. I tell him about the woman in the natural foods store who handed me a card and tried to help, about Brent, the brief lover who didn't. I recall a hotel room nine time zones away, a darkened space I could barely allow myself to leave. I talk about wanting help and not getting it, trying on my own to find it and failing in the bargain. I don't know how long I talk. I only know that when I run out of words, he is holding my hand.

He is facing me.

We are face-to-face.

279

His hand is on my face.

His gaze is moving closer.

When we kiss it is as if I've learned a new language that is instantly familiar. Its meaning comes clear through the alcoholic haze. It is not perfect. It is not magic. But it is love.

CHAPTER 19

2000

If you drink all the tap beers at Raleigh's, you get a free T-shirt. I've opted for a salad. We're sitting on the outside patio on a bright Sunday afternoon. Berkeley is beginning to wake up and stumble in for some standard pub grub. You don't come here for the food. You come here for the sports on the tube, the wood-paneled walls, the convenient location down the street from campus, the vines of ivy and bright flowers climbing the picket fences. It's not quite student life in an alcoholic nutshell, but it's close enough to have its charms.

It's our second date, if you count the drunken afternoon at the Missouri Lounge, and I do. Under the table he puts his foot atop mine. Every nerve in my body wakes up and sings an aria.

But we haven't slept together. Not yet.

Adam reaches into my salad bowl and poaches a walnut. "God damn it," I say. "Paws off."

"I don't like the sound of that."

"Deal with it."

"It's okay."

"What's okay?"

"Last night."

"I should hope so."

"It was great," he says. "I love touching you. I just worry that you don't like being touched."

Last night we lay entangled on my couch, my skirt rising toward my hips, his tongue tracing my neck. Then he tugged at my shirt and I froze. Just because he knows about my condition doesn't mean I'm ready for him to experience it in the flesh. The stubbly flesh, the flesh that will always feel rough no matter how hot I run the water, no matter how sharp the blade.

"I like it," I say. My voice is that small one, the little-girl cadence. It's an embarrassed and hushed tone. It sounds like a lie.

He takes his foot off mine and concentrates on his pastrami sandwich. I recognize that brand of concentration. It comes when you focus on what's in front of you but don't really see it. You look at it so long and so hard that it loses its focus and, thereby, its definition.

"I *like* it," I say again with more conviction. And the bitch of it is, that's not a lie. You can like something that scares you. You can like something that threatens to break down your barriers. You can like it, but it's not a comfortable feeling. It's your favorite color in such a bright shade that you feel blinded.

He's still staring at his sandwich. "Look at me," I say. His eyes flicker to mine. "I've revealed more of myself with you than I've done with anyone. I—"

I've seen every side of you.

"You don't know me," I say. "I mean, you're getting to know me, and I want you to get to know me more. But you have to understand that it's hard for me. All of it."

He rests his chin on his hand. His nails are blunt and unpolished, his fingers a shade darker than mine. "How come you never talk about your family?"

My nerves are no longer singing. They've dropped down into a lower register, a darker one. "I wouldn't say I never talk about them."

"Not to me."

I now know why I didn't like him when I first met him: He was a threat. He wanted too much. He came too close and only backed off when I asked. "There's a lot of things I don't talk about with you."

"I know, and I respect that. I'm just asking."

I reach over my wall and take his hand. He holds mine with careful warmth. His touch is present and real, something I can't ignore. "It's a long story," I say. "Maybe someday you'll meet them."

"I hope so."

Out of nowhere I'm sideswiped by a wave of desire. I want to push him against his chair, take him in ways that are illegal in at least six different states. "Let's get the bill," I say.

"Yeah?"

"Yeah. We're going home."

"Where'd this come from?"

For the first time in my life, I say to another human being: "I want to fuck you."

He signals to the waiter. "Check, please."

Inside my apartment he pushes me up against the wall, kisses me hard enough to hurt. He's already hard beneath his jeans, and for a moment panic dries my mouth. Then I kiss him back. *No reservations*, I tell myself. *Do it.*

Then we're on the couch, making out. There's magic in my mind, havoc in my heart. Part of me wants to keep it at this level, the kissing, the over-the-clothes caresses. His movements are

283

deliberate without feeling choreographed, savvy without making me feel like he's been here a million times before.

In other words, he's good.

When I'm really beginning to relax into his touch, to give myself over to the mouth that tastes of desire, he begins to tug at my sweater.

Freeze is not the word for it. I petrify. Under my clothes is a nation of concrete, its states united by a single desire: Do not tread upon us. My tongue dries again and my nipples, inexplicably, grow hard.

I wonder if he'll notice, pull back and ask . . . *What*? But he is too far down that tunnel to retreat. He places his hand at the small of my back and begins to inch underneath, toward my flesh.

"Wait," I say, and pull back.

He smiles. He's waiting.

"I want to read you something," I say. I disentangle myself and reach over to the bookshelf. I pull down a book I've never read, a slim volume of love poems by Pablo Neruda. I turn back toward him, flip through the pages, try to find some means of distraction. Maybe we'll sit here all day, reading, chaste. Perhaps by evening we'll have a greater understanding of the human heart's workings, an advanced grasp on the Spanish language.

Before I can choke out a single foreign word, he takes the book from me. He slaps it down on the coffee table, still open, the binding now forever creased. Then he takes me by both arms and leads me backward into the bedroom.

We half-sit, half-fall onto my futon. He circles my wrists with his fingers, and for a moment I feel his heat on my skin. Then he moves to my sweater sleeves and tugs. I think about the book on the coffee table, cracked open, forever changed.

He's a shadow in the darkened bedroom, its blinds closed against prying eyes. The shadow pulls the cloth from my skin. He reveals me one inch at a time, the uncovered parts of me blazing like the sun outside. When he has drawn the sweater over my head, we sit for a moment, unsure of what is to come next.

I think about how his flaws are revealed each day. He has no choice. Each time he speaks, his vulnerability is revealed. Yet somehow, he has come to terms with it. Perhaps one day I'll ask how it's done.

I remember Brent, his fast hands, wicked observations. The memory makes me want to pull my clothes back over my body, run fast and far. I push my skirt down over my knees. He takes care of the rest.

By the time I'm on my back, him positioned in front of me, I am shaking. I am shaking with excitement and fear, with anticipation and dread. I feel myself go tight, and I can't imagine how we will make love. I don't want this to fail. I don't want to be a failure. And I don't want to think in terms of success and failure. I just want to be close to him.

If love is vulnerability, then he is the heart of my heart.

He reaches down, repositions. He adjusts and moves forward. "Slow," I say, my voice familiar and yet not, startling as when you hear yourself on a recording. Does he hear himself differently? Does he perceive himself as the world does?

He presses forward. I tighten more, holding my breath. *Please*, I bargain with whatever deity is out there and listening, tapping my wish list on a clipboard. *Help me.*

The entry is slow and . . . painful? No. Slight resistance, but no pain. He moves his hips forward and then back. He is no longer a shadow. He is three-dimensional, real, flesh and blood, and he is here with me.

But love, being love, has its pitfalls.

He wants to meet my family. It's not as if we've been together that long: two months, to be exact. And it's been a good two months. I'm stopping short of saying a *great* two months because I don't think you can judge anything as great after such a small amount of time. But *good*, yes. It has been.

Still. He wants to meet Nails and Rooster and my brothers. He wants to get to know the parents from whom I've run and the brothers I've made strangers through neglect. We wrangle over it while sitting at Gaylords, my neighborhood cafe. Students bury their faces in texts and MacBooks; would-be revolutionaries scribble in journals. Baristas call out orders—double macchiato, extra hot; Mexican mocha, no whip—and an enthusiastic chess game broadcasts itself loudly from the corner.

"I'll stab your eyeballs out with a tuning fork," I say, prompting a startled glare from the orange-haired woman to my left. "Then you'll know the pain of meeting my parents. We'll even save on the gas money."

"I'm not sure what you're scared of."

"This isn't scared. This is being realistic."

"Come on. You think my family's any saner?"

I think about what he's told me: divorced parents, an overbearing older sister. A cute Cocker Spaniel who died before we got together. A house that had yet to be sold a year into the divorce. A rabbi brother-in-law who plays guitar, and—

"I don't know," I say. "I only know the facts."

"What else is there to know?"

"You haven't told me how you feel about your family."

"And you've told me how you feel about yours?"

Around me the cafe goes about its business. The students wield highlighter pens and headphones; the revolutionaries take a smoke break. The drinks are retrieved; the chess players slap the board with triumph.

"I'd tell you," I say, "if I knew."

"Come on. That's an easy answer."

"No. It's actually the hardest one I can think of."

I give my lower lip a little quiver, hoping he'll take my hand, all is forgiven and forgotten. He rests his chin in his hand and watches me, not saying anything.

"Speak," I say.

"I'm not a dog. I don't follow commands."

I could swear the orange-haired woman next to us represses a laugh.

"Neither do I," I say. "That's why I'm not having you meet my family. I'm not ready. I'm not ready for you to see them and to know what I grew up with. Okay? Is that what you wanted to know? Is that what you needed to hear?"

Now he takes my hand. His skin is warm and real, and I forget about trying to fool him or order him around. It's not going to work, and I'm glad for it. "Just the truth," he says. "It's all I ever want to hear."

A month later we're in Southern California. We're driving down Interstate 5 toward San Diego. We're in Adam's Miata, top down, hats and sunglasses and SPF 40 sunblock on. I'm taking my boyfriend to meet my family. This isn't necessarily a happy or tragic thing. It simply is.

When we made the decision to visit, I called Nails. "Where are you staying?" she wanted to know.

"Jonathan's," I said.

"The Schmuck doesn't have room for you?"

"I didn't ask."

"You like this guy?"

"Dad?"

"No. The guy you're bringing home."

"Adam? He's . . ."

I didn't know what to say. Any description would open my inner life to my mother, give her a glance into my feelings and needs.

"He's a nice guy," I said finally.

"Well," she said, "that's important."

"My mother still lives with Bill," I say now as we pass Camp Pendleton. "We're not going to her house."

He fiddles with the radio. Beach Boys, Cake, Cypress Hill. "How come you didn't want to stay with your dad?"

I think about Rooster's house: the newspaper stacks, the ketchup packets, the dusty stove and stained carpets. "Sometimes you just have to trust me," I say.

Nails looks different than the last time I saw her. That was years ago, and now the youthful freshness has faded from her face. In their place lines have set in, deep creases that each seem to showcase a sad story. Her hair is the same color as the woman who glared at me at Gaylords. She is missing a tooth and the rest seem jagged. Is this all new, or had I just never noticed?

She is the first to arrive at a barbecue hosted by Jonathan, who lives with a handful of friends in a rambling house with a pool. He's grown-up enough to live on his own. How did that happen? She greets Adam with a warm hug. "Your face," she says. "It's the map of Israel."

"Now that," I tell him, "is the seal of approval."

Nails, no stranger to excess, came laden with a carful of food. Hebrew National hot dogs and barbecue Lays, Tyson's frozen chicken wings and Fruit Roll-Ups. "Jesus," I say to Adam. "She bought out Costco."

"Hey," Nails says. "I left some things on the shelf."

"Like what?"

"Shrimp," she says. "I figured Mr. Israel over here doesn't eat it."

"I love shrimp," he says.

She makes for her purse. "I'll run to Costco then."

I put a hand on her arm. I feel a jolt of affection and want to pull back, run fast and far. "Leave it," I say. "Leave something for next time."

Next time.

Rooster arrives carrying two grocery bags, the plastic film clinging to the sweating contents inside. It's a pair of two-liter bottles of Diet Rite. "Really," I whisper to Adam while he's putting the sodas in the refrigerator, "he shouldn't have. And I mean that."

When he shakes Adam's hand, it's like a study in contrasts. One is young, boyish, vibrant, accessible. The other is my father. Somehow he has grown old, paunchy, graying, and balding. He is a little less scary, a little more unsure. When he kisses me on the cheek, I feel his lips, dry and hesitant, and there is an ache in my chest.

They're getting old.

The last to arrive is Middle. I haven't seen or spoken to him in years. It's not as if we had a fight. We don't know each other well enough to fight. He is tall, slender, prematurely thin on top. His cheekbones are pronounced, his eyelashes enviable to any woman. I can say objectively that my brother is an attractive person, but I have very little idea what lies under all that.

We all gather in Jonathan's backyard. This is Southern California in a desert-dry nutshell: brush instead of trees, concrete competing with a patch of lawn. It's alternately lush and lonely. Jonathan grabs a Dr Pepper. Middle pops a beer. Rooster pours himself some Diet Rite, and my mother clutches the lipstick-stained Starbucks coffee cup she brought with her.

I grab a Coke. The carbonation tickles my throat and burns my stomach. Adam pulls a beer from the cooler. Silence sets in like smog. Just when I think my lungs will burst, Jonathan saves the moment.

"To Adam," he says, raising his soda can in Adam's direction. I always loved that kid.

Later we find ourselves in the kitchen with Middle. He's on his third beer. "It's the only way," he says.

It's odd when you're so distant from a sibling. Common, but odd. You share DNA but not confidences, a history but not matters of the heart. Yet they know you in a way nearly no one else can: There is a wordless understanding, an agreement of sorts. Call it growing up together; call it what you will.

How does he see me? His homely older sister? A person from the past? Or a stranger whose presence fosters mixed emotions, uncomfortable as forgetting someone's name?

I reach for Adam's hand, but he's distracted. He seems to be examining my brother, studying him. Then Middle goes off to the bathroom—got to get rid of those beers somehow—and Adam turns to me.

"He's like you," he says.

Huh?

"Landa," he says, "inescapably."

We're in the DJ room at Jonathan's place, smoking hookah. Adam and I are staying in my brother's room. He's given us his bed and is sleeping on the couch.

My cell phone rings: the *Psycho* theme song. My mother.

"Are you okay?" she asks.

"Yes," I say. "I'm fine."

"You answered so quickly."

"I was right next to the phone."

"Anything wrong?"

I grew up with this sort of patter. Nails' version of being a concerned mother means haranguing you until you tell her something, anything, is wrong. Then she'll flip out on your behalf.

"*Fine*," I repeat, my voice growing sharp. Adam and Jonathan just keep smoking the flavored tobacco. Skittles, sweet and stinging to the tongue.

"Okay, okay. Just checking."

"You called to make sure I wasn't croaking?"

"Smartass. Keep that up and I'll make sure you do."

When did my mother and I become some edgy Abbott and Costello routine?

"What's up?" I ask. Nails never just calls to call. There's either some dirt to dig or some shit to sling. Either way, you're sure to end up with crap on your face.

"Your father," she says, and something about the tone of her voice makes me move outside the room. Even in the hallway, I can smell the sweet smoke.

I crouch against the wall, feeling the muscles of my calves lengthen. I consider sliding down to the well-worn carpet. I might as well settle in.

"Okay," I say, "Dad."

"That schmuck kept haranguing me the whole barbecue long."

"About?"

"He wanted me to talk to you about—"

And immediately I know what she's talking about. Hers is the same oddly hushed tone as everyone who's tried to help me and failed, because helping me isn't about making me aware of the hair. Helping me means letting me live as a normal person rather than a freak, allowing me to figure out what I need to do on my own.

I open my mouth to say, "Forget it," but that's not what comes out. I say, "I've got it under control."

"You don't even know what he wants me to talk to you about."

"Yes, I do," I say, "and he doesn't need to worry about it. Neither do you."

"I don't?"

"No," I say. "I'm taking care of it."

I run through my options as we drive northward on Interstate 5. There's the doctor, another phone book, another random choice. Another white gown, another terrifying exam. Another diagnosis and another fistful of prescriptions. Another chance, another hope, another moment to fear failure.

Then there are the cosmetic solutions. Electrolysis, waxing, perhaps even another crack at laser hair removal. Eyes screwed shut beneath dark glasses, fists curled under tensed legs. Inflammation, infection, hydrocortisone on U.S. shores this time. Jesus.

"You're quiet," Adam says.

"Enjoy it. It doesn't happen all that often."

"I'm not enjoying it. I get worried when you're quiet. It's like you're plotting my death or something."

I reach out my hand and tap his face lightly with my palm. *His* stubble is sexy, his smile amused. He turns to me and smiles, then turns back to face the road.

"You met my family."

"I did."

"What did you think?"

"What do I think? I think you downplayed how nuts they are. And I think I can understand a lot better where you come from."

"Yeah?"

"Yeah. And the same thing will happen when you meet mine. My balls are shrinking just thinking about it."

We drive on in silence for a moment. I stare out at the wash of dry land, brush and bush, desert. Atop that barrenness are malls. Cars. People living their lives as people tend to do, except they live in Southern California, and to most of the world that means existence as part of a movie.

"You're scared too," I say.

"Isn't everyone?"

"No. I think it's too easy to say that."

"I don't. Everyone's scared of something. That something is usually their families."

The desire to tell him about the conversation with my mother crashes in like a high-tide wave. After I finished talking to her, I went back and continued smoking with Adam and Jonathan. They didn't ask questions and I didn't offer explanations.

We pull off at a Starbucks. The heat is a wet rag stuffed in the throat, lit on fire. I'm feeling a dull dizziness as we walk toward the green-and-white umbrellas. He swings the door open for me, and the air-conditioning is a cool bath of relief.

We stand in line waiting to order. I count down from ten in my head. When I get to five, I will turn around and face him. When I get to one, I will speak.

I lose it at seven.

"I want to tell you something," I say without turning around.

"Will you look at me while you do it?"

And just then, it's our turn. He orders an Americano—I can't understand how he can drink that in this weather—and I get an iced Passion tea, no sweetener. We stand off to the side along with the rest of the Interstate 5 drivers and he tips my face up toward his.

"Let's go outside," I say.

"It's too fucking hot. Whisper it in my ear."

I stand on tiptoe. "Remember what I told you at the bar?"

"You've told me lots of things in lots of bars. You want to be more specific?"

Our drinks are up. We retrieve them and head back out into the inferno. Before we get into the car, he pauses and turns toward me. "What are you so ashamed of?"

"That thing I told you about at the bar that time. The first time we got together."

He grins. "Now you're talking."

"You know. About that thing I have."

He wipes the smile off his face. "Okay," he says. "I remember."

"I want to do something about it."

I expect him to hug me, but he doesn't. What he does is better: He gives me a high-five. Our palms smack together like some sort of ringing bell. We stand there for a second, connected and sweaty, celebrating.

After we get home I make a list:
Find doctor.
Quit job.
Get freelancing clients.

Make shit swing!

I get started with priority number one. The first order of business is taking a notebook down to Gaylords. I need some caffeine and a brainstorming session. Inside the place is packed, and I wind up sharing a table with a guy wearing a leather cap, harness, and Mickey Mouse T-shirt. It takes all kinds.

My pen hovers above the notebook. I'm not sure what to write. I don't know how to get this process started. I don't even have health insurance, haven't had it since I worked for the *Daily Republic. Get health insurance*, I write in the notebook. Okay. That's step number one. I should reward myself with a croissant to go along with my house coffee. I try to move on to step number two. *Get doctor.* I picture a supermarket shelf filled with little doctors, medical Beanie Babies in white coats. How to choose among them? Just reach out and grab.

The leather guy removes his cap, sighs, and runs his hand over his bald head. I wonder what sort of lists he's making. Then I notice a table's opened and I move. I settle myself into the chair, prop my legs on the seat next to me. Third step. Third step. I'm hit with a wave of annoyance. It feels so artificial, this list-making. The figuring-out, the planning.

But I might as well approach it logically. Going at it half-assed hasn't done me much good.

Third step.

Make appointment.

Fourth step.

Go.

Those are the two most difficult parts of this process: the follow-through. I can get online, check a few boxes and fill in a few more, get some basic health insurance. I can comb through a list and run some names through the internet and find a doctor who hopefully didn't get a medical degree at McDonald's University.

But making an appointment? Keeping it? Showing up? That's a fifth step: Panic.

"I'm proud of you," Adam says that night. We're cooking dinner in my little hallway of a kitchen, moving as nimbly as possible to avoid stepping on each other's toes. There's got to be a metaphor there, but I'm not interested in investigating it.

"Proud?" I say. My eyes are stinging from the onion I'm chopping. I wipe my hands on a dish towel, then rub my eyes with my fists like a little kid. A laser show of tie-dye pinwheels takes place beneath my eyelids. I rub harder, then stop.

"Yeah." He smashes garlic with the side of a knife, then minces it with a series of small movements. Then the knife slips and he cuts his finger.

"Maybe we should just have pizza tonight," I say, getting him a Band-Aid.

"Listen, Mario Batali, I've seen you draw blood too."

"Let's get back to how proud you are of me."

"Proud," he says, sucking his finger before centering the bandage on the wound. He wraps it around the tip of his finger, then turns away to rinse some cauliflower. We're making curry tonight. I never thought I'd do something like that: cook dinner with someone, talk about what *we* were doing. The world rarely fails to surprise.

"I'm proud," he says, "because you're getting your shit together. I'm proud because you're facing the stuff you don't want to deal with. You let me meet your family. You talk to me about this health crap you're facing. Now you're going to get treated."

Praise makes my stomach feel odd. Not quite queasy, just a

little unsettled. "Well," I say, "it's not as if I haven't tried before. And look at me."

He turns from the sink. "I look at you all the time."

"And?"

"And what do you think? You're fucking hot."

Now my stomach is doing flip-flops, a careening dive off a very high board. Fucking hot. Look at you all the time. God, in some ways it's easier to be ridiculed. At least you can trust that you know that person's a villain. When it comes to this, you don't know. This guy can just have a golden tongue and want to deploy it on me for some reason.

But why would he bother if he wasn't sincere?

I pick up a potato and begin to peel it. I use short movements, restrained yet rapid. I like cooking. You can get from Point A to Point B in an evening, and if it doesn't come off, there's always takeout.

"Thanks," I say.

"I mean it, you know."

"I do know."

"And it's hard for you to accept."

I crush the coriander with a mortar and pestle. I circle around and around the small piece of porcelain. I can smell the seeds giving up their scent. I suddenly feel defensive. I don't want to play the wounded woman here, the one who's felt broken until the right guy came along.

"You know, Freud," I say, "it's better if you just concentrate on the sex theories."

He washes spinach, wringing it out in the sink. He doesn't say anything.

"Are you mad at me?" I ask.

"A little."

"Why?"

"I give you a compliment, and—"

"You want to look at me?"

He turns from the sink toward me, still holding the spinach. "I give you a compliment and you turn it into a fight."

I lean against the counter, putting my weight on my palms. I rise on the balls of my feet. I'm not sure why I'm doing any of this.

"I'm not your enemy," he says.

"I never said—"

"You don't have to. There are days I can see it in your eyes. I love you, but you're incredibly defensive. You're—"

I love you. He said *I love you.*

I walk over to where he stands and hug him. "I can be defensive," I say against his chest. "I know."

"Thank you," he says into my hair.

Dinner quickly gets forgotten. An hour later we're putting away the half-prepared ingredients and getting ready to go out for pizza.

"I'll go with you," he says, tying his shoes. "If you want."

I'm in the bathroom brushing my hair. When he makes his offer, I stop and walk out, still holding my brush. "Serious?"

"Why not? Just tell me when."

"Isn't it going to be totally boring for you?"

"Yes," he says. "That's why you'll owe me a blow job."

Whoever designed the California Pacific Medical Center must have studied at the training academy of Boring and Bland. Never have I seen so many shades of ivory and cream, colors meant to calm, to soothe.

Thing is, it kind of *works.*

We crowd onto the elevator with a nun wearing a Bluetooth. "Fourth floor, please," I say to the sister, and she lights up a button with a touch. We all stand stiffly and face the front, hoping as generations of elevator-riders have hoped that no one will break the sacred silence.

Each floor brings a *ding* and a stop, a shuffling on and off. Each arrival and departure brings its own aberration. Could be the skin, could be the small intestine, could be that strange and simple fact of being human.

Eventually it's just us and the nun. The sister says nothing, just fingers the miniature space rocket above her right ear as we step out the door and onto cheap, nubby carpet.

You would think this would be where I start to lose it. Yet somehow I feel good. I bounce up to the front-desk receptionist and hit her with a big grin. I have no idea where I'm getting this energy, and I'm not questioning it.

She hands me a clipboard and a pen. She has drawn-on eyebrows, and they don't match. Sometimes I feel guilty for my nasty observations, but not today. Adam's already seated. I park myself next to him and slap his knee.

His mouth is crooked between his beard and moustache. He's amused.

"Something's got you all chipper."

"Chipper? What kind of douchebag word is that?"

He kisses me. "My kind of word."

Was it like this in Dr. Frye's waiting room all those years ago? Did I trounce among the uncomfortable chairs, gleeful, not realizing I was about to receive my first life sentence?

MEDICAL HISTORY QUESTIONNAIRE
Since this is your medical history and it will be used in evaluating your health, it is extremely important that the questions be answered as accurately and completely as possible. All information provided is kept confidential.

PLEASE LIST ANY KNOWN MEDICAL PROBLEMS YOU HAVE AT PRESENT.
Diagnosed with congenital adrenal hyperplasia in 1996. Symptoms: hirsutism, male-pattern balding, difficulty losing weight, irregular menstrual periods.

CURRENT MEDICATIONS
None at present. Previously took spironolactone and dexamethasone.

SIGNIFICANT PAST ILLNESS
None.

PAST SURGERY
None.

DRUG REACTIONS/ALLERGIES
Amoxicillin—causes rashes.

FAMILY MEDICAL HISTORY—MAJOR HEALTH PROBLEMS
Please complete the following information if your parents' medical history is known:

Father—None.

Mother—Possible congenital adrenal hyperplasia (never confirmed)

GENERAL HEALTH

Please indicate whether you have ever had a significant problem with any of the symptoms or conditions listed below:

High blood pressure—Yes

Depression—Yes

Anxiety—Yes

Thoughts of suicide—Yes

Nervous breakdown—Yes, I think

Sexual Problems (ex. pain with intercourse)—Yes
If yes, please comment: Difficulty with intercourse before beginning my current relationship.

How many times have you been pregnant? None

Number of miscarriages or abortions: None

When did your last menstrual period begin? I have not had a menstrual period in two years.

How long do your periods typically last? Variable—from a week to a week and a half.

How often do they occur? Very infrequently—every few years.

Do you have any problems related to your periods? Infrequency, which I believe is CAH-related.

"You said you don't snore," Adam says, pointing. "Tell the truth."

"Just during sex. That's normal."

We're punching each other's shoulders and generally annoying everyone in the waiting room when the door swings open. I hear my name.

This is it. Call it a moment of truth, call it a step in the right direction, call it a simple meeting between two people, one in the position to look at the other and say, *Here's what's wrong.*

The nurse leads me in. She's a wash of white capped by an olive-skinned countenance. Adam stays behind in the waiting room, thumbing through *Esquire*. It's either that or *Women's Health.*

Then there are the preliminaries: temperature, height, weight. I step backward on the scale because I know the number is larger than I'd like—*I'm* larger than I'd like—and why deal with it today? The nurse just smiles and shrugs, makes a few notations, leads me into an exam room, and closes the door.

I sit on a chair that feels more comfortable than it looks. I narrate the scene to myself: *Here we are. Moment of reckoning, come face-to-face with it.* If only there were a mirror so I could dramatically intone the words to myself. I address the cabinet that holds hospital gowns, the sink, the examination table. *You're going to leave your bra and underwear on and lie on that thing. The gown won't close in the back because they're designed for torture. His stethoscope will hunt you down like a predator.*

I'm immersed in my makeshift script when I hear a cursory knock. Dr. Clinton Young steps into the room. His handshake is firm and fast. He is that variant of middle age that somehow seems more vibrant than an adolescent: the fifty-five-year-old who still skis, jogs, and climbs Mount Everest before breakfast.

Where are the craggy, out-of-shape doctors who smoke menthols over your chart? That's who I want examining me.

"I've reviewed your chart," he says by way of introduction.

"Okay," I say. My voice sounds put-on, like the town whore trying to be the good girl. It's not working. For a minute I can't recall the chart he's referencing, and then I realize I've had my Santa Barbara medical records forwarded for his review. Dr. Young spreads the pages along the exam table, and we both hunker over them.

"Off the charts," he says. I feel what I always feel in these moments: guilt. Like I've done something wrong, screwed up my body and left the mess for someone else to repair.

"I'm an overachiever."

He doesn't laugh. He picks up his clipboard and clicks open a pen. "Your mother," he says. "Still alive?"

Yes, thank God. I mean no sarcasm here. It's a primal thing, primal and maybe something more.

"Any significant history of medical problems?"

It took her three years to get pregnant with me. I grew up hearing about all the lab tests she'd undergone, all the medications, all the work they'd done on her, and pictured her body as a construction zone, foundation of concrete, smell of fresh lumber, walled off from the world by an electrified fence and a warning sign.

"Your father?"

Healthy as hell. If I've ever seen the son of a bitch sick, I don't remember it.

"Siblings?"

Both fine. We're all fine, really. No mud-eating poverty, no crutches.

A series of scribbles and scratches. "Your father or brothers significantly taller than you?"

They're six feet, I'm five feet. I'm not tall enough to reach the top shelf, but not short enough to be a circus freak.

He puts down the clipboard. This is it. This is when he's going to say he's stepping out of the room for a moment, here's a hospital gown and a wrap for your waist, please be seated on the examination table after you've changed.

The questioning is one thing. I don't like it, but I can talk all day long. Just don't ask me to take my clothes off. Don't make me expose myself.

He reaches for a lab slip and starts to write. "The congenital adrenal hyperplasia diagnosis is pretty solid," he says. "I'm going to send you down for some blood work to establish a baseline. I'll call you after I get the results. Any questions?"

Just one: Why can't all doctor's appointments be this quick?

I'm practically waltzing within the gray walls of the basement lab. "Relieved?" Adam asks.

"Fuck yeah. He barely looked at me."

"This is a good thing?"

And like that, the balloon pops. The air leaks. Did the guy even look at me? Can the numbers tell the whole story? Am I hitting yet another dead end?

Adam sees the look on my face and grabs my hand. "Don't get upset," he says. It comes about thirty seconds too late. I'm already feeling the energy evaporating through my pores. Sometimes it happens like this. One moment you're brushing the ceiling—the next you're kneeling on the floor.

We're walking down Fillmore Street. It's the backbone of Pacific Heights, a neatly ordered jumble of boutiques, salons, bookstores, bars, and cafes. Somewhere along the way, Fillmore flattens out and leads into the actual Fillmore District, a place of jazz, urban renewal, and housing projects. You can walk Fifi here, but she'd better be wearing her bulletproof collar.

"Want to stop here?" he asks and gestures. The place is called The Grove, and it's a middle ground between swanky cafe and low-key bar. Women sit on outdoor benches wearing Ugg boots and huge Jackie O sunglasses, juggling cell phones and armloads of bags. Inside it's a ski lodge with huge, expensive chocolate chip cookies. We buy two and find seats among a raging river of white MacBooks.

"I'm not upset," I say. "I'm frustrated."

"That's legal."

"I mean, you're right. He didn't look at me. He looked at his clipboard and his watch, but not at me. And I was just relieved because I didn't want him to examine me."

"Look," he says, and bites into his cookie. "I said a dumbass thing. I mean, the guy knows what he's doing. He's a doctor."

"Please. Half the morons here are probably doctors." A guy wearing white iPod headphones shoots me a glare. "Look at *him*. He's probably an oncologist and doesn't take his earbuds out to tell his patients they're dying of ass cancer."

"You're projecting."

"Save it. Just because your mother's a shrink, that doesn't give you the goddamned right to lay me down on the couch."

"You're getting angry," he says, "when you don't even have anything concrete to get angry about."

"Nothing concrete," I say. "Is that right."

"That's right. How the hell do you know what he's going to come up with? How do you know how the tests will turn out? Why do you always sneer at the idea of a happy ending?"

"Happy endings exist in massage parlors. That's it."

In moments like this I despise him. I hate his sunniness and eternal optimism. He can shove his happy endings. What the hell does he know about struggle?

Then he opens his mouth to speak, and I remember.

I never notice his voice. Actually, I do. There's just nothing about it that bothers me. It's as much as part of him as his eyes and his nose, his ankles, and the soles of his feet. It's the way I found him, the way he was made. It exists in no realm of perfection. It has no overlap with what he *should be*. It simply is what is.

Maybe that's how he feels about me.

Maybe that's the happy ending.

A year after we started dating, six months after we moved in together, Adam goes down on one knee and opens a box.

"Is that real?" I ask.

"What do you think?"

"Where did you get it?"

"Where do you think?"

"Costco?"

"Bingo. Now will you say yes so I can get up?"

We have a late-night dinner at a French bistro whose bill is payable only in cash. He ducks around the corner to a no-name ATM—the kind that dings you for the simple pleasure of pulling out money—and I sit with my chin on my newly received rock.

Happy endings indeed.

I am taking three different medications: dexamethasone, spironolactone, and Yasmin, a birth-control pill. The combination is meant to bring down the values found in the lab results. "Still off the charts," Dr. Young said when he called, "but I can give you a way to fix them."

Fix them. Fix me. Yes, that's what I want. Fix me, repair me, sew me up and make me whole. No more secret sessions with blades and cosmetics. No more neurosis when I walk into a crowded room. No more worries when a camera flashes in my face.

Oh God. My wedding pictures.

Some brides want their Kotex to match the dinner napkins. Me, I just want to look like a woman at my wedding.

I'm not just getting married. I'm marrying Adam. "This means something," I say to him.

"I should sure as hell hope so."

I take a bite of steak tartare. "I know," I say. "It's kind of a *duh* statement. But it's . . . I don't know, a chance to think about things."

"Like what?"

The waiter comes over and pours more wine into each of our glasses. "Life, the universe and everything."

"I'm serious."

"I'm serious too. What doesn't it make me think about? There's the whole want-to-be-a-better-person thing, the worry that we're not going to be compatible, the fact that both our families are divorced. Little things like that."

He forks into some mushroom flan. "So?" he says.

We're sitting on the couch, surfing on our separate laptops. The front door is open and we can hear little kids playing outside, laughing over their hopscotch. It's one of those Saturday afternoons that feels like an indulgence, long and unhurried.

I go to Google and type *laser hair removal*. I'm not going to do it, of course. I'm just curious. The first of about four million results appears on my screen:

Looking for Your Best Laser Hair Removal Solution?

LaserHairRemoval.com is your best solution to get rid of your unwanted hair fast and permanent! Click or call us to get immediate answers . . .

Immediate answers. I like the sound of that.

Adam is concentrating, reading his political blogs or maybe *The Onion* online. Sometimes we do this, fall into our separate worlds, then we reconnect and find common ground. *"Soiwasthinking,"* I say, the words so murmured and blurred that even I hardly hear them.

He doesn't look up. "Well," I try again. "I was thinking that maybe . . ."

He arches his eyebrows.

"That maybe . . ." God, I'm frustrated with myself. Usually it's him who's like this, whose tongue-tied moments leave me hanging. I go quietly insane in these times, biting the inside of my cheek and looking at the trees outside to avoid screaming at him: *Just spit the shit out!* He just waits, tapping the pads of his fingers lightly against his keyboard.

Suddenly it's important that both our computers are closed. I push his shut and do the same to mine. Then I stand up and put my hands on my hips as if I'm making some sort of announcement. Maybe I am.

"I'm going to try it again," I say.

"Try what?"

I don't want to explain. Why can't he just know? "The laser stuff."

"That's kind of out of the blue."

"Well, yeah."

"You want me to go with you?"

This isn't where the story veers off into how love will save me, fix me now that I've found someone. This isn't a Cher song; it's not a soap opera. It's real life and we're both human, just like most everyone else out there.

He's not here to save me. But I do need him to be there.

"Yeah," I say. "Please come with me."

"Are you scared?"

They say you can't fold a piece of paper more than eight times. I'm testing that theory. The first fold holds promise, the sharp crease, the crinkle of the material. By the sixth fold, the effort seems pointless.

"Would you be?"

"Nah."

We laugh. Of course his answer is bullshit. Of course I'm scared. We're sitting in his little car in a parking lot in Walnut Creek. Walnut Creek would be like Berkeley if everything— streets, buildings, people—were scrubbed and power-washed. A few more Republicans, some extra popped collars, and name-brand khakis. The slight differences soothe me.

I loosen my grip and the paper tumbles to the floor of the car.

"Let's go," I say, and swing my feet out onto the pavement.

We're parked behind the building. A landscaped path leads through a courtyard and around to the front. I have a garden of my own now and can identify some of the foliage: lavender, rosemary, alyssum. Among rosebushes and ivy lies an expansive man-made pond. Fish swim in those brackish waters, big and friendly with harmless black eyes. They don't seem to mind when I stare.

At the front is a set of glass doors: *Encore Medspa*. The name is written in italics, a light hand. You could imagine someone sipping a mint lemonade as they penned those words, wearing a wide-brimmed hat and laughing.

Adam pulls the door open and we step into the lobby. Lots of mirrors and potted plants here, something unidentifiable on the Muzak. We take the stairs, though I would rather use the elevator. I don't want to arrive huffing and puffing. I want to be Kool Moe Dee when I show up for my face stapling.

We step into Encore's front room. More potted plants here, big ones with emerald-colored leaves curling over one another. Scented candles too, robust stalks that sting the air with cinnamon and sage. Strategic lamps and subtle canned bulbs in the ceiling provide tasteful lighting. I've become an expert on lighting. Whiter fluorescents somehow make my stubble seem less offensive, while yellowish tints bring it out in its full fury. Thank you, Encore, for bleaching my mirror image.

We're standing by the front desk when a middle-aged blonde emerges. One hand is wrapped around a wine glass, the other clutches a tissue. She's blowing her nose, and she literally *tweets* when she sees us. "Oh my," she says in a baby-bird voice. "I didn't realize anyone was *here*."

Her name is Ann, and I will grow to like her.

With a gesture she makes the tissue disappear. She has that kind of fine bone structure that you won't see anywhere in my family. A size two at most. "Let's get you all set up," she says.

Ann's very enthusiastic about getting me set up. She leads us
into a sitting area with cushy earth-tone couches and a rattan
coffee table, and she's humming what I could swear is the French
national anthem the entire time.

Thing is, the shit *works*. Her enthusiasm is contagious.
It's like going to the gym and flashing your pass, and as
they're swiping it they say, "Have a good workout, Allison." I
don't know about you, but I always get all jazzed up and say,
"Thanks!"

Ann gestures with the wine glass and asks, "Red or white?"

"Red," Adam says before I can even open my mouth to
answer. Well, I'm glad *he's* getting to enjoy this. They're getting
a huge kick out of him. I'm expecting them to offer him a
discount on a back-waxing, should he need it. For the record: He
doesn't.

She hands us twin glasses of cabernet. I rarely drink wine.
I can throw up on my own, thank you. This morning, though,
Folgers is just not going to cut it. The drink trails a burning path
down my throat to my stomach. I'm starting to understand the
meaning of liquid courage.

Ann wiggles away, then jitters back a moment later with a
Popsicle stick. "Numbing cream," she says. I remember this from
the last time. I hope the shit packs a punch. She gestures toward
a framed mirror. Adam follows me as I walk over. I want to turn
around and glare at him until he gets his ass back on the couch,
but I smile and say, "Want to help?"

He holds my hair back from my face as I swipe the cream
across every problem area: sideburns, upper lips, cheeks, chin,
upper neck. It is cool and rich, and for a moment it feels as if it
could solve everything. I've accidentally swiped the corner of my
mouth and it's already tingling, going numb.

311

A decorative fountain tinkles in the corner. This, of course, makes me want to pee.

I take a key attached to a box that says BOTOX. I fit it in the lock of the women's restroom. The door sighs as it swings open. A light clicks on. There are silk flowers in a vase on the sink, some Meyer lemon hand soap from a place called Sebastiani Spa, a jar of Bath and Body Works lotion. I remember that hiphop publicist in Suisun City, how her bathroom held a mixture of every type of potion. Has another reporter interviewed her, stepped into her air-conditioned cloistered designer town house, rifled through her cabinets? There is no medicine cabinet here, no secrets to make me feel better about my own.

I sit on the toilet. What the hell was Nails' breathing exercise? In for seven, hold for five, out for seven. It's not working. Damn it, *it's not working.*

We meet with Adrianne in one of the exam rooms. Adrianne will be the one stapling my face. She has olive skin and a short, practical haircut. Her voice is husky in a way that makes me think she might read every so often. I approve.

In the exam room, dark wood and marble accents take a back seat to various shades of ivory: a white vanity with a sink, ghost-colored bathrobe on a hanger on the door. A silver boombox plays classical music. A framed Chinese inscription hangs on the wall.

What does it say: *Abandon all hope ye hairy bitches*?

"We're going to do full face," Adrianne says. She wears a white lab coat, leans against one of the room's many shiny, hard surfaces. Somehow a wet washcloth materializes in her hand and she wipes the cream from my skin, leans close, and furrows her brow. "It's good that you shaved this morning. That'll really help the process."

Never have I used the word *shave* with Adam. I have no idea if he suspects that I do it, or how exactly he thinks I manage the facial hair. The word is a sweaty confession in the fluorescent room. No tasteful lighting here, just the hot, heavy glare of truth.

From the corner comes a hum: the laser machine itself. It's called a LightSheer Diode. Adrianne explains that its chilled tip cools the skin and makes the procedure less painful. "I actually want to talk about that," I say.

"Shoot," she says, and sinks into a chair next to a stack of *Glamour, Architectural Digest*, and *Self* magazines.

"I had a bad experience," I say, and wait for my throat to close. I'm almost disappointed when it doesn't. "It was years ago. I blew up."

"Folliculitis," she says—and I know I'm in the right hands. I nod. Adam catches my eye and he nods too. "There's been advancements since that time. You're going to be fine. We're going to keep a close eye. If there's any problem, we'll take care of it."

She sounds like she knows what she's talking about. Okay, Adrianne. Showtime.

Adam kisses me on the forehead and leaves the room. Adrianne smooths cooling gel on my face. Then she turns around and picks up . . . *oh God*. I know I need some sort of vision protection from the laser, but . . . "Some people don't like the goggles," she says, and tosses them back on the vanity. "Too claustrophobic. Try these."

They're a huge, dark pair of sunglasses: nothing I'd wear in the outside world, but not too likely to make me hyperventilate. I slide them on, the thick plastic earpieces asserting themselves above my earlobes. "Okay, hon," she says, and pats me on the shoulder. "Lie back."

It's a cool tip held to my face and a series of countdowns: *One-two-three, one-two-three,* Adrianne's voice interspersed with a series of beeps. It is a familiar feeling—a fishhook diving into my face and finding its catch—but the pain is fleeting, not searing. I hold my breath until Adrianne exhorts me to exhale. She starts at the sideburns and works her way toward the center of my face. When she reaches my lower lip, she asks me to put my tongue over my teeth. I imagine the laser working its way into my molars, a root canal, two procedures for the price of one. There is a bad moment when the cool tip is nearly up against my nostrils—I can't *breathe*—then it's over and gone.

She moves to my chin, where the hair is thickest. I expect this to hurt the worst. I am proven right. I screw my eyes shut under the ridiculous dark glasses. By the time I've taken my third deep breath, it's over. She's even given me a few zaps under my chin, toward the neck. I haven't felt them.

"Okay," she says. It's been maybe ten minutes.

I pull off the glasses and sit up, swinging my legs around to the side of the exam table. That's *it?* Bullshit. The last time stretched over the better part of an hour.

She's writing something on a chart, loading ice cubes into a plastic baggie. "You're done," she says. "How you doing?" The room smells like burning fur. My nostrils flare in triumph. I take the bag of ice and press it to my slightly swollen skin. I say, "That was *nothing*."

Nothing, but it works. Afterward, my face is slightly swollen, but no sign of folliculitis, no need to find soothing cream. Just an overwhelming urge to lean into the mirror and press at my skin, watch the zapped hairs come out in between my fingers.

It will take several treatments. It will not come quickly, nor will it come easily. It's just a beginning. But it is a beginning, not an aborted attempt, not a painful practice that led to absolutely nothing.

I'm starting to get bald patches on my face, places where the hair has been vanquished and hopefully will not return. I call up Dr. Young and he explains that now that I'm on medication, now that I'm not fighting against the hair growth at a medical level, the cosmetic treatments will have a better effect. I wish I had realized that before, but it really is better late than never.

A week after the procedure we go to a buffet for lunch. "Don't be shy," Adam says as I drop a small mountain of mushrooms on my iceberg lettuce and dive back for a second helping.

"Fuck you, Mr. Hairy Palms," I say, and a woman pushing a stroller freezes and frowns. I find myself pondering what I just said. Hairy palms, a punishment of legend for excessive whacking off. How did that tale come to be considered truth?

"Chewbacca had hairy palms," Adam says as we settle into a booth.

"Yeah?"

"And he's a good guy."

I spear a crouton. "How'd we get into this whackadoodle conversation again?"

The woman pushing the stroller wheels past me and sighs. I really don't belong in polite society.

"Because," Adam says, and finishes off a quarter of his salad in a single bite, "you can't judge someone by their exterior."

I've heard this argument so many times. And you know what? It's bullshit. "Yeah?" I say. "You think I can't be judged by how I look?"

"It wouldn't give someone the whole picture, no."

"You get enough."

"Is that so." He's learned to say it just as I do—flat, a statement, not a question.

"Yes," I say. "That's so." Then I pick up my plate and go back for seconds, because that's what you do at a buffet. It's spread out there for you, and you take advantage of it before it's gone.

Next to me is a woman who jiggles out of her fat-girl shorts—the kind with an elastic waist and soft, giving cotton. She's got a carb fiesta going on, her plate loaded with focaccia and macaroni and cheese, dappled with a few chocolate-chip muffins and even some spinach salad to even things out. Can I judge her by her exterior? Can I look at her, what she holds in her soft, chunky paws, and sum her fat ass up in a heartbeat?

Do you hate me? Should someone like me, someone who has run from eyeballs most of my life, have more forgiving vision of my own?

There's got to be a way to walk this balance beam.

Or is there?

Fact is, I didn't accept myself as the Bearded Lady. I still don't. If someone who looked like me cruised by right now, I would glance. Hell, I might—and I hope I wouldn't, but I can't guarantee it wouldn't happen—stare. A long and involved appraisal, a telegraph that says, *You stand out*.

I didn't want to stand out. I never did and I never will. I want to have a smooth face, maybe eventually a smooth body as well, a full hairline, the ability to lose weight. I'm not working to promote the Worldwide Federation of Bearded Ladies. I have no desire to strike a blow for stubble justice.

The worst part about being different isn't the ridicule. Hell, you expect that. You don't like it, but it's part of the package.

A shitty part, granted, the fruitcake at Christmas, but you make your peace, develop your coping mechanisms. You hire a therapist or six, run on the treadmill until your feet feel ready to drop from the rest of your body.

Maybe you stand in front of the refrigerator and eat past the point of satiation, push into that queasy country where food is not a bodily necessity but something to defeat. Could be you stick something in your arm, or your nose, or you find the same stranger in different bars in different cities, the same stranger with varying bodies and accents and ways of saying *Let's go back to yours*, and you wake up empty when you wanted to be full. Or you dig your nails into your arm until it bleeds, trap the inside of your cheek with your teeth, holding just past the point of pain. You release and repeat. You get by. You make do.

But that's not the worst part.

The worst part is people who think they're on your side. The woman who slides next to you onto a bench at a cafe: *It's important. You need to listen.* My electrologist friend at the Isla Vista Food Co-Op. The stoned theater director at a party crowing *It's the media. They tell us who's beautiful and who's not. They pressure us. They shove their concepts down our throats.*

I've heard plenty about *the media* and *their* ideas of beauty. I'll tell you this: The media never put a razor in my hand and said, *Use it.* No billboard or television show, no music video or magazine ad twisted my arm behind my back and said, *Make a change.*

I did it myself.

"It's a cult," I say to Adam, sitting back down at the table. "A new-age cult of self-esteem. People telling you that you *should* like yourself, that you're beautiful *just the way you are*. What if you know that's wrong? What if you *want* to change?"

All along I've wanted to change. From the moment Nails first twisted a tap and brought forth the steaming water meant to soften my facial hair, I've known I didn't want to look as I do. I want to be tall, skinny, hair-free. I want it because *I want it*, not because society tells me it should be so. I want it because it's what I've always wanted for myself.

My hormone levels are at normal. Normal looks great to me. Normal looks like a road trip down Highway 1, top down, wind blowing in your face. Creedence on the stereo, your baby's hand on your knee. Perfect like that.

I am stabilized. Between the medication and the laser hair treatments, my face is mostly smooth. I say mostly because there a few stray hairs, and I can live with those. As long as I can walk in a room and not wonder. If I can smile for pictures and mean it.

But if I stop taking my medication, the hair comes back. I will always need to do battle using chemistry as my weapon. I must be vigilant. I cannot let down my guard.

Eventually I will want to deal with my receding hairline, the weight, the infertility. Right now, it's enough to know that I can take care of the problem on the front line.

If you'd told me in the beginning that it would take years to figure out even how to fight, I might have shrugged and given up from the start. As it was, finding the right combination meant spinning the lock over and over.

You could have told me that and I might have believed you. Or maybe not. Could be that this was something I had to discover on my own, through fits and starts, giving up hope and picking it back up once more, running into walls before finding what looked like the right path. Even now, I'm still holding my breath.

EPILOGUE

2002

My mother's cat died today.

Simba was a sixteen-year-old diabetic with kidney disease, pancreatitis, and anemia—a chain reaction which eventually killed her. She was also a creature who knew nothing but love, a gray tabby with blue eyes and a sweet, willing personality. My mother called her the California cat. "She's mellow," Nails would say. "You can do anything with her."

You could too. You could pick Sim up and swing her around, pet her soft belly, press her ears back against her head and let them spring up again, then repeat the process. She loved it all, as long as she was being offered attention.

Two months ago she landed in critical care, intravenous fluids and insulin, hourly checks of temperature and heart rate, regular monitoring of the blood glucose. Total kidney failure, a shutdown. It was touch and go for days before they stabilized her, and when my mother finally brought her home, she was a weakened cat. Same outgoing personality, the same cat who would talk your ear off and warm your lap as long as you liked, but a cat whose condition was guarded nonetheless.

My mother got Simba during the Bill years. Jonathan picked her out at the Escondido Humane Society, a small dark kitten with a bright gaze. She was an older girl by the time Bill left and I was allowed back into the house. I stepped lightly those first few times in my mother's home, a place filled with memories, but none of me.

Simba welcomed me.

Now she's dead. She died early this morning with my mother by her side. Then Nails wrapped her in a towel to keep her body warm and drove her down to the vet.

This ended months of a complicated daily routine meant to maintain Simba's fragile health. The day began at 7:45 a.m. with an anti-nausea tablet, an appetite stimulant, and an antacid, with the rest of the morning bringing blood glucose tests and insulin, with IV fluid drips at lunchtime. With evening came the same pills as the morning, plus an antibiotic and blood-pressure medication. The day was capped off by another glucose check and fluid injection.

My mother did this every day, in and out, the effort and the thousands of dollars for the medications be damned. Each day she took that cat by the lovable scruff and gave her what she needed to survive.

Finally Simba's little body gave out. Enough was enough. I am crying; so is my mother, but we cry for different reasons. My mother cries because she has lost a pet—one of the most searing types of pain we will ever encounter. I cry because my mother has learned to care for someone.

Adam and I married a year ago. Rooster showed up in a suit that looked decently pressed and a tie that was new: his nod to the occasion. He sipped his sangria and put on the charm, chatting about his Toyota Supra and frequent-flyer miles. At the end of the night, he stepped over to where we stood on the dance floor, grinned at Adam, and told him, "Take a hike." Then the father of the bride danced with his daughter.

It was the picture-perfect moment. Then the glass shattered. He stepped back and got that confidential look. "I'm pulling for you guys," he said, "but sometimes people change."

"What?" Adam said when I told him later, as we sat in our living room changing our social-network statuses to Married and counting our loot.

"That's just him," I said. "What do you want?"

"For him to not act like an asshole at our *wedding*."

I opened the envelope marked ALLISON AND ADAM, FROM DAD (ALLISON'S) AND FATHER-IN-LAW (ADAM'S). It was written in my father's precise, lean-backward, all-caps handwriting, the dark black ink as formal and finite as anything I'll ever know.

There was a card and inside a check made out to the both of us, in the amount of $1,800. A multiple of *chai*, the number 18, a message for luck.

"Look at this," I tell Adam. "Look at this and ignore the rest."

In my head I hold a picture: a family. There's a mother and a father, siblings, friends, pets, a husband whose love buoys me when I cannot float on my own.

For just this moment, look at this. Just for now, look at this and ignore the rest.

ACKNOWLEDGMENTS

A book does not write itself, nor does only one person write it. I would like to thank The MacDowell Colony, WordSpace Studios, Playa Summer Lake, Kimmel Harding Nelson Center for the Arts, and The Julia and David White Artists' Colony for taking me in and offering me shelter, the Saint Mary's College of California MFA program for kicking my ass and waking me up, and The Writing Salon for empowering me to do what I love without getting arrested. All praise to my amazing agent, Marisa Zeppieri of Strachan Literary, for not just understanding my story but getting *me*, and to Woodhall Press for allowing me to enter the conversation. To my friends and family – you know you're amazing, but I'll tell you once more. Thank you for listening, for encouraging, for supporting, for being.

And to Wesley Gibson—brilliant rat bastard—for your proclamation of *sweetheart, go for it*. I did, Wesley. I did.

ABOUT THE AUTHOR

Allison Landa, whose work has been featured in *Business Insider, Parents Magazine, The Guardian US, The Washington Post,* and *HuffPost Personal* among other venues, wrote *Bearded Lady* as an account of life with Congenital Adrenal Hyperplasia. Landa teaches at The Writing Salon in San Francisco, has been a member of the San Francisco Writers Grotto, and earned her MFA in fiction writing from St. Mary's College of California. She has held artist residencies at The MacDowell Colony, WordSpace Studios, Playa Summer Lake, Kimmel Harding Nelson Center for the Arts, and The Julia and David White Artists Colony. She lives in Berkeley, CA, where she works as a writing teacher and coach.